The Liberative Cross

The Liberative Cross
Korean-North American Women
and the Self-Giving God

Hye Kyung Heo (Han)

☛PICKWICK *Publications* · Eugene, Oregon

THE LIBERATIVE CROSS
Korean-North American Women and the Self-Giving God

Copyright © 2015 Hye Kyung Heo (Han). All rights reserved. Except for brief quotations in critical publications or reviews, no part of this book may be reproduced in any manner without prior written permission from the publisher. Write: Permissions. Wipf and Stock Publishers, 199 W. 8th Ave., Suite 3, Eugene, OR 97401.

Pickwick Publications
An Imprint of Wipf and Stock Publishers
199 W. 8th Ave., Suite 3
Eugene, OR 97401

www.wipfandstock.com

ISBN 13: 978-1-4982-0064-6

Cataloguing-in-Publication Data

Heo (Han), Hye Kyung.

    The liberative cross : Korean-North American women and the self-giving God / Hye Kyung Heo (Han).

    xviii + 208 p. ; 23 cm. Includes bibliographical references and index(es).

    ISBN 13: 978-1-4982-0064-6

    1. Liberation theology. 2. Asian Americans—Religious life. 3. Asian American theology. 4. Theology, Doctrinal. I. II. III. IV.

BT265.3 .H40 2015

Manufactured in the U.S.A.   03/19/2015

For my mother, Cha Nam Han, and my father, Man Kuk Han, who live forever in my heart and inspire me to live as a true Christian, just as they once lived.

By viewing the cross from a social trinitarian perspective, we can retrieve a theology of the cross as the basic symbol of Christian faith to be liberating and life-giving for women.

Contents

Acknowledgments | ix

Introduction | xi

Abbreviations | xviii

1   Theology Always Lives in Context | 1

      Gadamer's Concept of "Fusion of Horizons" | 3

      Korean Women's Experience as a Theological Locus | 24

2   A Critical Evaluation of Feminist Theologies | 39

      The Maleness of God | 46

      God's Relation to the Cross | 64

      Revisiting Anselm's Atonement Theory in *Cur Deus Homo* | 76

3   Toward a Social Trinitarian Theology of the Cross: Moltmann's Social Trinitarian Theology of the Cross as a Contributing Resource for a Feminist Theology of the Cross | 91

      Luther's *theologia crucis* | 92

      Moltmann's Theology of the Cross | 102

      Moltmann's Social Doctrine of Trinity | 122

Contents

4 Social Trinitarian Understanding of the Cross and Its Praxis for Korean-North American Women in the Multicultural, Multiracial, Pluralistic Context | 136

>   Moltmann's Claim of Trinitarian Fellowship as "Prescription of the Nature of True Human Community" Faces Criticism | 137

>   Social Trinitarian Praxis for Korean-North American Women in the Multicultural, Multiracial, and Pluralistic Context Today | 152

Conclusion | 185

Bibliography | 191
Name Index | 209
Topical Index | 213

Acknowledgments

THIS BOOK IS THE outcome of my desire and effort to crystalize all my learnings throughout my long academic theological journey. My academic theological journey has been stimulated by Korean-North American women and their children who struggle to thrive as immigrants and citizens of this multicultural, multiracial land. As their pastor I have always felt obliged to theologically wake them to recognize the interconnectedness and interdependence of their existence regardless of gender, ethnicity, and race. Consequently, I have written this book to propose the social trinitarian theology of the cross as the most suitable symbol of Christianity to promote the dignity and value of Korean-North American women, as well as its praxis as their call to live in mutual, reciprocal relationship in this multicultural land.

    At this moment, as I am concluding this book, I cannot help thanking my God for the cross of Jesus Christ, the culmination of the self-giving love for the other, which reveals the essence of Trinitarian fellowship in mutuality, reciprocity, equality and generosity. I also thank Dr. Charles Fensham who, as a supervisor for my dissertation, has supported and encouraged me marvelously in the accomplishment of this project. I feel blessed and privileged by his scholarship that continuously inspires me to dig deeper and argue with depth and clarity. I was also privileged to have other outstanding scholars as my dissertation committee members. Special thanks are due to Dr. O'Gara who passed away while I was writing this thesis. Her advice to study Anselm and Luther in connection with Moltmann was certainly a great contribution to this project. I also benefited from Dr. Nik Ansell's outstanding scholarship, which helped me deepen my understanding of Moltmann's theology of the cross. I must also thank Dr. Dorcas Gordon, the principle of Knox College, who willingly joined my committee in place of Dr. O'Gara. Dr. Gordon has been my model, as one who truly lives a *perichoretic* lifestyle and shows how women can participate in building a

ACKNOWLEDGMENTS

society where they are free to realize their potential and to serve one another by using their gifts in freedom and trust. I am particularly grateful to Dr. Harold Wells, through whom I was introduced to Moltmann's theology of the cross. He taught me a very important principle for doing theology: Theology has to be biblical, contextual, life-giving and liberating.

This book is dedicated to my parents. My mother, eldress Cha Nam Han, is now in heaven. She is my heroine and mentor who lives forever in my heart and inspires me to live as a true Christian, just as she once lived. Although she is not physically able to see the completion of this project, I am sure she is now rejoicing as I write these final words of acknowledgment. My father, elder Man Kuk Han, also in heaven, was an egalitarian as a father of seven daughters. He always encouraged me, his youngest daughter, to study hard and become an influential pastor. I am also thankful to my parents-in-law, Seung Wook Heo and Jung Jae Lee, who have been praying for me in Korea. There are no words that can completely express my thanks to my husband, Rev. Dr. Chun Hoi Heo. He was the one to encourage me to take up the academic theological pursuit and has been my conversation partner on theology. To my two sons, Joshua Cha-young Heo and Isaac Ju-young Heo: "You have both grown to be handsome, strong, young men and Christian leaders while mother was studying." I thank my eldest son Joshua for making time to read his mother's thesis and correct mistakes, and Isaac for being his mother's "friend" and making her laugh with his brilliant jokes and sense of humor. I thank my dear siblings, all six sisters and one brother, who have been waiting so patiently and prayerfully for their youngest sister to reach the end of this academic journey. I must also thank my congregation members, both Korean ministry and English ministry of the Toronto Evangelical Church of the Word, for their prayers. I owe all my dedication and service to them.

Finally, I would like to shout with all my heart and all my strength, *Soli Deo Gloria*!

Introduction

Purpose

My theology of the cross is a contextual theology in the sense that the stimulus for this work is my unique experience as a Korean-North American immigrant woman pastor. In this thesis, I bring together both the first and the second generation Korean North American women in conversation with theologians of the cross and feminist theologians for the sake of a theology of the cross which is liberating and life-giving for them. Through conversing with those theologians who have endeavored to respond to challenges arising from every new situation by continually reinterpreting the Christian message, I attempt to render a merging of horizons for a redemptive praxis for both the first and the second generation North American Korean women.

My experience as Korean-Canadian is unique in that I am standing between the first and the second generation Korean-Canadians, and also between Koreans and non-Koreans. I was brought up in Korea and immigrated to Canada as a late teen. As an immigrant, I went through and overcame culture shock and language barriers, and came to share solidarity with the immigrants who suffer with various problems on personal, social, and spiritual levels. My unique "in-between" existence causes me to see the complexity of human relationships. Living in a multicultural, multiracial society, I have learned that Korean immigrants need to recognize the interconnectedness and interdependence of their existence regardless of gender, ethnicity, and race.

I have also come to see that the first generation Korean-North American women cannot be treated as a monolithic group of *han*-ridden people irrespective of their varied socio-cultural, religious, politico-economic differences. From my experiences as an immigrant and a woman pastor for the Korean-North Americans in the multicultural context, I have come to

INTRODUCTION

realize that it is not an appropriate way for today's context to construct a theology of the cross on the basis of the presupposition that Korean-North American immigrant women are one monolithic group of *han*-ridden people, or victims in the binary opposition between men and women or between the dominant and the marginal.

I have also noticed that Korean-North American women, living in a unique situation as immigrants or children of immigrants, tend to understand Christian tradition and symbols of faith in accordance with their existential experiences and the questions they bring to it. Many young Korean-North American women who have been educated in the multicultural context tend to appreciate the social aspect of Christianity more than their parents who tend to view Christianity as *cultus privatus* and practice it as a means of personal success and divine salvation which is heavenly and otherworldly. Living in the multicultural world, young Korean-North American women, and some of their parents who have learned new life circumstances in the multicultural context, raise an important theological question: "What does the Cross of Jesus mean to us and to others from different cultures in the world?" Their new life situation requires a new understanding of the cross of Jesus. Therefore, I take seriously into consideration the fact that human beings as "beings-in-the-world" have their existence and find meaning in a network of life. In this respect, both the first and the second generation Korean-North American women are challenged to move toward an understanding of the cross which would allow them to recognize the importance of mutuality and reciprocity in human relationships.

As a pastor of a Korean immigrant church for both first- and second-generation Korean-North American women, I share the same experiences with them. I accept it as a prophetic call to propose a theology of the cross which will challenge them to envision a new human community based on the values of equality, mutuality, and reciprocity in this world marred by sexism, classism, and racism. In response to this call, I propose a social trinitarian approach to the cross as one that reflects the essence of God in equality, mutuality, reciprocity, and community in diversity. The purpose of this project, then, is to propose the social trinitarian theology of the cross

Introduction

as the most suitable symbol of Christianity, which will promote the dignity and value of Korean-North American immigrant women and their call to live in mutual, reciprocal relationship in the multicultural context.

To argue the point that the very essence of God is to be in relation, mutuality, and community in diversity, I will critique Moltmann's social trinitarian understanding of the cross. According to Moltmann, the history of Jesus through his birth, life, death, and resurrection reveals the fellowship of the divine persons characterized by an infinite self-giving and reciprocal sacrifice of love.[1] This trinitarian self-giving, according to Moltmann, is both an outward movement toward the world and a reciprocal inward movement among the divine relations. McDougall explains it as follows:

> On the side of creation, the Father's self-giving of the Son involves a communication of the Father's eternal essence, his infinite goodness, into the world. Through the power of the Holy Spirit, the Father opens the exclusive fellowship that he shares with the Son to all human beings. On the divine side, this outward movement involves an inward self-donation among the divine persons where "in the sending of the Son, God . . . yields himself up." Here the Son responds to the Father's yielding himself up by taking up his own mission into the world. The Holy Spirit participates equally in this reciprocal self-giving of the Son and the Father as the mediator of their fellowship. The Spirit's self-giving inspires Jesus' proclamation, empowers his ministry, and accompanies him unto the cross.[2]

The reciprocal divine self-giving of the divine persons in the Trinity culminates at the event of the cross. The cross is a reciprocal sacrifice of love, in which "the communicating love of the Father turns into infinite pain over the sacrifice of the Son" and "the responding love of the Son becomes infinite suffering over his repulsion and rejection of the Father."[3] In this respect, the cross is not a one-sided sacrifice in which the Son plays the passive object or victim of the Father's will. Rather, it is *passio activa*: The Son undertakes the way to the cross deliberately.[4]

The cross, which is the pivotal symbol of Christianity, has become a problem for many feminist theologians today. They view the cross as a

---

1. Moltmann, *The Trinity and the Kingdom*, 75.
2. McDougall, "Return of Trinitarian Praxis?" 184.
3. Moltmann, *Trinity and the Kingdom*, 81.
4. Ibid.

Introduction

symbol of denigration and oppression. In contrast to their view, I argue from a social trinitarian perspective that the cross, as a symbol of the reciprocal sacrifice of love, is equally inclusive of both women and men and leans toward liberating faith and practice for Korean-North American women. The cross reveals God as the passionate loving God who exists by an infinite self-giving and reciprocal sacrifice of love and suffers in solidarity with the marginalized, the victimized, and the dehumanized. Thus, this social trinitarian approach to the cross invalidates the traditional descriptions of God that have underwritten the binary opposition between men and women, making one superior to the other.

Moltmann also employs the concept *perichoresis*, which portrays the tri-unity as the community and fellowship among three equal persons. He claims that the *perichoretic* trinitarian fellowship characterized by its mutuality and reciprocity not only describes divine community but also prescribes the true nature of human community. In agreement with Volf, I acknowledge that human beings can appropriate the peaceful and perfectly loving mutuality of the Trinity but only in a creaturely way within the conditions of history. I argue, however, that the self-giving love of the Trinity can be translated into the world of sin when human beings come to respond to their Triune God through the work of the Holy Spirit.

Methodology and Procedures

In doing a theology, it is necessary to respond creatively in every new situation and continually reinterpret the Christian message.[5] As Douglas Hall insists, contextuality conditions the manner in which the Christian message, centered on Christ and his work, is to be articulated and received. In this sense, the cultural and religious context of both the first- and the second-generation Korean-North American women needs to be analyzed. Whether they are aware or not, the first generation Korean-North Ameri-

---

5. Hall, *Cross in Our Context*, 47. See also Tillich, *On the Boundary*, 13–16. Tillich differs from Barth's position in that he admits that God's self–manifestation is dependent upon the way we receive this manifestation. This means that the reception of revelation is conditioned by human existence and we are in no position to construct a doctrine of revelation in itself apart from reception of it. For Tillich, the fact that we can ask about the connection between the revelation as an answer and human existence as question shows that the link between essential human goodness and God has not been completely destroyed. The fact that we must ask about it shows that we are estranged from such unity. See also Roberts, "Tillich's Doctrine of Man," 113.

Introduction

can women have been brought up with the nurture of Korean traditional religions in their spirituality and morality, and hold certain paradigms fostered by their traditional religions. They went through a paradigm shift in their worldviews as they converted to Christianity and live in a new life situation. Therefore, I will look into how Christianity as a new religion brought about a paradigm change in their view of salvation, human history, and value systems. They also received Christianity with a particular cultural understanding. In order to further unpack the fact that Korean women's spirituality has been culturally shaped, I also look into Gadamer's phenomenological hermeneutics, focusing on his ideas of "historically influenced consciousness" and "fusion of horizons."[6] In chapter 1, by employing Gadamer's phenomenological hermeneutics, I will analyze the experiences of Korean-North American women as a theological locus on the basis of the resources available in print, as represented in the attached bibliography, and my pastoral experiences in Canada since 1986. In so doing, I will also reflect on how first- and second-generation Korean-North American women view Christianity and ask christological questions concerning the relevancy of the Cross according to their different contexts.

The goal of my project concerns a new human community based on the values of equality, mutuality, and reciprocity which are dynamically revealed in the trinitarian relations. As a result, I take into serious consideration the attempts which feminist theologians have made to analyze and delegitimize theological patterns which have distorted Christian praxis. In the first section of chapter 2, I will critique various approaches that feminist theologians take toward exclusive, patriarchal language in order to renew the idea of God in a more inclusive way. Some feminist theologians attribute stereotypical feminine traits to God. Others uncover a feminine dimension in God by emphasizing the Holy Spirit as the feminine principle of the Godhead. Some feminist theologians replace the Trinity, Father-Son-Holy Spirit, with other triads of image which are neither masculine nor feminine, such as Creator-Redeemer-Sustainer. I critique these approaches in terms of what they contribute and what they lack. In the second section of chapter 2, I turn to the various ways in which feminist theologians view the cross and how some of them try to retrieve a theology of the cross that serves as a life-giving, liberating symbol of love for humanity including women. In the last section of chapter 2, I revisit Anselm's *Cur Deus Homo* and argue against feminist theologians that Anselm's theology of atonement does not lead to

6. Gadamer, *Truth and Method*, 277–309.

Introduction

what they term "divinely sanctioned child abuse." However, for the question of whether Anselm's theology of atonement empowers Korean-North American women today, I argue that its effect is limited and inadequate in relation to the challenges of Korean-North American women in today's multicultural world. Anselm's commitment to a static and hierarchical view of the created order may not empower Korean-North American women to reject their traditional views of women as inferior to men. Anselm is primarily concerned with personal regeneration, and thus he focuses on the cross, lacking emphasis on Jesus' personhood or actions.

To propose a theology of the cross, which will promote the dignity and value of the first- and the second-generation Korean-North American immigrant women and their call to live in mutual and reciprocal relationships in the multicultural context, I will explore Moltmann's social trinitarian understanding of the cross in chapter 3. In so doing, I will present it as a resource for a feminist theology of the cross, and thus prepare them for the trinitarian praxis in their multicultural North American context. Before critiquing Moltmann's social trinitarian understanding of the cross, I will discuss how Luther's *theologia crucis* in his Heidelberg Disputation (1518) could become a contributing resource to a social trinitarian feminist approach to the theology of the cross. In so doing, I will take a close look at the doctrine of *communicatio idiomatum* through which Luther explains how it is possible to conceive of God in the godforsakenness of Christ and to ascribe suffering and death on the cross to the divine-human person of Christ.[7] Moltmann critiques Luther's use of the doctrine of *communicatio idiomatum* and his two-nature Christology. Moltmann employs the Cappadocian concept of *perichoresis* to explain how the suffering of Christ on the cross is the trinitarian event. According to the concept of *perichoresis*, the divine persons are all subjects in relation to each other. It signifies the mutual interpenetration and indwelling of the Father, Son, and Holy Spirit which arise from the three persons' eternal acts of self-donation.[8] By virtue of this doctrine of *perichoresis*, Moltmann offers a solution to the misconception of the cross as the symbol of cruel victimization of those who are weak.

---

7. *LW* 34, 98. See also Wells, "Theology of the Cross and the Theology of Liberation," 152.

8. McDougall, "Return of Trinitarian Praxis?" 186. See also Moltmann, *Spirit of Life*, 217–21.

Introduction

The triune God, as Moltmann affirms, is not a closed circle but an "open Trinity," yearning for fellowship with God's own creation.[9] Human beings as *imago Dei* are called to mirror the trinitarian fellowship through emulating the *perichoretic* love of the Trinity in their relationships with others. Therefore, in chapter 4, I offer the contribution of a social trinitarian theology of the cross toward a feminist Christian praxis for both the first- and the second-generation Korean-North American women. First, I present the trinitarian fellowship which culminates at the cross to guide them as *imago Dei* to mirror the *perichoretic* relationship of the Trinity in various relationships with others. However, because of the gap between the Trinity and sinful, finite human beings, the trinitarian cycle of perfect self-giving love in reciprocity cannot simply be copied in this world marred by evil and sin. Therefore, it is the suffering love of the triune God which Korean-North American women are to emulate in this deeply flawed world of sin. It is *imitatio crucis* and *imitatio relationis* that they should hold true not only for social knowledge but also for social practice. Nevertheless, *imitatio crucis* and *imitatio relationis* would be impossible without the work of the Holy Spirit through which they come to respond to the triune God. The cross, as the culmination of the self-giving love for the other, reveals the essence of trinitarian fellowship in mutuality, reciprocity, equality, and generosity. On this basis, I propose that both the first and the second generation Korean-North American women participate in building a society where they are free to realize their potential and to serve one another by using their various gifts in freedom and trust. The social trinitarian understanding of the cross calls them to an ecclesial reform in the leadership and structure of the church, and a new approach to mission and interreligious dialogue.

---

9. Moltmann, *Crucified God*, 255. Also see Moltmann, *God in Creation*, 242.

Abbreviations

CD   Barth, Karl. *Church Dogmatics*. Vols. I and IV. Translated by G. W. Bromiley. Edinburgh: T. & T. Clark, 1956.

LW   *Luther's Works*. American ed. 55 vols. St Louis: Concordia (vols. 1–30); Philadelphia: Fortress (vols. 31–55), 1955–86

ST   Thomas Aquinas. *Summa Theologiae*. 60 vols. Blackfriars ed. New York: McGraw Hill, 1964.

1

Theology Always Lives in Context

IN EXPLORING VARIOUS UNDERSTANDINGS of the cross to find one that properly addresses both the first and the second generation Korean-North American women, I will first look into their socio-political, religious, and cultural circumstances. In doing a contextual theology, it is necessary to respond creatively in every new situation and continually reinterpret the Christian message. Douglas Hall in his book, *Cross in our Context* emphasizes the importance of contextuality by stating, "Entering into the specificity of one's own time and place is *the conditio sine qua non* of real theological work."[1] Contextuality, according to him, conditions the manner in which the Christian message, centered on Christ and his work, is to be articulated and received. In this sense, the cultural and religious context of the first generation Korean-North American women need to be analyzed because Korean traditional religions have played an important role in their lifestyles, worldviews, and value systems. Whether they are aware or not, especially first generation Korean-North American women have been brought up with the nurture of Korean traditional religions in their spirituality and morality, and hold certain paradigms fostered by their traditional religions. They go through a paradigm shift and come to view and judge the world as they convert to Christianity and live in a new life situation.

This concept of a paradigm shift is a concept borrowed from a philosopher of science, Thomas Kuhn (1922–96). In his book, *The Structure of Scientific Revolution*, Kuhn speaks of paradigms as patterns of understanding shared by members of a scientific community. Many scientists may resist and oppose a new theory or a discovery that breaks through

1. Hall, *Cross in Our Context*, 47. See also Tillich, *On the Boundary*, 13–16.

the old paradigm and exposes its inadequacy because it does not fit the established paradigm.[2] However, eventually a widespread shift may occur. The new paradigm will also pass away from its commanding position when another paradigm takes its place through a new theory or discovery. According to Kuhn, new paradigms make scientists look at the world from different perspectives.[3]

If we adapt Kuhn's theory of a paradigm change to the religious situation of Korea in the end of the nineteenth century when Protestant Christianity was first introduced to Korean people, they needed a new paradigm of salvation to adapt to a situation in which they were emotionally and spiritually bankrupt on both a national and private level. At the time, they faced a socio-political crisis and found that the existing paradigms of traditional religions like Buddhism, Confucianism, and Shamanism were unable to accommodate the drastic changes occurring in modern society. The traditional religions lacked a historical consciousness and did not have a scientific approach to the rapidly changing world. When Korean people encountered Christianity, they accepted it in hope that it would meet their needs. Kyoung Jae Kim affirms that they found in Christianity the elements they needed and looked for:

> the personal faith in a Sovereign God, the faith in Christ who deals with sin and suffering, the faith in the Holy Spirit who supports the community of freedom, love, and justice, the eschatological faith in the kingdom of God, and the dynamic organization and activity of the Christian church. All these are dynamic elements making Christianity the sort of creative institutional organism that the other religions were not.[4]

Kyoung Jae Kim explains further how the early converts understood and accepted the new salvation paradigm of Christianity. For instance, in turbulent situations when they were attacked by foreign countries and finally colonized by Japan, the suffering Korean people accepted and depended on the absolute God as the Lord, the One who ruled the world with divine freedom, justice, and mercy. They also accepted and believed that evil would finally be judged. Kim also insists that "the eschatological faith in the Kingdom of God" which puts much emphasis on the transcendental other

---

2. Kuhn, *Structure of Scientific Revolution*, 151–52.
3. Ibid., 121.
4. Kim, *Christianity and the Encounter of Asian Religions*, 143.

world or heaven often caused believers to fall into the danger of escapism, escaping particularly from the present realty to "the futuristic next world."[5]

By employing Kuhn's theory of paradigm change to the religious situation of Korean people, we come to see how Christianity as a new religion brought about a paradigm change in their view of salvation, human history, and value systems. When they accepted Christianity, they did not receive it in a vacuum but with a particular culture-shaped understanding. In order to unpack further the fact that Korean women's spirituality has been culturally shaped we will now turn to Gadamer's phenomenological hermeneutics, focusing on his ideas of "historically influenced consciousness" and "fusion of horizons."[6] The argument in this chapter will proceed as follows: Since religion plays a major role in shaping culture, I will first look into how the pre-Christian traditional religions like Buddhism, Confucianism, and Shamanism were fused with one another to create a unique form of spirituality in the Korean mind. I will also investigate how the traditional religions as "prejudice" (used here in the same way Gadamer uses this term without pejorative implications) shaped the understanding of Christianity. Finally, I will discuss how their immigration life experiences in the multicultural context of North America influenced their understanding of the Cross.

Gadamer's Concept of "Fusion of Horizons"

People encounter new religions with particular cultural understandings. Before Christianity was introduced to Korea, Korea had been a religiously pluralistic society where traditional religions, Buddhism, Confucianism, and Shamanism thrived together. Even though there had been conflicts and tensions between them, the traditional religions influenced one another and formed a religious seedbed for Korean people. This phenomenon can be explained by Gadamer's fusion of horizons. Gadamer, following Heidegger, thinks of humanity as "the being-in-the-world," immersed in historical traditions.[7] The world for Heidegger and Gadamer is neither the cosmos as the natural environment nor objective reality in opposition to subjective self-consciousness. It is rather like a huge web of life in which human beings have their existence and find their meaning. Therefore, the

---

5. Ibid., 51–52.
6. Gadamer, *Truth and Method*, 277–309.
7. Palmer, *Hermeneutics*, 124–25.

world is a life-world for humanity. This life-world is where they draw their own experience and understanding.

According to Gadamer, human beings as "beings-in-the-world" are found and influenced by their historical reality.[8] They always find themselves within a particular situation. It means that they are not standing outside a situation and are, therefore, unable to have any objective knowledge of it. All self-knowledge, therefore, arises from what is historically pre-given and underlies all subjective intentions and actions. It both prescribes and limits every possibility for understanding any tradition.[9]

In this regard, Gadamer uses the unique term, "prejudice." For him, the term, "prejudice" is not an arbitrary or illogical judgment that people make to understand the objective world but rather a *vor-struktur* (fore-structure) of understanding or a condition of understanding which constitutes the historical reality of their being.[10] Understanding, according to Gadamer, does not begin from a neutral standpoint but unavoidably from some initial presupposition and expectation. Understanding, true or false, is prejudiced because the subject of history does not possess a pure consciousness but is affected by history. The reality of history (*Die Wirklichkeit der Geschichte*) is then the unity between history and an understanding of it, which Gadamer calls *Wirkungsgeschichte* (effective history).[11] This history, *Wirkungsgeschichte*, at both the personal and cultural level, affects the individual's understanding of the world. Gadamer calls this phenomenon *Wirkungsgeschichtliches Bewusstsein* (historically effected consciousness).[12] It means that it is impossible for people to totally remove themselves from their cultural, historical backgrounds. They understand different cultures, traditions, and beliefs on the basis of past experiences and prejudices.

Gadamer calls this historically determined situation of understanding a "horizon." It marks the limit of everything that can be seen from a particular point of view. However, it also implies that we can see beyond our immediate standpoint. Gadamer writes:

> Every finite present has its limitations. We define the concept of 'situation' by saying that it represents a standpoint that limits the possibility of vision. Hence an essential part of the concept of

8 Gadamer, *Truth and Method*, 276–77.
9. Ibid., 302.
10. Ibid., 265–71.
11. Ibid., 300–307.
12. Ibid., 301.

situation is the concept of the "horizon." The horizon is the range of vision that includes everything that can be seen from a particular vantage point. Applying this to the thinking mind, we speak of narrowness of horizon, of the possible expansion of horizon, of the opening up of new horizons, and so forth.[13]

According to Gadamer, then, human beings exist with a horizon (*horizont*), a historically-determined situation of understanding. By "horizon" Gadamer does not mean that we are sealed off from others because of our cultural, historical, and linguistic conditioning; rather we understand horizon as fluid and even open to new expansions. The horizon of understanding is neither static nor unchanging. It changes and is constantly in the process of formation. As it is constantly forming, the fore-structure (*vor-struktur*) of understanding is continually changing by merging into new horizons with new experiences and knowledge. Gadamer insists that this process of fusion is continually going on in traditions, because "there old and new are always combining into something of living value . . . "[14] In this ongoing process of fusion, neither old nor new remains unaffected: it never achieves any final completion or complete elucidation.

Another aspect of Gadamer's concept of fusion of horizons is that understanding is always linguistically mediated.[15] He remains faithful to Heidegger's idea that the truth of being, as disclosed in an act of understanding, is only possible in language, and language is finite and situated. Truth is, therefore, rooted in the historic-linguistic context in which it is uttered. For Gadamer, it is the linguistic community that determines the meaning of a text by virtue of holding itself open and listening to the tradition. Therefore, the fusion of horizons consists most concretely in a fusion of language. In this respect, translation is an extreme form of interpretation which offers a model of the process of the fusion of horizon where two alien languages are to be integrated.[16] Consequently, all understanding requires interpretive mediation and involves some form of translation.

Gadamer's concept of the fusion of horizons is significant for the argument of this thesis because it offers a useful hermeneutical structure from which I will demonstrate the fusion of pre-Christian religions and the enculturation of Christianity in Korea, including the process of translation

13. Ibid., 302.
14. Ibid., 306.
15. Ibid., 389.
16. Ibid., 386.

of the Scriptures. In the following section I will demonstrate how, over the centuries, Korean traditional religions like shamanism, Buddhism, and Confucianism have visibly fused together to create a syncretic religio-cultural horizon for the Korean people. Christianity also has been fusing with these older traditions to a certain degree to form a unique Korean Christian spirituality.

In light of this concept of Gadamer's fusion of horizons, we will raise and answer these questions in the first section of this chapter: How have the pre-Christian religions fused to form a unique spirituality of Korean people? In what ways have the pre-Christian religions functioned as "prejudice" for understanding Christianity?

Examples of the Religious Fusion of Traditional Religions, Buddhism, Confucianism, and Shamanism

In this section, I will demonstrate how Korean traditional religions have influenced one another in pre-Christian history and shaped Korean women's spirituality and perception of God. Although Korea has been a mono-racial, mono-lingual society, it has always been a religiously pluralistic society where traditional religions, Mahayana Buddhism, Confucianism, and Shamanism have thrived together.[17] They were fused or grafted with one another and created a unique form of spirituality in the Korean mind.

Buddhism was introduced through China to Korea in the fourth century and brought a paradigm shift in the ancient Korean mind. Kyoung Jae Kim insists that even though Buddhism brought a drastic change in their worldview and value system, within their religious mind there still lived the pre-Buddhist traditional religions like Shamanism and *Pungryudo*.[18] These

17. The newest religion, Catholicism, arrived at this fertile land of religions in the late eighteenth century and Protestantism a century later.

18. Kim, *Christianity and the Encounter of Asian Religions*, 105. Kim explains that *Pungryudo* was the henotheistic religion of the ancient Korean people believing in the heavenly God, the God of light and life, called *Hananim*. They never tried to make an icon of *Hananim*, and never propagated dualism. But in the development of village life, from hunting to agriculture (the high mountain belief), the transcendental *Hananim* belief changed into a more concrete, theophanic religion, a more inherent form. It was necessary to have spiritual beings in daily life to meet the requests for blessing of children, fertility of agriculture, healing sickness, long life, avenging the spirit of the dead, and so on. They needed the powers of spiritual beings that are accessible on earth, not in heaven, here in the village, not on the high mountain. To meet this demand, *Pungryudo* was fused with polydemonic Shamanism.

religions were fused or grafted with the new coming religion and created a unique form of Buddhism. Korean Buddhism never hesitated to fuse with the traditional religions of the land or other philosophies.[19]

Kyoung Jae Kim looks into the religious fusion of Buddhism with *Pungryudo* and Shamanism, a fusion which is observed in some distinctive practices and beliefs such as the Buddha Land belief, *Pal-gwan-hoe*, and *Sam-sung-gak*.[20] The first example of the religious fusion of Buddhism with *Pungryudo* is the Buddha Land belief. The high mountains of Korea became special places where Buddhas manifested themselves, and thus Buddhism was indigenized as a Korean religion, no longer a foreign religion imported from outside.[21] The second example of the religious fusion of Buddhism with Shamanism is shown in the rite called *Pal-gwan-hoe*. *Pal-gwan-hoe* was originally a Buddhist assembly where people made a special vow to keep away from eight sins during the time of confession. The eight vows were not to kill, not to steal, not to commit adultery, not to lie, not to drink, not to sit at the head table, not to put on perfume, not to enjoy songs and dance. However, the spirit behind *Pal-gwan-hoe* changed in the *Shilla* (57 BC–935 AD) and *Koryu* dynasties (918–1392 AD). The rite became a ceremony to worship the various spirits, like the spirits of the sky, mountains, rivers, and warriors. As the ascetic character of the Buddhist assembly almost disappeared, shamanistic ecstasy and polydemonic worship flourished. *Pal-gwan-hoe* eventually turned into a shamanistic rite seeking personal blessing.[22] The third example is demonstrated in the establishment of *Sam-sung-gak* within the temple compound. *Sam*(three)-*sung*(deities)-*gak*(house) is a shrine serving three deities. This is a typical fusion of Buddhism with Shamanism. The building structure of Korean

19. Ibid., 74.

20. Ibid.

21. Ibid., 79. Ui-sang was the one who proposed Buddha Land doctrine in the Buddhist history of Korea. Ui-sang in 661 AD well versed in Mahayana Buddhist texts went to T'ang (China) to study *Hua-yen* Buddhism, He studied for eight years under Master Chihyen (602–688 AD), who was the second Patriarch of Chinese *Hua-yen* and teacher of Fa-tsang (643–712 AD) who was the celebrated third Patriarch. The sky God belief of the *Pungryudo* regarded the high mountains as sacred because God descended on them. In *Hua-yen* Buddhism, O-Tai (five ledger) stands for east, west, north, south, and the middle. In each station its special Buddha is positioned. This five-position belief in *Hua-yen* thought is that the Ultimate Reality is everywhere. In Korea it was merged with similar belief of *Pungryudo*, and the Buddha Land faith developed in the *Shilla* (BC 57–935 AD) and *Koryu* (918–1392 AD)

22. Ibid., 83.

Buddhist temples is composed of the main *dharma* hall called the *Dae-ung-jeon* dedicated to Sakyamuni, *Myung-bu-jeon* for funeral rituals, and the *Sam-sung-gak* for prayers of blessing for the present life. Interestingly, the deities depicted in wall paintings in the *Sam-sung-gak* originally had nothing to do with Buddhism. They were deities of Shamanism among others such as *Chil-sung, Sam-shin,* and *Dok-sung*.[23]

We have observed that by fusing with the traditional religions Buddhism has become an indigenous religion in Korea. However, by turning into a personal blessing-seeking religion, according to Kyoung Jae Kim, Korean Buddhism in the end of *Koryu* dynasty (918-1392 AD) lost its creative power to address societal problems. The Korean people were prepared to accept another religious paradigm, which was Neo-Confucianism. The *Cho-sun* dynasty (or *Yi* dynasty, 1392-1910 AD) adopted Neo-Confucianism as the socio-political ideology and oppressed Buddhism. The result was that Korean Buddhism further developed into and remained in the form of a personal blessing-seeking religion through its fusion with Shamanism and embattlement with the Neo-Confucian opposition.

Confucianism had been influencing the life and value systems of the Korean people for a long time, even before the official introduction of Buddhism in the fourth century. Classical Confucianism as a practical moral philosophy emphasized moral principles and the proper order of social relations in human life. It was basically a way of self-discipline emphasizing loyalty, filial piety, benevolence, righteousness, propriety, wisdom, and sincerity. It served Korean people as the ruling ideology of the nation, particularly for the edification of law systems, government structures, social

---

[23] Ryu, *The History and Structure of Korean Shamanism*, 271. According to Tong-Shik Ryu, the *Chilsung* deity is a fusion of ancient *Hananim* belief, *Toksung* deity is a transformation of Hwan-Woong, and The *Sam-shin* deity is a form of Tankun. Tankun is the founder of the ancient Cho-sun, the first kingdom of Korea. According to the Tankun myth, he is born of Hwan-Woong, a god and a woman who used to be a bear. Hwan-Woong always had a heart for humanity so his father Hwan-In sent him to the top of Tae-Baek Mountain and began to rule with a god of rain, a god of wind, and a god of cloud in the over 360 matters including harvest, life, sickness, judgment, good and evil, etc. At the time, there were a tiger and a bear who always wanted to turn to a woman, so they prayed. They were given a condition to turn into a woman, which was, to stay in darkness, eating twenty cloves of garlic and a bunch of wormwood only. The tiger failed but the bear persevered and finally turned into a woman after twenty-one days. She wanted to have a child, so she prayed. Hwan-Woong saw her and turned into a man and made her bear a son, whom she named Tankun. Tankun established a kingdom called Ko-Cho-sun (meaning Ancient Cho-sun) and ruled as the first king in 2333 BC for 1500 years and died at the age of 1,908, and he became a mountain god.

norms, and the training of the government elite even before Buddhism was introduced in Korea.

If Confucianism was only a moral philosophy and not a religion, why did it become such a great obstacle against Christianity when it was first introduced to Korea in the eighteenth century? According to Kyoung Jae Kim, in Neo-Confucianism, which was the political ideology in the Yi dynasty, there is no room for rationalizing a belief in deities or the spirits of ancestors.[24] However, ancestor worship (*je-sa*) was practiced among Koreans under Neo-Confucianism. Ancestor worshippers strongly believed that the spirits actually returned to the altar to eat the food laid out for them on their memorial days. The rite of ancestor memorial was only possible because of the shamanistic belief that the departed continued living in the nether world. Kyoung Jae Kim explains clearly why ancestor worship (*je-sa*) has been a great obstacle for Korean people to accept Christianity in this way:

> Ancestor worship was not just a religious rite for Korean society . . . It was the absolute symbol of the Confucian controlling ideology. In other words, the abolition of ancestor worship meant the destruction of the conservative feudalistic social structure from its roots. Ancestor worship was the worship of the spirits of the ancestors, showing gratitude for their continual oversight over the affairs of their descendants. This belief was the indigenous way of life in fusion with the shamanistic beliefs. From the religious angle of Confucianism, ancestor worship certainly had some aspects of superstition.[25]

Thus, ancestor worship (*je-sa*) can be seen as a fusion between the horizons of the shamanistic belief in the immortality of spirits and the Confucian philosophy of gratitude toward ancestors. As we have seen in the case of ancestor worship, some kind of religious fusion also has taken place among dominant religions both consciously and unconsciously. Religious fusion occurred even though they have replaced one another due to socio-political changes. In the following section, I will discuss how these traditional religions served as "prejudice" or fore-structure of understanding as Korean women accepted a new religion, Christianity.

---

24. Kim, *Christianity and the Encounter of Asian Religions*, 144.

25 Ibid., 144. For the ancestor worship, the descendants gather usually at the oldest son's home and prepare the table with certain choicest food for the spirits of ancestors on every memorial date, new year's day, full moon day, and etc.

The Liberative Cross

Traditional Religions Served as "Prejudice" or Fore-structure of Understanding Christianity

The Korean general public by the end of the nineteenth century was ready to accept Christianity. The Protestant missionaries were well accepted especially by the grassroots, the lower class people, and children.[26] From the socio-political perspective, the Christian gospel served as a liberating gospel for those who were shackled under the feudalistic Confucian ruling ideology in the latter part of the nineteenth century. Kyoung Jae Kim insists that Christian teachings, which promote human rights by abolishing class barriers and extending women's human rights, helped Korean women to accept Christianity as a gospel liberating them from oppression.[27]

Christianity was also easily understood by Koreans because of the fertility of the religious soil in Korea. All the traditional religions served as foundations for their hermeneutical pre-understanding. When Christianity was introduced, biblical words had to be translated into the Korean language. According to Gadamer's concept of linguistics, understanding is achieved through the medium of language, and understanding means interpretation, and interpretation is a process of the fusion of horizons.[28] In the process of translating the Bible, missionaries and Korean Christians had to borrow certain words which had been born and used by the previous religions to translate biblical words like the Holy Spirit, salvation, redemption, repentance, rebirth, heaven, mind, power, and so on. It was a challenging but doable task because these words had been already used in religious context. Kyoung Jae Kim affirms that when the words were used in the new

---

26. The Protestant missionaries came to Korea about a century later than the Catholic missionaries. Already in the end of eighteenth century, there were Catholic believers and they rejected ancestor worship. This kind of action was condemned by their families and society as serious violations against the filial piety. Severe persecution broke in 1785, 1791, 1801, 1839, 1846 and 1866, which led to the death of about 10,000 martyrs. Among those who died martyrs were a considerable number of outstanding lay leaders. Also, the loss of one Chinese and twelve French missionaries from the Paris Foreign Missions Society was a big blow to the Church. Out of them 103 martyrs were canonized on May 6th, 1984 at Yoido, Seoul, by the Pope John Paul II. For more information about the martyrdom in the Catholic Church in Korea, see Finch, "The Pursuit of Martyrdom in the Catholic Church in Korea before 1866," 95–118.

27. Kim, *Christianity and the Encounter of Asian Religions*, 117.

28. Gadamer, *Truth and Method*, 389.

Christian context, a new dimension and reality were given to these words and concepts.[29]

It is noteworthy that the translation of the biblical God as *Hananim* demonstrates the case very clearly. John Ross, the first missionary who translated the Bible into Korean stated the case for his translation in this way: "The *Hananim* is so distinctive and so universally used that there will be no fear in the future translation and preaching."[30] The concept of *Hananim*, which had its origin in Korean culture, was prominent in the success of communicating the Christian concept of God.[31] Etymologically, *Hana* means high and big. *Nim* is the suffix attached to the name or the title of a person to show respect. Therefore, *Hananim* means to Koreans the highest God. H. B. Hulbert distinguishes the *Hananmim*-faith from Shamanistic faith in this way: "*Hananim* is entirely separated from and outside the circle of various spirits and demons that manifest all nature. *Hananim* has never been worshipped by the use of any idolatrous rites . . . As a rule, the people do not worship *Hananim*. He is appealed to by the Emperor only."[32]

Hananim also means the one and only God. This concept did not signify the triune God, but Koreans easily identified *Hananim* with the unique God of the Old Testament.[33] *Hananim*, as God beyond the heaven of the natural world, was God who punished the evil and rewarded the good. The emperor on behalf of his people interceded to *Hananim* to liberate them from troubles and sufferings. Because of this concept of *Hananim*, they could easily understand the Old Testament God.

The word *Hananim*, as I demonstrated above, became a point of contact in understanding the Christian God. This word, however, did not explain fully the Christian God, as it lacked the concept of Trinity and the Mediator Christ. Thus, Bible study and catechesis was required along with

---

29. Kim, *Christianity and the Encounter of Asian Religions*, 119.

30. Ross, *History of Corea*, 356. See also Y. Kim, "Christianity and Korean Culture," 142.

31. Y. Kim, "Christianity and Korean Culture," 142.

32. Hulbert, *The Passing of Korea*, 404–5. H. B. Hulbert (1863–1949) as a Methodist was one of the first American missionaries to Korea. He wrote a few books such as *The Passing of Korea*, *The History of Korea*, and *Korean and Dravidian*. He was buried in Yang-hwa-jin, Korea where his one year old son had been buried.

33. There was a debate whether to adapt *Hananim* or *Haneu(l)nim*, because *Haneul* signifies the heavenly abode. They eventually chose *Hananim* over *Haneu(l)nim*. However, the Catholic Church still uses *Haneu(l)nim* because it is the literal translation of *Chun-ju*, which is the Chinese term for the Lord of Heaven.

translation in order to transform the indigenous god into the Christian God in the minds and hearts of new believers. Initially, Koreans had inherited a vague *Hananim* into their culture. Through scriptural study, Koreans eventually came to have a vivid understanding of *Hananim* and the Cross of Christ through which God showed God's suffering love for God's creation.

Christianity and Syncretism

We have observed above that in Korea, over the centuries, the horizons of Shamanism, Buddhism, and Confucianism have visibly fused together to create the syncretic religio-cultural horizon of the Korean people. Such fusions took place often through competition, conflict, and persecution among them, and we have identified this phenomenon as Gadamer's "the fusion of horizons." This process of borrowing and blending between religions is also called syncretism. The majority of Korean Protestant Christian believers unconsciously carry with them certain syncretic elements in their Christian teachings and living. Nevertheless, as Harold Wells observed during his extended study tour in Korea in 1997, they are quite unwilling to acknowledge any truth or wisdom to be found in the traditional religions they renounced at the moment of conversion.[34] He rightly points out that it may be out of their ardent declaration of Christian faith which causes them to keep the exclusivist tendency; however, such tendency has often caused non-Christian Korean people to consider Christianity as a foreign religion in conflict with traditional culture and also misunderstand it as a religion of arrogance and domination.[35] This situation raises the question: "To what degree should we, Korean Christian believers, be open to a possible fusion of horizons?"

Traditional religions like Buddhism, Confucianism, and Shamanism are very different from Christianity in terms of their views of life and understanding of salvation. The polytheism of Shamanism and a belief in some kind of life in the nether world after death in the practice of ancestor worship are very different from the teachings of Christianity about the Triune God, eternal life, and human redemption through the death and the resurrection of Jesus Christ. Furthermore, the Christian eschatological

---

34. Wells, "Korea Syncretism and Theologies of Interreligious Encounter," 60. Wells in this article writes that he made this observation during his study tour in Korea shortly before he wrote the article which was published in 1998.

35. Kim, *Christianity and Encounter of Asian Religions*, 125–26.

understanding of history is not compatible with the eternal cycle of Buddhism. The heteronomy-based soteriology of Christianity stands in tension with the autonomy-based salvation of Buddhism. Therefore, we cannot help but ask, "To what degree and nature is this fusion of horizons possible between Christianity and Buddhism, and Christianity and other traditional religions?"

A fusion of horizons between Christianity and other traditional religions has happened to a degree. It is proven by the fact that some elements of other traditional religions are easily detected in Korean Christianity. Moffat, an American missionary and church historian who dedicated his lifelong career to mission in Korea observed how Christianity had adjusted to traditional religions and culture without losing its peculiarity: "Korean Protestants taught social justice, respected science and learning as high value like Confucianism, sought for purity and promised the next life like Buddhism. They also taught that prayer will be answered and miracles will happen like shamanistic religion."[36]

Historically speaking, Korea, located in between the two super powers of China and Japan, suffered from frequent invasions, causing poverty and disease. For this reason, their hopes were naturally aimed toward prosperity, health, and long life. Consequently, the blessing-oriented shamanistic faith functioned as a "prejudice" or a fore-structure of understanding God when they accepted Christianity. Material blessings and physical healing have been major topics of the sermons preached by Korean pastors. For instance, Dr. Yong-gi Cho, who planted and established the Yoido Full Gospel Church as the largest church in the world, preached the "three-beat blessing" based on 3 John 2: "Dear friend, I pray that you may enjoy good health and all may go well with you, even as your soul is getting along well."[37] The message which promised salvation of the soul, physical health, and material blessing was very well received by people. It was powerful enough to bring about a paradigm change in their outlook and attitude toward life, from fatalism to proactive living.

Often we find shamanistic elements disguised as Christianity among Korean believers, elements such as fortune telling and the healing of diseases by exorcism. Because they have culturally experienced spirits and

---

36. Moffat, *The Christians of Korea*, 52.

37. Dr. Yong-gi Cho with the emphasis on God's blessing for Christian believers established the Yoido Full Gospel Church in 1958 and it reached to the membership of one million by 2007.

physical healing through exorcism, the supernatural miracles of healings and spiritual experiences of Christianity were easily accepted. Under the influence of Western enlightenment scientism, Rudolph Bultmann, in his project of demythologization for existential hermeneutics, proposed a view acceptable to modern Western people.[38] He considered miracles not as actual occurrences but as mythological expressions, a view considered acceptable by many modern Western people. However, for Korean people, the miracle stories were perceived as signs pointing to the all-powerful God who worked through the name of Jesus.

However, while claiming that the general tendency and nature of Korean Christianity is to be a private religion, I do not deny the historical fact that Christianity played an important role in national enlightenment and modernization. Among those who accepted the Christian message were the Christian pioneers who acknowledged their social responsibility and proactively participated in rebuilding the country in the areas of education, medicine, politics, economics, visual arts, architecture, music, and so on.

With regard to the question of to what degree Korean Protestant believers should allow the fusion of horizons with other traditional religions, we need to identify the fundamentalist, progressive, and liberal camps among the early Korean Protestant theologians who had great impact on the Protestant churches in Korea. First of all, Korean Christianity has been largely influenced by fundamentalism whose primary spokesperson was Hyung-Nong Park.[39] As a promoter of the reformed traditional theology of John Calvin, Park's theological position is grounded in his conviction of the total depravity of human beings, the absolute sovereignty of grace, the irresistible changing power of the Holy Spirit, and the dichotomy of nature and super-nature. He did not accept traditional religions as a stepping stone to the Christian gospel. Instead, he considered them as idol worship and

---

38. Bultmann, *Interpreting Faith for the Modern Era*.

39. Hyung-Nong Park (1897–1978). His name sounds more like Hyoung-lyong Park. Hyung-Nong Park was born in Pyungbuk province of Korea. He inherited a puritanical pietism at Soongshil University, from which he graduated in 1926. He then went to Kumrung College, Nanking, China, and continued at Princeton Theological Seminary where he majored in dogmatic theology. Afterwards, he went on to graduate study at Louisville Seminary where he gained a degree. Upon his return to Korea, he taught at Pyung Yang Seminary. His one of the best known publications is *Dogmatic Theology* (1964). He is known as the key leader of Christian conservatism and promoter of Calvinism in Korea.

heretical non-truth to be conquered by the gospel. Consequently, he treated the traditional religions as nothing but weeds and thistles to be pulled out.[40]

Park's view of the traditional religions to be conquered by the Christian gospel has been the most influential among the Korean Presbyterian churches which comprise the majority of conservative Protestant Christianity. This exclusivist approach never acknowledges that the Scriptures are the products of an encounter between the self-revelation of God who brings salvation and the responding human situation. Thus, it does not accept the hermeneutical circle of understanding operated in Gadamer's fusion of horizons. Due to this exclusivist tendency of a major part of the Korean Protestant Church toward other religions, Christianity is often regarded as a foreign religion in conflict with the traditional culture.[41] In addition, the conservative Korean Protestant Christian believers are intolerant of other theological positions, insisting that only their theological position is biblically based and sound.[42]

In the opposite end of the spectrum, we find some Korean theologians who call themselves pluralists. They view the pre-Christian religions as more or less equivalent paths to truth and salvation. Consequently, they are very open to syncretistic borrowing. For example, Hyun Kyung Chung, a Korean feminist theologian and Nam Dong Suh, a *Minjung* theologian see nothing but good in the mixing of insights and wisdom from the Asian religious heritage.[43] Hyun Kyung Chung depicts Jesus as a shaman who releases *han*[44] from Korean women.[45] Nam Dong Suh in his *Minjung* theology

---

40. Park, *A Review of Modern Theological Problems*, 300. See also Kim, *Christianity and the Encounter of Asian Religions*, 121–24.

41. Kim, *Christianity and the Encounter of Asian Religions*, 125–26

42. Karl Barth was rejected from Park's circle of theology as "new theology," because his Christology differs from that of Calvin in his understanding of predestination.

43. Chung, *Struggle to Be the Sun Again*. See also Suh, *A Theology of the Changing Era*.

44. *Han* is caused when one's goals are blocked and intensified for an extended period of time by external oppression and the feeling of abandonment and helplessness. *Han* produces sadness, resentment, aggression, helplessness. C. S. Song, a Taiwanese theologian pointed out, an experience of *han* is particularly evident where domination-subordination has persisted for centuries. See Park, *The Wounded Heart of God*, 71.

45. In Hyun Kyung Chung's depiction of Jesus as a shaman who releases Korean women's *han*, I find two problems. First, she takes the Scriptures as reference only while she takes the women's life situations as text. For Korean Christian women, the Scriptures play an important role as the authoritative resource for spiritual power to overcome life problem and as their guidance for moral life. Secondly, it will not necessarily be helpful for younger Korean-North American women as they are no longer exposed or aspire to Shamanism.

(a theology of and for the oppressed) contends that the particular events of salvation in the past, including the exodus and the life and cross of Jesus, should be seen simply as a reference for interpreting the events of today. Suh believes that the living God is not confined to the tradition of the past or the scriptures, but God is found in the suffering *minjung*,[46] in their soul and body. Whatever actually liberated people from oppression and injustice, whether it is from Christianity or other religions or from secular activity, he viewed it as a work of the Spirit and part of the *missio Dei* in which we are called to participate. Suh, therefore, favors a "confluence" of the great Korean religious traditions.[47]

With regard to Suh's Pneumatology and Christology, Harold Wells points out a few problems.[48] He correctly argues that Suh emphasizes a universal, liberative work of the Spirit; however, Suh's idea of the Spirit is clearly not the Spirit of Christ, and therefore, not Trinitarian in character. Suh also sees the cross and resurrection of Jesus Christ as a reference only. Kyoung Jae Kim also correctly criticizes Suh's Christology as he states: "The story of Jesus is not just an example of another *minjung*'s story, but it is a story that has the power to save. The converging model does not fully appreciate the ultimacy of the cross and resurrection event of Jesus Christ, and its unique power in transforming the old into the new." [49]

In the middle of these two extremes is Chai-Choon Kim (1901-1987),[50] the founder of Chosun theological seminary (1939) which devel-

---

46. *Minjung* means for Koreans those who are oppressed politically, exploited economically, marginalized sociologically, and despised culturally.

47. Suh, "Historical References for a Theology of Minjung," 155–82. See also Suh, *A Theology of the Changing Era*. Also K. J. Kim discusses this matter in his book, *Christianity and the Encounter of Asian Religions*, 133.

48. Wells, "Korea Syncretism and Theologies of Interreligious Encounter," 67.

49. Kim, *Christianity and the Encounter of Asian Religions*, 135.

50. Chai-Choon Kim (1901–1987) was born in North Ham-Kyung Province, Korea. He represents the progressive reformed theology of the Protestant Church. Like Hyung-Nong Park, he also studied the Reformed theology of Calvin in the United States of America. However, they are different from each other in their theological positions, and created two major camps of theology in Korea. Kim, Chai-Choon finished theological studies at Chung-San theological Seminary in Tokyo (1928), then went on to Princeton Seminary (1929). At Chung San school, he was influenced by the liberal atmosphere and the neo-orthodox theology of Karl Barth and Emil Brunner. While he was at Princeton, he encountered the fundamentalist conservative theologians; yet, he felt that he was unable to agree with the current theology there, so he went to Western Seminary. There he majored the Old Testament studies (1929–1932) and took a master's degree. Then he returned home to devote himself to theological education in Korea (1939–1970).

oped into today's Hanshin University. Chai-Choon Kim, a contemporary with Hyung-Nong Park, accepted the neo-orthodox theology of Karl Barth and Richard Niebuhr's "Transforming Christ"[51] as the model of his incarnation theology and culture transformation theology. Chai-Choon Kim stated his views on the history and culture as follows:

> As for history, Christianity is putting the redemptive history of God's kingdom into history so that human history is transformed into God's kingdom . . . We have received God's commission to transform Korean history into God's kingdom . . . Therefore, we should endeavor to make the Christian spirit to be the transforming soul in the fields of politics, economics, education, and culture of Korea.[52]

Chai-Choon Kim's theory of the kingdom of God emphasizes that history is the work of God alone, yet is to be carried out by humankind. The kingdom of God, in his view, is transcendental yet immanent; it is a present and yet a futuristic life reality. It is the rule of God. Kyoung Jae Kim names this view of the kingdom of God "a paradoxical synergism."[53]

Chai-Choon Kim evaluates the traditional religions of Korea, like Buddhism and Confucianism, as a piece of God's word worked out by the Holy Spirit, though incomplete and dim. He stated as follows:

> Not mentioning Shamanism, the Koreans have had some religions such as Confucianism and Buddhism for nearly 1500 years. For good or bad, these religions have formed Korean minds and established the norm in Korean society. However, the first missionaries to Korea regarded the Korean mind and the culture as vacant. Whatever was there, they thought it not worthy of consideration but of destruction . . . We do not regard other religions as products of demons, but as piece of God's word being worked out by the

---

He received an honorary doctorate from Union College, British Columbia, in Canada (1958), which is called today The Vancouver School of Theology, in recognition of his contribution toward theological education in Korea. See Hwang, *The Life and Theology of Chang-gong, Kim Chai Choon.* See also Kim, *Christianity and the Encounter of Asian Religions*, 128.

51. H. Richard Niebuhr (1894–1962) presents in his book, *Christ and Culture*, five paradigms for understanding the variations among Christians and their responses to culture. Five paradigms are "Christ against Culture," "Christ of Culture," "Christ above Culture," "Christ and Culture in Paradox," and "Christ Transforming Culture."

52. Kim, *Christianity and the Encounter of Asian Religions*, 129, quoting *The Collected Work of Kim Chai Choon*, 4:303–4.

53. Ibid.

Holy Spirit. It is dim and not complete as if one sees it in a moonless night but now it can be made clear and complete in Christ.[54]

Chai-Choon Kim's view of religions as a "piece of God's word" here seems to reflect Barth's position in his discussion of "other lights" in his fourth volume on reconciliation in *Church Dogmatics*. In this section on reconciliation, Barth raises the possibility of there being "other lights." He distinguishes "lights and words" from the self-declaration of God in the prophecy of Jesus Christ[55] but includes them in God's self-revelation.[56] In this later writing, Barth seems to show a more positive attitude toward natural knowledge of God. However, he distinguishes between the validity of natural revelation, which he considers possible, and the natural theology of fallen man, which he will not allow.[57] Barth asserts that God has in fact always declared and revealed Godself to the Gentiles from the creation of the world.[58] In his discussion of "other lights," Barth indicates that there is much in other religions which is both true and edifying, not only for the adherents of the particular religions but also for Christians.[59]

54. *The Collected Work of Kim Chai Choon*, 7:341–42.
55. Barth, *CD* IV/3:152.
56. Ibid., 127, 134, 143.
57. Bromiley, *Karl Barth in Creative Minds in Contemporary Theology*, 40.
58. Barth, *CD* IV/3:127–28.
59. Barth, *CD* I/2:299–303. See also Scott, *Karl Barth's Theology of Mission*, 16. Barth in his early writings affirms and negates the human being's ability to know God. He contends that the truth that only God makes God known is a truth that humans are able to know; but they can know it only if God reveals it to them. Because revelation tells us clearly that only God can reveal it to them and save humanity and that God has done this only in Jesus Christ, religion must be seen as the human being's attempt to do what only God-in-Christ can do and has done. Therefore, Barth declares a verdict on all religions: "Religion is unbelief." Having announced the verdict, Barth draws his practical conclusions concerning the relationship between the gospel and other religions. According to him, in no way may theologians or missionaries seek relationship between Christian revelation and the religions; in no way may they look for questions in the religions from which revelation supplies the answers; in no way may they see "points of contact." The relationship between the Christian message and the religions is an "either-or." Barth's intense response, "Nein" to Brunner's possibility of "points of contact," however, needs to be understood in the context of the German Confessing Church in its struggle against the German Christians who "affirmed the German nationhood; its history and its contemporary political situation as a second source of revelation." Cf. Barth, *The German Church Conflict*, 16. Therefore, it was Barth's strong refusal to the ideology of the German Christians during the Third Reich, and a warning that they were repeatedly inclined to control and manipulate the knowledge of God that went under the name of general revelation. See also Almond, "Karl Barth and Anthropocentric Theology," 435–47. Almond

Theology Always Lives in Context

Unlike Hyung-Nong Park who regards religions like Buddhism and Confucianism as "weed" to be pulled out as the product of demons or the creation of humankind, Chai-Choon Kim acknowledges that they are "a piece of God's word being worked out by the Holy Spirit." A great contribution which has been made by Chai-Choon's tolerant "fulfillment theory" is that it enables the relationship between the gospel revealed in Christ and the traditional religious culture of Korea. However, According to Kyoung Jae Kim, Chai-Choon Kim by his "fulfillment theory" maintains the Christian gospel as the active, powerful, transforming subject and the traditional culture as the passive object to be transformed. Thus, he does not leave room for mutual influence between the Christian gospel and traditional culture.[60]

Another influential theologian to consider is Tong-Shik Ryu,[61] a Methodist theologian who is a generation younger than those mentioned above, is known as a pioneer of indigenized Christianity in Korea. Ryu, following the principle of hermeneutical circulation, enables both the Christian gospel and traditional culture to come together as subjects by his grafting model.[62] He compares the traditional culture to the trunk and the gospel to the scion, presupposing mutual interdependence and mutual contribution between them. As the scion is grafted into the trunk to become one organic branch, so a successful indigenization of the gospel is incarnated into the culture and becomes an inseparable entity. Ryu makes the following remark that the hermeneutical circulation of the gospel and culture has to be made continually in a different cultural context:

---

observes that in his later years Barth would do more justice to Brunner than was possible in 1934 when the question of natural theology was inextricably tied to the threat of Nazism.

60. Kim, *Christianity and the Encounter of Asian Religions*, 131.

61. Tong-Shik Ryu (1922–) is the representative mission theologian who has delved into the question of indigenization in the Korean Church. He was born in Hwang Hae Province in 1922. He graduated from the Methodist Seminary in Seoul and graduated from the Divinity School of Boston University with a master's degree in New Testament Studies. Then he joined the Ecumenical Institute in Geneva, where he was introduced to both world mission and the lay movement. He translated Kraemer's *Lay Theology* into Korean (1963). He received a doctorate at Tokyo University by submitting a dissertation entitled *The History and Structure of Korean Shamanism* (1975). He has taught at the Methodist Seminary and Yonsei University in Seoul. Some of his representative works are his *Korean Religions and Christianity* (1965), *The History and Structure of Korean Shamanism* (1975), and *Pungryudo and Korean Theology* (1988).

62. Kim, *Christianity and the Encounter of Asian Religions*, 136.

> If the gospel in the scriptures is the word of God grasped in Judean culture, then Western theology is the understanding of the gospel through Graeco-Roman culture. Though the word of God is transcendental by itself, it has to be incarnated in order to work out salvation . . . Therefore, though the gospel should be illuminated as the universal truth in the light of eternity, it needs a subjective cultural eye to capture it in order to make it a real and living truth. The subjective eye can be formed within concrete culture and history; therefore, each nation receiving the gospel has to have its own theology . . . The Jews had their own eye to see the word of God, so did the Westerners. Likewise we Koreans have ours. The eye here refers to its national spirit . . . Theology serves the mission of the church. So theology has to be subjective and from that standpoint it can begin a dialogue with the gospel. In other words, it translates the gospel from the point of national spirit.[63]

In light of this thought, Ryu contends that just as Hellenized Christians used the Greek concept of *logos* to understand Jesus, Asians, nurtured in the soil of *Tao-te-ching*, can understand Jesus in terms of *Tao*.[64] For the Hellenized Christians, the concept of *logos* offered a horizon for understanding the gospel. When they accepted the gospel standing on their horizon, their lives were changed and the concept of *logos* acquired another meaning. Ryu points out that far from the traditional sense of the word, now *logos* meant Jesus. Likewise, Ryu contends, the *Tao* concept which underlies the oriental thought can be appropriated as a foundation for understanding of the Scriptures.[65]

Ryu, however, does not suggest that Israel should be replaced by Asian religions nor does he propose that the Old Testament be replaced with Buddhist or Confucian Scriptures. In this respect he is very different from the pluralistic Chinese theologians like Po Ch'en Kuang, Hsieh Fu Ya, and Hu Tsan Yun whom Kwak Pui Lan, a Chinese American feminist theologian, mentions in her book, *Discovering the Bible in the Non-Biblical World*.[66] From a pluralistic perspective, these Chinese theologians argue

---

63. Ryu, *Tao and Logos*, 39–40.

64. Ibid., 26–27. *Tao* means the "way." The word is often used in the sense of "the path of life" or "the way of nature and its power." See Lao Tzu, *Tao Te Ching*.

65. Ryu had already used the term, "horizon" twice in his article, "Tao and Logos" which he had written in 1959 a year before Gadamer's *Truth and Method* was published.

66. Kwak, Pui-lan, a Chinese-American feminist, argues for the open canon in her book, *Discovering the Bible in the Non-Biblical World*, 10. She supports her position by citing Chinese theologians such as Bo Chenguang, Xie Fuya and Hu Zanyun who argued

that since the Bible contains the important classics of the Jewish people which preceded Jesus, they should include their own Chinese classics in Chinese Bible. They suggest that the Chinese Bible should include parts of the Hebrew Scriptures, the New Testament, Confucian classics, and even Taoist and Buddhist texts.

Ryu is different from these pluralistic Chinese theologians mentioned above in the sense that he simply acknowledges the value of Korean spiritual heritage in relation to the gospel. The approach of Ryu's inculturation or incarnation allows the hermeneutical circle, which means that the gospel transforms the culture while at the same time the understanding of the gospel is transformed through an encounter with the other religious cultures.[67]

Yet, we need to answer this question which remains unsolved: whether the particular salvation experiences of Christianity and other traditional religions can come together for a fusion of horizons. Kyung Jae Kim, reflecting on Ryu's grafting metaphor, points out that grafting is possible only with similar species. He states: "Genetically, it is possible to graft an apple with a pear; but it is not possible to graft it with a chestnut . . . ."[68] What is implied here is that there are limits to what can be grafted if religious traditions are to avoid the loss of their unique identity and message. Consequently, wholesale syncretic efforts to reach homogeneity through simplistic synthesis should never be encouraged. With this regard, Harold Wells sternly suggests:

---

that many Chinese classics such as the *Analectis* of Confucius, the Mencius, and the Book of Songs are comparable to the books of the prophets, the Psalms, and the Book of Deuteronomy in the Hebrew Scriptures. Since the Bible contains the important classics of the Jewish people that preceded Jesus, he could see no reason why Chinese Christians should not include their own classics as Scripture. They suggested that the Chinese Bible should include parts of the Hebrew Scriptures, the New Testament, Confucian classics, and even Taoist and Buddhist texts. See Bo Chenguang, "Zhongguo de jiuyue," (Chinese Old Testament), 240–44, See also Xie Fuya, "Guanhu zhnghua Jidujiao shengjing de bianding wenti" (On the issues of editing the Chinese Christian Bible), 9–40; and Hu Zanyun, "Liangbu kiuyu" (Two Old Testaments), 67–71.

67. For a discussion of inculturation and incarnation, see Arbuckle, *Earthing the Gospel: An Inculturation Handbook for the Pastoral Worker,* 22. See *Christianity and the Encounter of Asian Religions,* 141. See also Wells, "Korean Syncretism and Theologies of Interreligious Encounter,"68.

68. Kim, *Christianity and the Encounter of Asian Religions,* 141. Ryu also does not believe that salvation experiences of Buddhism, Confucianism and Christianity can come together naturally for a fusion of horizons. Thus, he limits grafting at the level of life producing realities in the justice, freedom, love, power, health, and so on instead of the level of doctrines. See Tong-Shik Ryu, *Tao and Logos,* 14.

> For Christians, progress toward a positive and tenable syncretism will need to be based, first, in a very clear christological position . . . If Christian faith is to remain recognizably Christian and hold fast to its 'good news', any syncretism must be a Christ-centered syncretism. That is, Jesus Christ, crucified and risen, will remain its governing center and criterion of truth. Much can be borrowed and blended . . . there are limits to what can be 'grafted', or shed, if any religious tradition is to avoid loss of identity and of its unique message.[69]

Wells here rightly contends that any syncretism must be a Christ-centered syncretism. However, the term syncretism has caused much confusion because of its frequent use in a pejorative sense. It is often used with a negative connotation that when religions encounter each other, one particular religion loses its creative elements and is merged with another in a process of mutual influence, of borrowing and blending. Many Christians are concerned about this kind of reduction or dilution of the content of Christian faith. For this reason, I argue that instead of the term syncretism, which has often caused confusion, Gadamer's category of the fusion of horizons should be used to explain how Christianity has been incarnated in different cultures. Perceiving syncretism in a pejorative sense, Kyoung Jae Kim chooses to use the term "fusion of horizons" instead of syncretism. He states:

> Fusion of horizons between religions makes each religion hold to its own characteristics. It is like making harmony in an orchestra, each instrument producing its own sound . . . the fusion of horizons in the encounter of different religions means a creative enlargement of one's experience. But it is not always a peaceful fusion of horizons of major leading religions that took place.[70]

In a similar sense to this understanding of the fusion of horizons, Carl Starkloff proposes the phrase "the syncretic process." He defines it as "a dynamic built into human nature and a process of all human social and religious interaction."[71] Starkloff acknowledges it as "connatural with, not the heritage of sin, but of a laudable desire of humans for unity within diversity."[72] Therefore, he argues that Christianity from the beginning has always been incarnated in different cultures, and that these cultures

---

69. Wells, "Korean Syncretism and Theologies of Interreligious Encounter," 73.
70. Kim, *Christianity and the Encounter of Asian Religions*, 107.
71. Starkloff, *Theology of the in–between*, 11.
72. Ibid., 11.

invariably have religious dimensions which interact with the gospel story of the life, death, and resurrection of Jesus. In this sense, we can attest that there is no pure theology because, as Tillich argued, "the reception of revelation is conditioned by human existence."[73]

So far, in this section, employing Gadamer's concept of "Fusion of Horizons," I demonstrated how traditional religions, often through competition, conflict and persecution among them, have influenced each other and fused to create the syncretistic religio-cultural horizon of Korean people. I also demonstrated how this phenomenon has brought about a common characteristic in all religions, and Christianity also has become *cultus privatus*, a means of personal wellbeing and prosperity. Despite the fact that Korean Protestant believers unconsciously carry with them certain syncretic elements in their Christian beliefs and living, many of them show exclusivist attitudes toward other religions. By looking into three basic theological camps, fundamentalist, progressive, and liberal in terms of their views of other religions, I argued that the fundamentalist view of Christianity held by Hyung-Nong Park has made notable influences on Korean Protestant believers. Many Protestant believers are so greatly influenced by his view of other religions that they perceived them as idol worship and heretical nontruths to be conquered by Christianity. Their exclusivist attitudes toward other religions certainly has caused non-believers to perceive Christianity as a Western religion with an imperialistic attitude.[74] As a way to counter this exclusivist tendency, I argued that they need to understand syncretism in a broader sense, as a process of incarnation of the gospel in different

---

73. Tillich, *On the Boundary*, 41. Tillich criticizes both naturalistic and supranaturalistic theologies because both failed to set up the structural frame between humanity and God. The naturalistic theology emphasizes the humanistic and ignores the revelation, and the supranaturalistic theology does not find the ontological connection to God but separation. Tillich differs from Barth's position in that he admits that God's self-manifestation is dependent upon the way we receive this manifestation. This means that the reception of revelation is conditioned by human existence and we are in no position to construct a doctrine of revelation in itself apart from reception of it. For Tillich, the fact that we can ask about the connection between the revelation as an answer and human existence as question shows that the link between essential human goodness and God has not been completely destroyed. The fact that we must ask about it shows that we are estranged from such unity. See Roberts, "Tillich's Doctrine of Man," in Kegley and Bretall, *Theology of Paul Tillich*, 113.

74. I take up the topic, interreligious dialogue from a social trinitarian perspective in chapter 4. I discuss what kind of attitudes Korean-North American women are to have toward people of different religions and culture in this pluralistic North American context.

cultures. Christianity from the beginning has always been incarnated in different cultures. Therefore, there is no one "pure theology" or "pure gospel," which the exclusivists believe they alone hold.

Korean Women's Experience as a Theological Locus

In this section, I will look into how the pre-Christian religious traditions have functioned as a "hermeneutical pre-understanding", or a "prejudice", for the understanding of God among Korean women in general. I will also analyze their experiences as a theological locus on the basis of the resources available in print, along with my experiences as a pastor for Korean-North American immigrants and their children for three decades.

A typical portrayal of Christianity drawn by Korean feminist theologians is negative in tone. For instance, Ai Ra Kim who immigrated to the United States of America in 1962 to marry her husband in San Francisco stated the following in her book, *Women Struggling for a New Life*:

> The Korean immigrant churches became my saviors, supplying the fixed and rigorous apologetic principles legitimating my self-denunciation, principles such as woman's submission to man (Eph 5:22–25) and women's silence in public (1 Cor 14:31–35), derived from the Bible. Also, the church's hierarchical system and structure enhances and justifies women's subjugation to men. The more I was involved in the church and adopted the church's patriarchal teachings and doctrines, the more easily could I placate my quest and yearning to claim my own personhood. In this case, as Karl Marx proclaimed once, I became addicted to "religious opium" prescribed by the church . . . The church, implicitly and explicitly, supplies the justifying principles of women's self-demolition. By legitimating women's inferior status, it perpetuates institutional sexism at home, in the church, in Korean immigrant community, and in society.[75]

Ai Ra Kim accuses the Korean immigrant churches of supplying the justifying principles of women's self-abnegation. Ai Ra Kim's testimony is a typical case of conservative Protestantism which uphold patriarchal teachings and systems as God-ordained. However, it is noteworthy that the situation has changed very much since she wrote the book, and how women are treated in the church often depends on the denominational standing and

---

75. Kim, *Women Struggling for a New Life*, x.

the pastoral leadership in individual churches. At any rate, it is ironical that we still hear that some churches are perpetuating sexism in North America which supposedly promotes egalitarianism.

The Christian identity lies in an act of identification with the crucified God. In order to maintain the relevance of Christian faith we must be able to translate our Christian identity into praxis in the changing world. A theology of the cross is a challenging enterprise because it needs to answer new questions raised in continually changing situations. In the process of coming up with a theology of the cross which recognizes and promotes mutual, reciprocal relationships among people of different genders, races, and cultures, I will, first of all, look into how the social milieu of Korea has changed in women's socio-economic status. It is very important to look into the socio-economic change of women in Korea because the immigration society in North America is directly and/or indirectly affected by the changes of their home country.

The main working force of the Korean-North American immigrant society is comprised of people born in the 60's, 70's, and 80's. The women who were born after the late 60's are very different from the previous generations in terms of how they view themselves, which predominantly has to do with how they were brought up. In the late 60's, the South Korean government, alarmed by the way in which the rapidly increasing population was undermining economic growth, began a nationwide family planning program. The government encouraged married couples to have only one or two children, stressing families to "Have a single child and raise it well." As a result, the fertility rate (the average number of births a woman will have during her lifetime) fell from 6.1 births per female in 1960 to 4.2 in 1970, 2.8 in 1980, 2.4 in 1984, and 1.21 in 2005, recording one of the world's lowest birth rates according to the United Nations.[76]

It is true that the older generation still show a strong preference for sons because of their traditional Confucian value system. Sons are expected to take care of their parents in old age and carry on the family name. However, today in South Korea, young married couples are more preoccupied

---

76. According to the information given by United Nations Department of Economic and Social Affairs, Population Division (2007), "United Nations Population Prospects: 2006 revision, Table A. 15," (New York: U.N.), Retrieved 7 December, 2009, fertility rate below the replacement level of 2.1 births per female has triggered a national alarm, with dire predictions of an aging society unable to grow or support its elderly. Recent Korean governments have prioritized the issue on its agenda, promising to enact social reforms that will encourage women to have children.

with their professions than family name, and, therefore, tend to be uninterested in raising big families. For this reason, the preference for sons has nearly vanished. Having been raised in nuclear family units with the best care possible, many young Korean women do not think that they have been discriminated against or victimized just because they are female.

Another drastic social change is that today South Korea is transforming into a multicultural and multiracial country. Up until the late 1990s, Korea has been one of the world's most ethnically homogeneous nations. Foreigners were often rejected by the Korean society or faced discrimination. However, the word "multiculturalism" is increasingly heard in Korea today. In 2007, Stephen Castles of the International Migration Institute argued:

> Korea no longer has to decide whether it wants to become a multicultural society. It made that decision years ago—perhaps unconsciously—when it decided to be a full participant in the emerging global economy. It confirmed that decision when it decided to actively recruit foreign migrants to meet the economic and demographic needs of a fast-growing society. Korea is faced by a different decision today: what type of multicultural society does it want to be?[77]

Korea once viewed its homogeneity as its greatest strength, establishing a country of shared values and fraternity. Thus, homogeneity was considered a cornerstone, helping Korea survive adversities throughout their tumultuous history. However, because of their immersion in homogeneous traditions and culture, Koreans often show exclusivist attitudes toward those who are racially or culturally different from them.[78]

The women who have immigrated to North America from the late 1980s till now are the ones who have benefited from the recent changes in family structure, economic growth, and gender views in South Korea. As they immigrated to the multicultural, multiracial North America, their existence became even more complicated by the foreign culture, language, and many other social factors such as race, class, ethnicity, religion, sexuality, and age.

---

77. Castles, "Will Labour Migration lead to a Multicultural Society in Korea?" Global Human Resources Forum 2007/ International Migration Institute.

78. "Multiculturalism in Korea," *Joong Ang Daily*, August 26, 2010.

Theology Always Lives in Context

The Social Context of Korean-North American Women

The first generation immigrant women tend to adapt to new cultures and environments more easily than the men do. Large numbers of Korean-North American immigrant men experience loss of self-esteem. They are used to living in a patriarchal society, respected as the family provider, the father, and the husband; however, living in this egalitarian foreign land, they feel like nobody, insufficient and incapable as they depend on others because of the language barrier. Women, on the other hand, continue to live in the foreign country as they did in their homeland, as the family supporter, but also often act as a money earner despite their language barrier. Furthermore, women are more adept in adapting to living in new environments. There are many second generation Korean women who have entered the main-stream society as professionals in medicine, law, business, media, and etc. Another social issue that occurs is the challenge of intercultural and interracial marriage among the second generation.

All these social factors make us realize that Korean-North American immigrant women cannot be treated as a monolithic group of *han*-ridden people,[79] irrespective of their varied social-cultural, religious, political and economic differences. Besides, they should not be treated as victims in the binary opposition between men and women, or between the dominant and marginal. From the social, gender analysis of the *Sitz im Leben* of Korean-North American immigrants, I will propose a theology of the cross that is inclusive and holistic, one which recognizes diversity as well as the interconnectedness of women to others, and embraces the need of interdependence regardless of gender, generation, ethnicity, or race.

The Religious Context of Korean-North American Women

The self-worth of the first generation Korean-North American women has been greatly influenced by the traditional religions of Korea. Therefore, we need to discuss how these religions have functioned as ideologies constructing and reinforcing the androcentric, hierarchical mentality of the

---

79. *Han* is defined by a Korean *Minjung* theologian, Nam Dong Suh, as "a common denominator of the feeling of the powerless *minjung*." Andrew Sung Park, a Korean American theologian, defines it as "frustrated hope." See Park, *The Wounded Heart of God*, 16. See also Suh, "Towards a Theology of *Han*," 58.

Korean mind, and in turn how this mentality has crept into the Christian church and been endorsed as God-ordained.

First of all, ancestor worship, which is the major ritual of Confucianism, reinforced male dominance.[80] It strengthened the identity of the family's lineage by reuniting the ancestors with the living family members. The first son in the family played the role of a ritual priest. All men including even young boys participated in family rituals of ancestor worship, but women were totally excluded. The only part women played in ancestor worship services was that of men's assistants for preparing food and setting up the ritual tables.

The goals and identities of Korean women were determined by Confucian ideology. In the name of the Confucian "harmonious order," women were oppressed and disdained.[81] Two major principles of Confucianism which govern the interactions between women and men are *namnyo-yubyol* (male and female are essentially different) and *namjon-yobi* (men are honored and women are abased).[82] In his essay, "Thunder over the Lake: The Five Classics and the Perception of women in Early China," Richard W. Guisso insists that these principles were rooted in the Five Classics. He states:

> The female was inferior by nature. She was dark as the moon and changeable as water, jealous, narrow-minded, and insinuating. She was indiscreet, unintelligent, and dominated by emotion. Her beauty was a snare for the unwary male, the ruination of states.[83]

Because of the ignorance and inferiority of women, they were supposed to be subject to three men in their lives. As daughters, they had to obey their fathers and brothers; as wives they had to obey their husbands, and as daughters-in-law, they had to obey their parents-in-law. In the

---

80. Choi, *Korean Women and God*, 38–40.

81. Confucianism teaches heaven, husband, king, parents, and men are in the superior, higher position, while earth, wife, servant, children, and women are in the inferior, lower position. This hierarchy is seen by Confucianism as indispensable to maintain the cosmic order. While persons in the inferior positions should be obedient to their superiors, persons in the superior positions are obliged to use their power to take care of their inferiors. Each seems patterned to work for the good of the whole, but when Confucianism weds the ruling ideology, it serves only to legitimate the power of those in the superior positions. See Choi, *Korean Women and God*, 36–37.

82. Chong, "Women's Social Status during the Yi Dynasty," 12.

83. Guisso, "Thunder over the Lake: The Five Classics and the Perception of women in Early China," in Guisso and Johannesen, *Women in China*, 59. See also Choi, *Korean Women and God*, 37.

Theology Always Lives in Context

androcentric, hierarchical society, women suffered from an extreme emphasis on male genealogy and patriarchal community values. Because one of the primary functions of women was to provide for the male genealogy, in many cases, sonless women were dismissed from the position of being a wife and replaced by a woman who could bear a son for the husband.[84] Hee An Choi, a Korean-North American theologian rightly affirms that these ideologies were the primary cause of *han* in women.[85] This abusive form of Confucian ideology accentuated women's unconditional submission and at the same time ignored men's abusive power.

Secondly, Korean Buddhism also had patriarchal religious structures and rituals even though most religious Buddhist rituals and services were practiced and supported by female seekers. Just as female seekers practiced their daily devotions in a shamanistic context, they did the same in Buddhism. They not only had similar images of gods in Shamanism and Buddhism, but also similar attitudes of fidelity and loyalty to both religions. Korean women went to pray at the Buddhist monasteries and consulted with the monks whom they believed could cure them through the use of spells and magic medicines. Likewise, Buddhism, by adapting to the Korean cultural and religious milieu, became a folk religion which provided a means to conquer personal misfortunes and natural disasters. This form of Buddhism flourished not because of its profound philosophy but because it was able to provide for the needs of shamanistic women.

Even though Korean Buddhism mainly functioned as a folk religion for women, it carried in it a misogynist ideology which caused women to believe that they were inferior to men. In Buddhism, women were not able to imagine themselves as equals to men because Buddha historically appeared as male.[86] Women often saw themselves as deserving of pain and suffering from the sins of their past lives, which they had to endure in their current life. They accepted womanhood as something they needed to rid themselves of through the completion of their *karma*.[87]

Lastly, though Shamanism was once the main religion for Korean women, it was incapable of liberating women from an androcentric

---

84. Peterson, "Women without Sons: a Measure of Social Change in Yi Dynasty Korea," in Kendall and Peterson, *Korean Women*, 37–43.

85. Choi, *Korean Women and God*, 39.

86. Ibid., 33.

87. *Karma* is the concept of "action" or "deed", understood as that which causes the entire cycle of cause and effect, which is called *samsāra*.

worldview. Shamanism is polytheistic with more than eighteen thousand gods.[88] Many shamanistic gods are female, and they are worshiped as equals to male gods. For instance, *Sam Shin* (the grandmother god of birth) is the most powerful and famous female god in Korea. *Sam Shin* shows very independent power and strong character even in Korea's patriarchal culture. It is believed that *Sam Sin* brings into existence all human beings on earth and protects babies from diseases and bad spirits for a hundred days after birth. There are many gods closely connected with women's living spaces such as the storage space, the gate, and the kitchen. Shamanistic gods are believed to live in these places where they protect people from negative events and bad fortunes as long as they are treated favorably. Women make sure to treat these gods well as they are believed to be easily angered and irritable. Shamanistic rituals like *gut*, which are designed to appease gods, demonstrate how women live in an inevitably dependent reality, controlled by their protectors whether by men or by gods.[89]

As argued above, the pre-Christian religions in Korea carry in them misogynist ideologies suppressing and oppressing Korean women. How about Christianity? We need to see whether Christianity has liberated the Korean women or reinforced the misogynist ideologies which have oppressed them.

In early Korean Christian history, women and children were the first recipients of the gospel. From the socio-political perspective, the Christian gospel of Jesus' vision of *basileia* served as a liberating gospel for those who were doubly shackled under conservative feudalistic Confucianism and Japanese colonization. The Christian gospel took part in changing Korean society by promoting equal human rights, which included the abolition of class barriers and the extension of women's rights to public education and participation in public services. The Christian message of egalitarianism attracted girls and women from lower social classes first. The church was the only public place where they were allowed to sing and pray aloud, freely expressing their feelings.

The gospel, which was first accepted by women and children, gradually reached even high ranking men of knowledge. The collapse of socio-political structures which was brought about by Japanese colonization caused

---

88. Kim, "Korean Shamanism: A Bibliographical Introduction," in Yu and Guisso, *Shamanism*, 12.

89. Chung, "*Han-Pu-Ri*," 54–55. By the shamanistic ritual, *kut*, the shaman honors *han*-filled ghosts who have been ignored, and asks their forgiveness and reconciles the people with them.

a loss of hope and dignity among the Korean social elite. Consequently, some intellectual men trying to find a breakthrough in despair began to pay attention to the new religion of Christianity. Once intellectual men of higher classes began to join the church, the shifts of leadership took place from women to men and from men of lower classes to intellectual men of higher classes. Thus, social stratifications crept into the early Korean church. This was later reinforced by patriarchal injunctions given in the household codes (Col 3:18—4:1; Eph 5:21–33; 1 Tim 2:10–15; Titus 2:4–5).

In light of these developments, I draw on the work of Elisabeth Schüssler Fiorenza, who helps us recognize that patriarchal structures are not inherent to Christian community. A parallel can be easily identified between her reconstructed life and practice of women discipleship in the earliest churches and the situation of the early Christian church in Korea. In her first book, *In Memory of Her*, Fiorenza insists that it was the post-Pauline and pseudo-Pauline tradition that eliminated women from the leadership of worship and community. For instance, in the first and most precise form of the domestic code given in Colossians 3:18-4:1, she finds that the writer of the Colossians not only spiritualizes and moralizes the baptismal community understanding of the tradition of discipleship in Galatians 3:28, but also makes this Greco-Roman patriarchal household ethic a part of the Christian social ethic. She insists, however, that such a reinterpretation of the Christian baptismal vision did not happen before the first century, and, therefore, had no impact on the earlier Jesus' traditions.[90]

Fiorenza points out that the patriarchal-societal ethos, in the long run, replaced the genuine Christian vision of equality. This phenomenon is observed in the letter to the Ephesians as well as in the Pastoral Epistles. Ephesians 5:21-33 takes the household-code pattern and reasserts the submission of the wife to the husband as a religious Christian duty. In the Pastoral Epistles, we find further patriarchalization not just of the Christian household but also of the church as "the household of God."[91] In both 1 Timothy 2:10-15 and Titus 2:4-5, a woman/wife is to learn in all quietness and submission, as her status requires. She points out that the Pastoral Epistles advocate a patriarchal order to accommodate the patriarchal Roman society that the church was reaching out to. Therefore, ministry and leadership were dependent upon age/gender qualifications, not primarily upon one's spiritual or organizational resources or giftedness.

90. Schüssler Fiorenza, *In Memory of Her*, 252.
91. Ibid., 290.

The Liberative Cross

Fiorenza concludes that the Pastoral Epistles, by merging the leadership of wealthy patrons with that of the local officers of the Christian community, stratified church leadership according to patriarchal status and seniority.[92] The patriarchal order of the house, when applied to the order of the church, restricted the leadership of wealthy women and maintained the social exploitation of slave-women and men even within the Christian household community. Furthermore, the prohibition of the leadership of women was reinforced by theologizing and legitimizing the creation story of the Bible (1 Tim 2:12-15). Not only was Eve secondary in creation; she was first to sin. The stress on patriarchal submission by the early church certainly has brought about the genderization of Christian ministry.[93]

In light of Fiorenza's reconstructed life and practice of women disciples in the earliest churches, I have argued that a parallel situation is found between the earliest churches of Christianity and the early Christian church in Korea. The early Korean converts to Christianity brought with them their old habits and ideologies into church. The church, in order to accommodate the intellectual men of higher classes, juxtaposed these old habits and ideologies with patriarchal teachings in the Bible and produced a unique system through which classism and sexism have been perpetuated. Consequently, it is not too farfetched to claim, "Patriarchal Confucianism dominates even today in some of the Korean North American churches."

Among the first generation immigrants are many Korean Protestant Christian women who are influenced by conservative faith and strong puritan ethics.[94] They regard their conservative or even fundamentalist faith as 'orthodox.' However, their theology and praxis demonstrate that they have been influenced by Korean traditional religions. In this respect, I will argue that the traditional religions as "prejudice" have shaped their understanding of God and practice of beliefs. For instance, there is a unique mentality in their practice of piety which considers certain places and certain times of day more spiritual. Korean women, before Christianity was introduced to Korea, used to practice a ritual of prayer early in the morning before sunrise. Believing that "heaven" will be moved by their piety,[95] they set apart a

---

92. Ibid., 291.

93. Ibid., 315.

94. Lee, "American Missionary Movement in Korea 1882–1945," 387–402.

95. "Heaven" literally meaning *"tien"* in Chinese or *"chun"* in Korean pronunciation was believed to be "One" (*hanamin*) above all the Shamanistic gods dwelling in their living space.

certain period of time to pray in the early morning for family fortunes and the healing of diseases. For the ritual, women washed themselves and set a bowl of freshly drawn well-water in a designated area, praying and kneeling before it until sunrise. If an urgent situation were to emerge, these women would go up to a Buddhist monastery in mountains and pray for many days. When Christianity was introduced, they found a better alternative to these unique religious practices. Instead of praying to "Heaven" at their private places alone, they ran to church and prayed to the almighty God whom they believed would answer all their prayers with God's power and wisdom. Instead of going to a Buddhist monastery in mountains, they now turned to the Christian prayer centers built in mountains. Their religious piety was Christianized as they converted to Christianity. They prayed to God instead of "Heaven." They prayed not only for their personal matters like healings and family fortunes, but also for the forgiveness of their sins and salvation of those who persecuted them for their faith. They also prayed for their country to be liberated from Japan, and later in the history they began to pray for the economic growth of Korea as well. In this way, the traditional, religious practices of piety were fused with Christian practices of piety and further developed to form a unique spirituality of Korean Christian women. Many immigrant churches in North America today hold prayer meetings in the early morning before sunrise. They hold not only daily early morning prayers but also special seasonal prayers around New Years, Easter, and Christmas for forty days. Korean women in general tend to consider early morning prayers as more spiritual and powerful. They also tend to consider the churches and pastors who do not offer the early morning prayers as less spiritual and less powerful.

Another example of the influence of pre-Christian religions on women's spirituality is the way in which they easily perceive the immanence of God. Korean women, before the introduction of Christianity, served Shamanistic gods who dwelt in individual living spaces like the inner room, the kitchen, the garden, and the well. As a result, they had no problem with understanding an immanent God who dwelled among them, who struggled together with them and shared in their life. Because the Shamanistic deities are easily angered and irritated when they are not treated well, some Christian women who are not well versed in the biblical knowledge hold the imagery of an angry and fickle God ready to punish them whenever they do wrong. Fear of punishment and misfortunes instead of gratitude for God's grace becomes a ruling factor in their spiritual life.

The Liberative Cross

While Korean women easily relate to the immanent God, Hee An Choi argues, it is very hard for them to accept the almighty Father God as their own God. I find her argument hard to accept but I will let her argue first to make her point. Hee An Choi supports her argument by pointing to Korean history. Korea was frequently invaded by neighboring countries throughout history and most recently had a civil war (1950-53 AD) which caused many men to be killed. She argues that the almighty God was perceived as one who was not with them but with their oppressors. Furthermore, because of the wars, children were raised by mothers only. Consequently, it was difficult for them to imagine a Father God who would listen to them or seek to understand.[96] What motivated children to obey the commands of a father, according to her, was fear rather than love. Likewise, they feared the Father God and obeyed God out of fear. She concludes that this conception of God fails to heal women's pain, but instead accentuates their suffering. Women's conception of God was formed from their experiences of suffering and *han*.

In order to overcome this unrelatability to the almighty patriarchal God, Hee An Choi makes the innovative proposal that God should be viewed as family, mother, and daughter instead of Father God. She states how Korean women relate to God as immanent and part of their living family as follows:

> Faced with cruel poverty and oppression, the family held together and provided an absolute ground of trust and faith. God shared their poverty, suffering, and oppression as family. God as family is compassionate and merciful. God is there with and for them every day and night. God shares their every tear. God dies with them and revives them from poverty, colonial oppression, and male violence. God and women are together every day.[97]

She also contends that this model of God as family can encompass all the blood related family members and even neighbors who share their everyday lives, communicating, understanding, crying and laughing. She adds this God as family can empower women to overcome the patriarchal world, bringing peace to their lives and hope for abundant life.

I see Choi's alternative suggestion to view God as family instead of the almighty Father God has potential to overcome the weakness of the almighty patriarchal God. However, her weakness is found in that she built

---

96. Choi, *Korean Women and God*, 106.
97. Ibid., 108.

Theology Always Lives in Context

her theology on a specific group of women who were victimized by the historical tragedies and have experienced the Japanese colonization and the Korean War and their after effects. She stereotypes Korean women as *han*-ridden and builds a theological framework around the *han*-ridden woman's experiences thereby excluding those who have grown without the experience of *han*. Therefore, Choi builds a theological framework on experiences that not all share.

In addition, I disagree with her argument that Korean women universally find it difficult to accept God as the almighty Father because of their historical realities and tragedies. In fact, in many cases the helpless realities, like poverty and oppression, caused Korean women to hope for and desire an Almighty God who was able to empower them to face their daily struggles. Protestantism was well accepted by Korean people by the end of the nineteenth century when it was first introduced. At the time, they faced socio-political crisis and found the existing paradigms of traditional religions unable to accommodate the drastic changes in modern society. When they encountered Christianity, they saw that it was capable of meeting their needs. I agree with Kyoung Jae Kim as he argued, "In the turbulent situation of our people, the suffering people could depend on the absolute God as the Lord, the One who rules the world with God's freedom, justice, and mercy."[98]

Choi contended that Korean women have had a very hard time accepting the almighty Father God because such a God was perceived as one who was not with them but with their oppressors. Contrary to her argument, the almighty Father God has served as a powerful conception of God to Korean Christian women. In my experience as pastor I find two prevailing motifs of faith among the Korean women I minister to. They are *Christus Victor* and the atonement theory of Anselm of Canterbury. Both motifs picture God as the almighty Father God. The women seek both empowerment from God, to overcome their helpless circumstances, as well as God's forgiveness for their sins, which they often believe to be the cause of punishment in the form of conflicts, struggles, and illness. Consequently, they accept very easily the imagery of *Christus Victor*, the image of God as one who fights against and triumphs over the evil powers of the world as well as reconciling the world to Godself (2 Cor 5:19).[99] The deliverance

---

98. Kim, *Christianity and the Encounter of Asian Religions*, 51–52
99. Aulen, *Christus Victor*, 76.

of humankind from the power of death and the devil is at the same time deliverance from God's judgment.

Another powerful aspect of God that is well accepted among Korean women is the substitutionary atonement of Christ. The almighty God forgives sins through the death of Jesus Christ. The almighty Father's sacrifice of the Son for humanity has been understood by Korean women as good news. Those who had been doubly fettered throughout history through invasion by foreign superpowers and oppression within the patriarchal system of their own country understood very well what it meant for a powerful king to sacrifice his only son for the benefits of his subjects. For them, the ones in power were usually exploiters and oppressors, but the almighty God was introduced as one who sacrificed the only Son for their benefits. Thus, they understood and accepted God' sacrifice as an amazing, immeasurable grace which they could never be able to repay with human efforts. Consequently, Anselm's substitutionary atonement theory was the most popular hermeneutical lens through which Christian Koreans explained the gospel when Christianity was first introduced to Korea.[100]

This image of God as the Lord who is responsible for the welfare of his subjects, and who in turn deserves honor, was well accepted by Korean women who had been familiar with that feudal system in Korea. Recently, Anselm's position has been strongly criticized by feminist theologians. In the next chapter I will discuss why feminist theologians reject Anselm's theory of atonement.

The first generation Korean-North American immigrant women who have grown in the Korean religio-cultural context show a very conservative outlook which confines Christian faith to *cultus privatus*. They are strongly influenced by these two traditional views of the theology of redemption in Christ, *Christus Victor*, and Anselm's substitutionary theory of atonement. Consequently, they emphasize personal moral living and heavenly salvation but are less concerned with the common welfare of all people and the socio-political problems of the world. When the believers take Christianity as *cultus privatus,* they are often tempted to use biblical images of God in a distorted way for their personal advantage. For instance, some followers of the charismatic movement use the *Christus Victor* motif of atonement in a distorted way. They hold a strong dualistic view of the world as being

---

100. In his *Cur Deus Homo* 1.8, Anselm of Canterbury reflected the feudal medieval worldview and presupposed his understandings of law, offense, reparations, and social obligations. God and humans are related like feudal lords and their serfs. Any act of disobedience dishonors the lord, and satisfaction must be given.

divided between good and evil, always considering God to be on their side, while considering anything that is against them to be on Satan's side. Serious problems may arise if distortions such as this dualistic view occur in the conception of Christ as Victor. For example, women with dualistic views may see themselves as always right, not needing to repent. The social implication for such distortions is an absence of self-examination and repentance, or judgment and even violence in extreme cases. It is also important that first generation Korean-North American immigrant women learn that those "orthodox" doctrines which American and European missionaries introduced to them as absolute are actually the products of temporal social changes in Europe. Therefore, such "orthodox" doctrines need to be critiqued whether or not they can presently give answers to the questions arising from the North American multicultural context.

The Need for a New Understanding of the Cross as a Prophetic Call in the New Context

Having been brought up in the multicultural North American context, second generation young Korean-North American women do not relate to God in the same manner as their parents do. They have been educated in multiculturalism and tend to appreciate the social aspect of Christianity more than their parents. Their parents, however, tend to view Christianity as *cultus privatus* and confess Jesus as their comforter, counselor, healer, and the Savior. Consequently, for their parents, the churches are the comforter, problem solver, and eliminator of sufferings. These roles are important for the parents; however, they tend to forget that Christian believers are also called into the world to be involved in social justice for the common welfare of humanity.

Many first-generation Korean-North American women have come to North America with the dream of a more prosperous life and better education for their children; therefore, they tend to shun the theology of the cross and turn to the theology of glory.[101] They view Christianity as a means

---

101. A theology of the cross implies that God is made known not in strength but in weakness and in death. We participate in the death of the Crucified God not by elevating to positions of strength but by entering in the life–giving love of the suffering God. Seeking the fulfillment of a personal dream only to be rich, to be powerful, and to be popular by means of the Christian faith for one's own glory is exactly opposite to what a theology of the cross attests. It is in fact a theology of glory. See Hall, *The Cross in Our Context*, 75–79.

of personal success or as a means to divine salvation which is heavenly and otherworldly. A good number of the second generation Korean-North American men and women, however, leave the church silently once they reach adulthood and achieve the dreams and aspirations of their parents. For the second generation, Christianity as *cultus privatus* is not as persuasive and attractive to them as it was to their parents. Living in the multicultural society, they come to raise a new question: "What does the Cross of Jesus Christ mean to us and people of different cultures in the world?" Definitely, what they need today in their multicultural world is a new understanding of the Cross that would allow them to envision a new human community based on the values of equality, mutuality, and reciprocity between men and women and between different races and cultures. Therefore, I take it as a prophetic call to present a theology of the cross which will offer an appropriate answer to the question raised by second generation Korean-North Americans, what the cross means to people living today in this multicultural world. At the same time, this theology of the cross I present as a prophetic call will also challenge first generation Korean-North Americans to come out of their ghetto mentality which focuses on only "my" personal interests, forgetting altogether the fact that human beings as "beings-in-the world" find their meaning in relationships. With this prophetic call in mind, I will take the next step into critiquing various attempts which feminist theologians have made to expose oppressive theological patterns within theology and tradition.

2

A Critical Evaluation of Feminist Theologies

IN THIS CHAPTER I will critique, from my perspective as a social Trinitarian Korean-North American woman pastor, various theological attempts made by feminist theologians to expose oppressive theologies and their traditions. Recognizing Korean-North American women's varied experiences of power I aim to retrieve a theology of the cross which provokes them to live in this global world as people fully aware of their need for interdependence and reciprocity, regardless of gender, ethnicity, and race. Clearly, the goal of my project concerns a new human community based on the values of mutuality and reciprocity which are dynamically revealed in the Trinitarian relations.[1] I agree with Elizabeth A. Johnson as she stated:

> The goal is not the reverse discrimination, with women dominating men; that would be the same problem in reverse. Rather, the dream of a new heaven and a new earth takes hold here, with no one group dominating and no one group being subordinated, but each person in his or her own right participating according to their gifts, without preconceived stereotyping, in genuine mutuality. It is not envisioned that everyone be the same, but that the uniqueness of each be equally respected in a community of brothers and sisters.[2]

A social Trinitarian understanding of the cross, I propose, signifies and promotes a relation marked by voluntary giving in love, trust, and respect

---

1. I discuss the concept of the *perichoretic* trinitarian fellowship in chapter 4 in relation to the social Trinitarian praxis.

2. Johnson, *Consider Jesus*, 98. See also her book *She Who Is*, 68.

instead of competing or dominating with the spirit of superiority.³ In this view, I will critically evaluate the theological works of feminist theologians centered on two main issues: first, the male-centered language and symbolism of God, and second, God's relation to the cross.

To retrieve the central Christian symbols of God and salvation which have been life-giving and liberating for women, feminist theologians take seriously both radical feminist criticism and the cultural and religious traditions formed by Christianity. H. G. Gadamer, in this sense, offers an important perspective for feminist theologians as they attempt to understand the traditions adequately and forge new contextualized interpretations.⁴ Feminist theologians recognize that it is impossible to work outside the effective history of tradition that offers them the subject matter. They have to be aware that traditions have been interpreted and reinterpreted from the context upon which the interpreter stands. In their discussion of biblical and historical texts and the way these texts have been interpreted through centuries of preaching and teaching, feminist theologians attempt to expose the distortions of these interpretations and the continuing effects these interpretations have on the practical life and self-understanding of women in order to emancipate them from the negative effects of these distortions.⁵

Phyllis Trible and Elisabeth S. Fiorenza, for instance, have seen the "counter-voices" arguing for the Bible as theoretical and practical witness against traditional sexist interpretations. First, Trible employs a complex hermeneutical method to show that "scripture in itself yields multiple interpretations of itself" in its continuing interaction with the world.⁶ She writes:

> As the Bible interprets itself to complement or contradict, to confirm or challenge, so likewise we construe these traditions for our time, recognizing an affinity between then and now. In other words, hermeneutics encompasses explication, understanding, and application from past to present.⁷

---

3. I will discuss in details the topics, the social Trinity and the social trinitarian praxis in chapters 3 and 4.

4. Gadamer, *Truth and Method*, 277–309. See also Ricoeur, *Interpretation Theory*, 39–95.

5. Carr, *Transforming Grace*, 101.

6. Trible, *God and the Rhetoric of Sexuality*, 4.

7. Ibid., 7.

A Critical Evaluation of Feminist Theologies

Trible acknowledges that the Bible overwhelmingly favors male metaphors for deity, but at the same time she shows that the Bible is a potential witness against all the very same androcentric interpretations. She explores the female imagery of God that shows the equality of female and male in creation, in disobedience, in erotic joy, and in mundane crisis. Trible concludes that female imagery is not a minor theme but "with persistence and power it saturates scripture"; some texts about male and female yield "the grace of sexuality, not the sin of sexism.[8]

Elisabeth S. Fiorenza, employing historical-critical hermeneutical theory, questions whether the New Testament authors have conveyed history in an androcentric way at all. She points out,

> The New Testament does not transmit a single and androcentric statement or sexist story of Jesus, although he lived and preached in a patriarchal culture . . . In the fellowship of Jesus, women apparently did not play a marginal role even though only a few references to women disciples survived the androcentric tradition and redaction process of the gospel.[9]

Fiorenza suggests that Galatians 3:28 was not an abstract ideal, but a political reality in the early church.[10] According to her, the early Christian writings were pastorally engaged writings, and in them we witness how ecclesial patriarchalization occurred for the early church's survival. She argues that Christianity was not originally patriarchal because the Jesus movement and the early Christian missionary movement were countercultural, radically egalitarian, and inclusive. Patriarchalization was a gradual process that was accomplished only over the course of several centuries and in the context of a real struggle about the question of women in the church.[11] She states,

> Only an egalitarian model for the reconstruction of early Christian history can do justice to both the egalitarian traditions of women's leadership in the church as well as to the gradual process of adaptation and theological justification of the dominant patriarchal Greco-Roman culture and society.[12]

---

8. Ibid., 201–2.

9. Schüssler Fiorenza, "Interpreting Patriarchal Traditions," 52. See also Schüssler Fiorenza, *In Memory of Her*, 105–59.

10. Schüssler Fiorenza, "Interpreting Patriarchal Traditions," 53.

11. Schüssler Fiorenza, *In Memory of Her*, 97–323.

12. Schüssler Fiorenza, "You Are Not to Be Called Father," 318.

These biblical and historical studies which Trible and Fiorenza render, albeit in different ways, are against traditional sexist interpretations. The work of Trible and Fiorenza undercuts the claim that the doctrines of God and Jesus Christ are intrinsically patriarchal, and that they necessarily legitimate the subordination of women.

Feminists share the same goal to promote the full humanity of women; however, they do not share the same methodological approaches. Carol Christ divides feminist scholarship into "reformist" and "revolutionary" approaches. Feminist "revolutionaries" like Mary Daly, Carol Christ, and Daphne Hampson use the experience of women not only as a corrective but as a starting point and norm. Free of the authorities of Christianity, feminist revolutionaries attempt to create new symbols and traditions on the basis of their own perceptions of reality.[13] Abandoning traditional Christian symbolism, revolutionary feminist theologians argue for and turn to the image of goddess, or great Mother, which embodies and affirms female characteristics.[14]

Mary Daly critiques the symbolism of Christianity and the way it has legitimated the subordination of women and reinforced women's internalized inferiority. Her critique of Christianity centers around the understanding of God as "father": God as the supreme patriarch in heaven rules his people on earth and thus legitimates the male-dominated order of society. She suggests that the male symbols of God, or the "ultimate symbol" of "the all male Trinity," the "procession of a divine son from a divine father," are not adequate symbols for women.[15] In laying out the framework of her feminist critique of the major symbols of Christianity, Daly accuses male theology as being a cerebral "methodolatry" that renders the questions of women into "nonquestions" and data about women into "nondata." In contrast, she makes such "nonquestions" and "nondata" central in rejecting Christian symbols for their devastating effects on women. Daly argues that the feminist experience itself is a source of liberating spiritual experience for women.[16] Daly sums up profound sociological and psychological ef-

---

13. The revolutionary feminists like Mary Daly, Daphne Hampson, Carol P. Christ declare that feminism represents the death knell of Christianity as a viable religious option for women. See Christ, "Why Women Need the Goddess"; Daly, *Beyond God the Father*; Hampson, *Theology and Feminism*.

14. Budapest, *The Spiral Dance*; Christ, *Diving Deep and Surfacing*; Goldenberg, *Changing of the Gods*.

15. Daly, *Beyond God the Father*, 13–63, 44–68, 69–71.

16. Ibid., 11–12, 69–97.

A Critical Evaluation of Feminist Theologies

fects of patriarchal God symbolism in her aphorism, "If God is male then male is God."[17]

Daphne Hampson, agreeing with Daly, declares feminism as a viable religious option for women. According to Hampson, women operate out of an essentially different mode of thinking than men do. Feminism which supports and affirms women's mode of thinking is opposed to Christian thought which, she believes, advances an exclusively male mode of thinking.[18] In the similar line of thought to Daly, Carol Christ argues that the symbolism of goddess, or great Mother, is necessary for the full religious affirmation of women's power, bodies, will, and collective bonds with one another.[19] She also argues that whether innately or because of historical experience, women are heirs to different knowledges and visions, as well as a different approach to reality and to God. These kinds of knowledge, she insists, have always been erased, repressed, suppressed, excluded, and subjugated by male institutional control, and subordinated to exclusive male language for God.[20]

I argue here that by adhering to exclusively female images of God or Goddess worship, feminist revolutionaries actually suggest a reversal of patterns of domination rather than genuine transformation. A reformist feminist, Rosemary Ruether rightly criticizes them for separatism, reversal of domination, perpetuation of the nature/culture split in female/male symbolism, assignment of goodness to females and evil to males, and failure to work toward synthesis and transformation. She also argues that the "new feminist religions" including the cult of the Great Mother claimed by feminist Goddess devotees emerged historically from a patriarchal culture, and how it "has to do with putting kings on thrones of the world, not with liberating women or slaves."[21]

Feminist revolutionaries have left Christianity, considering it destructive and exclusionary. Their radical critique has great influence on women today. Having taken their critique seriously, Christian feminists struggle with Christian symbols and the transformation of these symbols. They

---

17. Daly, *Beyond God the Father*, 8. See also Daly, "Feminist Post-Christian Introduction," 38.

18. Hampson, *Theology and Feminism*, 54.

19. Christ, "Why Women Need the Goddess," in Christ and Plaskow, *Womanspirit Rising*, 273–87.

20. Ibid.

21. Ruether, "A Religion of Women: Sources and Strategies," 310.

recognize that both historically and in the present, Christian symbols of God, Jesus, sin, salvation, the church, and the Holy Spirit have been life-giving and liberating for women. Therefore, reformist feminists such as Rosemary Ruether, Elisabeth Schüssler Fiorenza, Elizabeth A. Johnson, Dorothee Sölle, Letty Russel, and Elisabeth Moltmann-Wendel stay within the Christian tradition and expose oppressive theological patterns and reconstruct basic symbols of Christian faith to be equally inclusive for both women and men, emphasizing liberatory faith and practice.[22]

In search for a theology of the cross which offers adequate resources to resist the structures of violence and promote the full humanity of women, we first of all need to unmask the hidden dynamic of domination in the Christian tradition's language and symbolism, and retrieve alternative wisdom suppressed or lost in history. How should the symbol of God be spoken anew to promote women's sense of dignity and self-esteem?

We need to retrieve a liberating truth for women from Christian theology not only for the purpose of liberating them from the constricting theological implications and praxis, but also for the reason of the very viability of the Christian tradition for the present and coming generation. In terms of the viability of the Christian religion, Elizabeth A. Johnson, citing Wolfhart Pannenberg, affirms that religions die when they lose the power to interpret the full range of present experience in light of their idea of God:

> The truth of God is tested by the extent to which the idea of God takes account of currently accessible aspects of reality and by the ability of the idea of God to integrate the complexity of present experience into itself. If the idea of a God does not keep pace with developing reality, the power of experience pulls people on and the God dies fading from memory.[23]

Today, recognition of women's equality and human dignity has emerged as a subject which tests whether the God of the Christian tradition is able to take account of, illumine, and integrate the currently accessible experience of women. Therefore, we need to look seriously into the exclusive, patriarchal symbols and language about God because they function to debilitate women's sense of dignity and self-esteem.

---

22. Ruether, "Christian Feminist Theology: History and Future" in Haddad and Esposito, *Daughters of Abraham: Feminist Thought in Judaism, Christianity, and Islam*, 69.

23. Johnson, "The Incomprehensibility of God and the Image of God Male and Female," 445. See also Pannenberg, "Toward a Theology of the History of Religions," 65–118.

A Critical Evaluation of Feminist Theologies

With regard to the power of symbolism, Elizabeth A. Johnson convincingly states:

> The God-symbol is not only a visual phantasy but a focus of a whole complex of conscious and unconscious ideas, feelings, emotions, views, and associations, very deep and tenacious. For women, speech about God couched exclusively in male terms does not point to the equal participation of women and men in the divine ground. Male images allow men to participate fully in it, while women can do so only by abstracting themselves from their concrete, bodily identity as women. Thus is set up a largely unconscious dynamic that alienates women from their own goodness and power at the same time that it reinforces dependency upon men and male authority.[24]

Exclusive, literal patriarchal speech about God has played a role in justifying social structures of dominance, such as the androcentric world view. Therefore, Johnson affirms that structural change and linguistic change go hand-in-hand.[25]

One example of how male-centered language and symbol systems have influenced in shaping and creating a world where male-centeredness is taken as universal is clearly shown in the debate of my English-speaking Korean young adult congregation members on whether a female member could be cast as God for Christmas plays. Whether arguing for or against, both parties have strong theological backup and do not easily give into the other. What is implied in the mindset of those who oppose female casting is the conviction that God is male because God was incarnated in the form of male Jesus and Jesus himself called God father. The reason this theological debate about the gender of God is important is because it usually leads to the anthropological, ecclesial issues on whether women are equally treated in the civil and religious world.

Feminist theologians take the bias seriously and attempt to analyze and delegitimize theological patterns which have distorted Christian praxis. I will, therefore, look into different approaches feminist theologians take toward exclusive, patriarchal language in order to renew the idea of God in more inclusive way. Feminist theologians take different approaches to the notion of the maleness of God. First, some of them attribute stereotypical feminine traits to God. Secondly, others have uncovered a feminine

---

24. Johnson, *She Who Is*, 38.
25. Ibid., 40.

dimension in God by emphasizing the Holy Spirit as the feminine principle of the Godhead. Thirdly, they replaced the Trinity, Father-Son-Holy Spirit with other triads of image which are neither masculine nor feminine, such as Creator-Redeemer-Sustainer. I will critique these approaches in the following section in terms of what they contribute and what they lack.

The Maleness of God

We must keep in mind certain principles as we assess various attempts which feminist theologians have made to analyze and delegitimize theological patterns which have distorted Christian praxis. First of all, we need to remember that God is neither basically masculine with a feminine side nor feminine with a masculine side. Consequently, in worship and prayer, I argue, God needs to be spoken of in various images and symbols both male and female in order to relativize undue emphasis on any one image. Female images of God disclose the relative character of male images and restrict any claim to ultimacy. Secondly, God is beyond all names, and the essence of God is unknowable. Ineffability of God demands a proliferation of images.[26] In respect to the richness of God, it is necessary to utilize a full complement of God images, both masculine and feminine as well as both personal and impersonal. However, we should neither literalize metaphors for God nor forget the dissimilarity in every analogy we make between God and humans. According to Augustine, God is greater than all our conceptions of God, and our conceptions of God are greater than all our expressions of God. In other words, it is easier to say what God is not than what God is. Therefore, even when we think we have understood God, we have not completely understood God. By the beginning of the sixth century, these insights had been explicitly formulated into the principle of the threefold way of arriving at knowledge of God: the way of affirmation, negation, and immanence or transcendence.[27] According to this *apophatic* approach known as negative theology, or *via negativa*, every statement we make about God must be negated; we must say what God is not as well as what God is. For instance, if we assert that God is just or wise, we must add that God is not just or wise as measured by human justice and wisdom. If

---

26. LaCugna, "The Baptismal Formula, Feminist Objections, and Trinitarian Theology," 239.

27. Armstrong, "Negative Theology," 176–89.

we say that God is father, God is also unlike a father because God is neither male nor female.

Aquinas carries forward the tradition of divine incomprehensibility from the early Christian centuries and further develops the *apophatic* theology. He differentiates between various types of words we use to describe God.[28] Metaphors like "God is a rock" involve some form of concrete bodiliness as part of what they mean. Relational terms like "God is our savior" name God on the basis of a divine relationship between God and creatures. Substantial terms like "God is good, living, and wise" predicate an attribution which is proper to God's own essence. These words are all used to name God, but they cannot either singularly, or taken all together, name what God is *in se*. In order for the word to be true, in every case we must go through the same simultaneous movement of affirmation, negation, and letting-go in a transcending movement of affirmation.

Feminist theologians employ this principle of negative theology to argue that it is improper to equate the divine fatherhood with the divine essence. They insist that it is one aspect of God's way of relating to us. They also remind us of our propensity to literalize metaphors of God and forget the dissimilarity in every analogy. Divine fatherhood, therefore, should never be understood in terms of maleness. When we use father as an analogical term for God, we must remember that analogy works by dissimilarity and not similarity between human and divine fatherhood. Therefore, all the symbols for God, either mother or father, intrinsically demand their own negation: None of them grasps the transcendent. They affirm God's intimacy to the human community and people in their experiences.[29]

Keeping in mind these principles, we will assess various attempts which feminist theologians have made to analyze and delegitimize theological patterns which they believe have distorted Christian praxis.

Is God Male?

The Scriptures were formed in patriarchal cultures; therefore, they usually depict God as father, mighty warrior, jealous husband, righteous king, and so on. However, we also find feminine images of God in the Scriptures. For instance, God is depicted as mother: giving birth (Deut 32:18), nursing

28. Johnson, "Incomprehensibility of God," 452. See also Pesch, *The God Question in Thomas Aquinas and Martin Luther*, 9.

29. Ibid., 441–80. See also Carr, "The God who is Involved," 314–28.

(Hos 11:3-4; Isa 49:15), crying in labor (Isa 42:14), comforting (Isa 66:13), and a mother who weaned her child (Ps 131:2). God is also depicted in metaphors from other female experiences such as sewer (Neh 9: 21), a woman baking (Luke 13:18-21), a midwife attending birth (Ps 22:9-10, 71:6; Isa 66:9), and the owner of money who searches for a lost coin (Luke 15:8-10). God the creator is depicted as father and mother, begetter and birth-giver (Job 38:28-29). These explicit references to God in female and male imagery as birth-giving woman, loving mother, victorious warrior and compassionate father enable us to comprehend in a greater measure the mysterious goodness of God's ways with us. These images and personifications are not considered as feminine or masculine aspects of the divine but expression of the fullness of divine power and care for God's creation. The best example is given in the parallel parables of the shepherd looking for the sheep and the woman searching for the lost coin (Luke 15:4-5, 8-10). Both parables orient us to God's redeeming action in images that are equivalently male and female.

Trinity and God-Language

As observed above, God is depicted in both male and female images in the Scriptures. However, almost every Korean-North American immigrant church, no matter what denomination it belongs to, would be disturbed if God were addressed in any other way but as God the Father, the Son, and the Holy Spirit, or if God were presented in a female image. There is no doubt that the use of only masculine images and metaphors in worship and in theology has created for them the impression that God is male. At the same time, the use of only masculine images and metaphors for God implies that they still remain in their traditional view of genders that male is superior to female. At any rate, this one-sided way of referring to God in masculine images and metaphors contributes to the religious legitimization of patriarchy in the sense that masculinity is assumed to be normative for all human beings.

Because God is named Father, Son, and Spirit, the Trinity has been regarded as contributing to conception of a male God. Undeniably, it has been used to legitimize patriarchy and justify the subordination of women to men. However, does this mean we should reject all Father-Son language

A Critical Evaluation of Feminist Theologies

and choose non-sexist, inclusive, and emancipatory language instead?[30] Feminist theologians, acknowledging the power of language, turn their attention to the Father-Son-the Holy Spirit language in the Trinity. In order to bypass the masculinity of Trinitarian images, they take three different approaches. One highlights the so-called feminine characteristics of the Holy Spirit. Another replaces Father-Son-the Holy Spirit with other triads neither masculine nor feminine. A third takes a holistic approach by turning to the biblical Sophialogical tradition to reject exclusively male metaphors for God language.

First of all, as a corrective to overcome the inherent patriarchy in the Trinity, some have suggested feminine imagery for the Holy Spirit. In history, Gregory of Nazianzus found the image of the Triune God in the original nuclear family: Adam, Eve, and Seth. In this social analogy of the nuclear family, he found eternal Fatherhood, eternal Motherhood, and eternal Childhood.[31] In the Scriptures, some feminist theologians point out, the Spirit is portrayed as the creative maternal God who brings forth life in creation (Gen 1:2) and also brings about the incarnation of Christ, new members of the body of Christ in baptism, and the body of Christ through the *epiclesis* of the Eucharist (ἐπίκλησις, invocation or calling down from on high of the Holy Spirit the power of the blessing of the Holy Spirit upon the Eucharistic bread and wine).

Elizabeth A. Johnson critiques various attempts at identifying the Spirit as "feminine." First of all, she critiques Yves Congar who identifies the Spirit as the feminine person in God. Johnson affirms, in developing the idea of the Spirit as the feminine person in God, Congar describes ways in which the Spirit brings forth, loves, and educates as a mother does, by daily presence and communication that operates more on an affective than intellectual level.[32] In so doing, Johnson argues, "The author effectively reduces women's identity to the one role of mothering, an utterly important one to be sure, but just as certainly not the only role women exercise in the course of a lifetime. Nor is its execution devoid of the exercise of intellect."[33] Secondly, Johnson looks into Leonardo Boff's position which holds that the

---

30. Sallie McFague's model of God as Friend is nonsexist. The Inclusive Language Lectionary Committee's use of "God the Father (and Mother)" is inclusive. Ramshaw-Shmidt has proposed a partially nonsexist Trinitarian formula of "Abba, Servant, Paraclete." See also Collins, "Naming God in Public Prayer," 291–304.

31. Moltmann-Wendel and Moltmann, *Humanity in God,* 100–106.

32. Congar, "The Motherhood in God and the Femininity of the Holy Spirit,"155–64.

33. Johnson, *She Who Is,* 52.

Holy Spirit is the person in the Trinity who appropriates the feminine in a unique way. The Holy Spirit, he affirms, has maternal traits which accord primarily with love and self-giving. In analogy with the incarnation of the Word in Jesus, the Spirit, Boff contends, divinizes the feminine in the person of Mary for the benefit of all women:

> The Spirit, the eternal feminine, is united to the created feminine in order that the latter may be totally and fully what it can be—virgin and mother. Mary, as Christian piety has always intuited, is the eschatological realization of the feminine in all of its dimensions.[34]

Boff here attempts to give women direct access to the divine, as men have enjoyed with their physical similarity to Jesus. However, as Elizabeth A. Johnson points out, his attempt is not really liberating for women:

> In spite of this, however, his option for uncritical Jungian ground where the feminine is equated with darkness, death, depth, and receptivity and the masculine with light, transcendence, outgoingness, and reason, even while allowing that neither set of qualities is limited to men or women alone, coupled with his limitation of this feminine dimension to the Spirit alone within the Godhead, insures an outcome that is not liberating for women.[35]

Accordingly, while these attempts have been made to alleviate sexism by imaging the Holy Spirit as feminine, the outcome is not liberating because Boff and Congar build their theory upon stereotyped understandings of women's characteristics and roles. Johnson explains:

> Nurturing and tenderness simply do not exhaust the capacities of women; nor do bodiliness and instinct define women's nature; nor is intelligence and creative transformative agency beyond the scope of women's power; nor can the feminine be equated exclusively with mothering, affectivity, darkness, virginity, the Virgin Mary, or the positive feminine archetype without suffocating women's potential.[36]

As argued by Johnson above, when the Spirit is considered as a feminine aspect of the Godhead, while the Godhead is still understood within a patriarchal framework, the result is not a view of God that may liberate, empower, or develop women as *imago Dei* in all their complex dimensions.

---

34. Boff, *The Maternal Face of God*, 101.
35. Johnson, *She Who Is*, 52–53.
36. Ibid., 53–54.

A Critical Evaluation of Feminist Theologies

Therefore, attempting to understand the Spirit as feminine, in order to add a feminine aspect to the Godhead, is an inadequate measure to liberating women because this understanding is founded upon overarching androcentric frameworks. In the frame of a subordinationist Trinitarian theology, Johnson correctly points out that the association of feminine imagery solely with the Spirit would only reinforce the subordination of women in church and society.[37] Consequently, when the Spirit is viewed as the feminine person of the Godhead, it should never be taken to indicate the sex of God but rather to indicate the essential relationality of God, or to represent a diversity of divine activities and attributes.[38]

Another approach to challenge a male-imaged God is to suggest a substitute for the unique personal name, Father, Son, and Holy Spirit, eliminating both the masculinity and the femininity of the Trinity. For this reason, Feminist theologians have come up with inclusive, non-sexist language. Gail Ramshaw-Schmidtt has proposed a partially nonsexist Trinitarian formula of "Abba-Servant-Paraclete."[39] Letty Russell conceived the Trinity as "Creator-Liberator-Advocate" who calls human beings into partnership with divine care for the world.[40] There is also the "Creator-Christ-Holy Spirit."[41] The most common triad suggested is "Creator-Redeemer-Sustainer."[42]

Susan Brooks Thistlethwaite contends that the strength of the economic Trinity as Creator-Redeemer-Sustainer lies in how it contains the history of God's relationship with the world. She emphasizes the relationality of God's nature by employing Moltmann's conception of the Trinity from the perspective of history. The Trinitarian history of the relationship of the persons of the Trinity is "open, inviting, unifying, thus an integrating unity."[43] The unity of the divine persons in Trinity is not imposed by some prior conceptuality but emerges as the triune God comes to embrace humanity. Thistlethwaite insists that the Trinitarian history of God's activity in creating, in redeeming, and in sustaining subverts concepts of domina-

---

37. Johnson, "The Incomprehensibility of God," 458. See also LaCugna, "God in Communion with Us," 105.

38. LaCugna, "God in Communion with Us," 105. See also Johnson, *She Who Is*, 55.

39. Collins, "Naming God in Public Prayer," 291–304.

40. Russell, *The Future of Partnership*, 25–43.

41. *Word and Sacrament*, United Church of Christ Office of Church Life and Leadership, 47.

42. Thistlethwaite, "On the Trinity," in Thistlethwaite and Engel, *Lift Every Voice: Constructing Christian Theologies from the Underside*, 125.

43. Ibid.

The Liberative Cross

tion and subordination that have characterized theological reflections on the Father, Son, and Holy Spirit.

However, LaCugna points out that the problem with "naming" God "Creator-Redeemer-Sustainer" is that it can contribute to the impression that "there are 'three' (that is numerically three) some things or some ones, each of whom is responsible for different aspects of redemption."[44] LaCugna correctly points out that this functional or modalist Creator-Redeemer-Sustainer language does not adequately reflect the language of Scripture that portrays God as creating through the Son (Col 1:16; Heb 11:3; John. 1:1-3) and by the Spirit (Gen 1:1-2), or how God redeems us through Christ (2 Cor 5:19; Eph 1:7; Col 1:14).[45] Most importantly, LaCugna insists, because persons are more than what they do, such functional or modalist language is not in every case an exact equivalent to the uniquely personal name, "Father-Son-Spirit."[46] Distinguishing the divine persons by their function does not sufficiently highlight the personal and relational character of God as God in *se*.

Thirdly, in order to overcome the inherent patriarchy in the Trinity, Elisabeth Fiorenza and Elizabeth Johnson turn to the biblical Sophialogical tradition which is rooted in the experiences of the Spirit and understands the ministry and life of Jesus in terms of Sophia. Fiorenza maintains that a Sophia-Christology pervades the early Christian missionary movement.[47] The God of the Christian missionary movement is not God who leaves Jesus in the power of death, but God who raises him "in power" so that Jesus may become "a life-giving Spirit." (1 Cor 15:45). The wisdom theology of the Christian missionary movement identified the resurrected Lord not only with the Spirit of God but also with the Sophia of God. It sees Jesus as the divine Sophia herself. Fiorenza finds this Sophia-Christology in the pre-Pauline hymns (Phil 2:6-11; 1 Tim 3:16; Col 1:15-20; Eph 2:14-16; Heb 1:3; 1 Pet 3:18-22; John 1:1-14). She contends that these hymns proclaim the universality of salvation in Jesus Christ through language derived from Jewish-Hellenistic wisdom theology and from contemporary mystery religion. For example, the *kenosis* passage of Phil 2:6-11 proclaims that through

---

44. LaCugna, "The Baptismal Formula, Feminist Objections, and Trinitarian Theology," 243.

45. LaCugna, "God in Communion with Us," 105.

46. LaCugna, "The Baptismal Formula, Feminist Objections, and Trinitarian Theology," 243.

47. Schüssler Fiorenza, *In Memory of Her*, 189–99.

A Critical Evaluation of Feminist Theologies

Jesus' exaltation and enthronement, Christ-Sophia has received his-her lordship over the whole cosmos as well as over heavenly and earthy powers.

Elisabeth S. Fiorenza affirms that exalting Christ-Sophia as the Lord over the whole cosmos is done in a language alluding to the Old Testament (Isa 45:23) and the contemporary Isis cult. According to her, "Like Isis, Christ-Sophia is given a name 'which is above all names' and worshiped by all the powers in the cosmos. Just as Isis' true acclamation is 'Isis is the Lord,' the true Christian acclamation is 'Jesus Christ is the Lord.'"[48] In the religious milieu of the Hellenistic world ruled by merciless powers and, above all, by blind fate, Christians proclaimed Christ-Sophia as the ruler of the principalities which had previously enslaved the world. Furthermore, the Christian missionary movement, which proclaims Christ-Sophia as the ruler of principalities, implores Christians to seek liberation from the powers of this world and participate in the divine world.

Fiorenza, in her *Jesus: Miriam's Child, Sophia's Prophet*, points out that the Gospel of John does not introduce Jesus as the Son of Divine Sophia but the begotten Son of the Father. She sees throughout the Gospel John, Jesus characterized as Wisdom Incarnate:

> Like Sophia-Isis, Jesus speaks in the revelatory "I am" style, and with the symbolisms of bread, wine, and living water s/he invites people to eat and drink. Like Sophia, Jesus provides the pattern of narrating the life and mission of Jesus. Like Sophia, Jesus was sent. Jesus-Sophia came into his/her own but was not received by his/her own people and therefore has returned through his/her exaltation to the world of G*d. Wisdom mythology sees all-important for understanding the life and fate of Jesus. The logos title of the prologue therefore seems not to lessen but to increase the possibility that the Fourth Gospel understands Jesus as making Sophia present in and through her/his work.[49]

Fiorenza argues that by introducing father-son language in the very beginning of John (John 1:14-18) and by using it throughout the Gospel, the whole book reinforces the idea of logos and son as being congruent to the biological masculine sex of the historical Jesus. Consequently, the Fourth Gospel not only dissolves the tension between the feminine gender

---

48. Ibid., 190.
49. Schüssler Fiorenza, *Jesus: Miriam's Child, Sophia's Prophet*, 152.

of Sophia and the masculine gender of Jesus but also marginalizes and silences the traditions of God as represented by Divine Sophia.[50]

Like Fiorenza, Johnson also points out that what is ascribed to Hokma/Sophia in the Old Testament and the apocryphal wisdom books is now ascribed to Jesus in the New Testament.[51] She explains why the Gospel of John substitutes word/logos for wisdom/Sophia in the prologue: "By the end of the first century, word was the term used to signify the apostolic kerygma; *sophia*'s use was increasingly problematic due to its adaption by budding Gnostic groups."[52] Johnson also considers the thought of the Hellenistic Jewish philosopher Philo to have had a major influence. Philo affected the milieu in which late first-century theological reflection took place. In his work on the relationship of Sophia to logos, Philo adopted the dualistic pattern of Greek thinking. He held that the symbol of the female signified whatever was evil, tied to the world of the senses, and irrational or passive; by contrast the symbol of the male represented the good, the world of the spirit and rationality, and active initiative. Within this framework it would be inconceivable that divine Sophia could remain feminine. Johnson quotes Philo:

> For pre-eminence always pertains to the masculine, and the feminine always comes short of it and is lesser than it. Let us, then, pay no heed to the discrepancy in the gender of the words, and say that the daughter of God, even Sophia, is not only masculine but father, sowing and begetting in souls aptness to learn, discipline, knowledge, sound sense, and laudable actions.[53]

Johnson points out how this outlook easily led to replacing the female symbol with the male symbol. In addition, it was necessary to replace the feminine Sophia with the masculine symbol of Logos because of the gender of Jesus.[54]

In arguing all the above, Johnson's point is that Christian reflection, before the gospel of John, did not find it difficult to associate the historical Jesus, as well as the risen and exalted Christ, with Sophia. However,

---

50. Ibid., 152–54.

51. Johnson, *She Who Is*, 94–98. See also Johnson, "Jesus the Wisdom of God," 261–94.

52. Ibid., 97.

53. Ibid., 98. See also LaPorte, "Philo in the Tradition of Biblical Wisdom Literature," 103–41.

54. Ibid., 98.

the replacement of Sophia by Logos in the prologue of the Gospel John brought about a growth of sexism in the Christian communities. It eventually changed the Christian communities, leading them toward patriarchal ecclesial structures, preventing women from practicing in certain ministries in which they had originally served.

Johnson affirms that by linking the historical Jesus with wisdom/Sophia, the Christian communities were enabled to attribute cosmic significance to the crucified Jesus and to see that Jesus was not simply a human being inspired by God, but was related to God in some special way. Since Jesus the Christ is depicted as divine Sophia, it is neither unthinkable nor unbiblical to confess Jesus the Christ as the incarnation of God imaged in female symbol. She further comments, "Sophia in all her fullness was in him so that he manifests the depth of divine mystery in creative and graciously saving involvement in the world."[55]

According to Elizabeth Johnson, the prologue of the gospel John is essentially a wisdom text; therefore, there is no necessity in discussing the incarnation solely in terms of Logos.[56] Johnson argues that "Jesus is Sophia incarnate; Jesus is Logos incarnate. This inclusive Christological reflection makes room for female image and it has the potential to contribute in theory and practice to the appreciation of the dignity of real women."[57] Wisdom Christology reflects the depth of the mystery of God and points the way to an inclusive Christology in female symbols.

Using the concept of Sophia in her social Trinity, Johnson speaks of the one God as Holy Wisdom or simply as Sophia-God. In developing the Sophia Trinity, she explains why she uses female images to speak about the Trinity:

> It is not essential for the truth of God's triune mystery to speak always in the metaphors of father, son, and spirit, although virtually exclusive use of these names over the centuries in liturgy, catechesis, and theology has caused this to be forgotten . . . I believe that we need a strong dose of explicitly female imagery to break the unconscious sway that male Trinitarian imagery holds over the imaginations of even the most sophisticated thinkers.[58]

55. Ibid., 99.

56. Elizabeth A. Johnson cities, among others, Brown, *The Gospel according to John I–XII*, 523; and Dunn, *Christology in the Making*, 214.

57. Johnson, "Jesus the Wisdom of God: A Biblical Basis for Non–Androcentric Christology," 289.

58. Johnson, *She Who Is*, 212.

The Liberative Cross

Johnson, therefore, affirms that the Trinity needs to be presented as a symbol of the mystery of salvation in the midst of the world's suffering by using female images. She uses Sophia in relation to each of the three persons of the Trinity: Spirit-Sophia, Jesus-Sophia, and Mother-Sophia.[59] In using Sophia in this way, she is not adding a fourth person to the Trinity or replacing any one of the three with Wisdom. By the concept of Sophia Trinity, Johnson emphasizes that at the heart of holy mystery is not monarchy but community; not an absolute ruler, but a threefold *koinonia*. She also contends that "the very essence of God is to be in relation, and thus relatedness rather than the solitary ego is the heart of all reality."[60] The Trinity understood in this way, she believes, resonates with the feminist values of mutuality, relation, and community in diversity.

Fiorenza's understanding of the life and lordship of Jesus in terms of Sophia, as well as Johnson's Sophia-Trinity, is a great attempt at overcoming the weakness of traditional descriptions of God which have reinforced systems of male domination and led to the dehumanization of women.[61] However, I see that the basic problem causing patriarchal, androcentric mentalities and systems is deeper than language. As LaCugna points out, amending religious language in liturgy or theology may raise consciousness about exclusion implicit in language, but it does not immediately overcome all exclusiveness or literalness.[62]

For this reason, certain feminist theologians take a different approach at retrieving Jesus' teachings about God as father and his calling of a new, non-patriarchal faith community of equal disciples. Those who attest to invoking God as the Father defend their position by referring to Jesus' referral to God as "Father." Their argument goes like this: Because Jesus called God Father, God must be called Father. If God had wanted to reveal "Himself" as a Mother, God could have done so. It is true that Jesus called God Abba (Mark 14:36). "Abba" was a startlingly personal and intimate revelation of God by Jesus. We, by addressing God as "Abba" also use a term of intimacy, which was a characteristic feature of Jesus' own prayer. In the Pauline Epistles, we are told that we have gained access to God, whom Jesus called Abba, through the Spirit (Rom 8:15; Gal 4:6).

---

59. Ibid.

60. Ibid., 216. See also Wells, "Trinitarian Feminism: Elizabeth Johnson's Wisdom Christology," 339.

61. Wells, "Trinitarian Feminism," 339.

62. LaCugna, "God in Communion with Us," 107.

LaCugna, however, argues that we cannot deduce the masculinity of God directly from the fact that God was called Abba by Jesus. LaCugna rightly insists:

> Great care is required to move from a term of invocation and prayer to a divine attribute. "God the Father" in the sense of "Father of Jesus Christ" is a specific and personal way to name God, not an indefinite name for the divine essence.[63]

Consequently, Jesus' relationship to God must not be understood as a Father-Son relationship in the biological or patriarchal sense. As a result, Jesus' presenting God as Abba constitutes a liberating subversion of patriarchy which can no longer claim divine sanction but stands revealed as a sinful human structure.[64]

However, this Fatherhood of God has been used to support both sexist theologies of complementarity and patriarchal God-language. LaCugna makes the important point that if we understand "God the Father" as an indefinite name of divine substance, we are led to the downfall of the Arians who understood "father" as a synonym for the divine substance (*ousia*).[65] According to Arius, God as "Father" is the source of all reality, and God as "Father" is unbegotten, eternal, and without beginning. Besides, Godhood could neither be shared with nor imparted to anyone, not even to Christ. If the Father had a Son of the same nature and/or substance, there would be two gods. Arius, therefore, regarded Christ as a creature, higher than other creatures but still less than God. If "father" is understood as a synonym for the divine substance (*ousia*), then the logic perfectly makes sense. Consequently, LaCugna contends that their view of "Father" as a generic, non-relational name for God altogether removed God from the world and prohibited any relations with humanity. Consequently, the premise of Arianism could not evoke praise from Christians whose faith was centered on Christ.[66]

Over against the view of the Arians, LaCugna argues, the Cappadocians (Basil, Gregory of Nyssa, Gregory of Nazianzus) saw the title Father as a way to secure the essentially relational and personal nature of God.[67]

---

63. LaCugna, "The Baptismal Formula, Feminist Objections, and Trinitarian Theology," 240–42.

64. Schneider, *Women and the Word*, 48.

65. LaCugna, "The Baptismal Formula, Feminist Objections, and Trinitarian Theology," 240–42.

66. Ibid., 242.

67. Ibid., 240.

According to the Cappadocians, "Father" as *agennesia* (unbegottenness) means "Father in relation to the Son" (Begetter). However, she contends that "Such words as begetting and unbegotten, or generate and ungenerate, do not tell us what the essence of God is; they name an aspect of God's face turned toward the world."[68] Likewise, the title "Father" does not give any information about the nature or qualities of divine fatherhood." LaCugna affirms that God is Father in a personal sense: God is Father of Israel by election, and God is Father of Jesus Christ by generation.[69] If we refuse to use "Father" as a personal name for God, she argues, we actually concede that God the Father is male, just as patriarchy had claimed.[70] Consequently, the problem, LaCugna insists, is not that God is imaged as Father, but that Fatherhood has become the root-metaphor for God, thereby replacing the proclamation of God's reign with the institution of patriarchy.[71]

In contrast to seeing the doctrine of the Trinity as the culprit lying behind patriarchal religion, I concur with LaCugna's assertion that studying the theological and historical development of the Cappadocian doctrine of the Trinity can help us find a strong foundation for the vision of equality and mutuality among human beings in society.[72] The Cappadocians postulated personhood in relation to another as the supreme characteristic of God. They asserted that divinity, or Godhood, originates with personhood (someone toward another), not with substance (something in and of itself). Personhood is being-in-relation-to-another. For example, the Son is defined by origin from the Father: the Son is begotten from the Father. The Holy Spirit likewise originates from the Father: The Spirit proceeds from the Father. The identity and unique reality of a person emerges entirely in relation to another person. Although God the Father's personhood is defined as "to be from no one" (Unoriginate), it is precisely the economy of Christ and the Spirit that introduces the all-important qualifications:

---

68. Ibid., 241.
69. Ibid., 240.
70. Ibid., 243.
71. Sallie McFague, *Metaphorical Theology*, 45–52.
72. LaCugna, "God in Comunion with Us," 90. The Cappadocian doctrine of Trinity with its emphasis on the total equality, mutuality, and interpenetration among the divine persons, has appealed to some feminist and liberation theologians as a way to ground a vision of equality among human persons in society. See, for example, Wilson-Kastner, *Faith, Feminism and the Christ*; Boff, *Trinity and Society*; Farley, "New Patterns of Relationship: Beginning of a Moral Revolution," 627–46.

the unoriginate God is by nature originating and related. God by nature is outgoing love and self-donation.[73]

The idea of a shared divine *arche* proposed by Gregory of Naziansus is noteworthy here because, as LaCugna contends, "it entirely eliminated any remaining traces of an Arian subordination of the Son to the Father monarch."[74] The divine unity was no longer located in the Father-God who was prior to or greater than everyone and everything else. Instead, the divine unity and divine life were located in the communion of equal, though unique, persons, not in the primacy of one person over another. In this way, Trinitarian monotheism preserved the principle of shared rule and eliminated the idea that any person can be subordinated to another. LaCugna strongly affirms, "This is the kernel of the radical theological and political proposal of the Cappadocians that is relevant to the program of feminism today."[75] In chapter 3, I will look into *perichoresis*, an important term which Moltmann borrows from the Cappadocians to describe the mutual interpenetration and the indwelling of the Father, Son, and Holy Spirit.[76] The term, *perichoresis* allows an understanding that there is no subordination in Trinity. For now, however, I contend by agreeing with LaCugna that the Cappadocians can challenge the Christian imagination to renounce biological, cultural and commonsense notion of fatherhood, including the patriarchal ideal of the self-sufficient father.

Is the Subordination of Woman to Man Inherent in the Trinity?

Those who believe in the theology of complementarity argue for a parallel between the relationship of God the Father and God the Son with the relationship of men and women: God the Father is the source of the Son, and by analogy, man is the source of woman. God the Son is said to be obedient and even submissive toward God the Father, hence women are to be obedient and submit to men.[77] The theology behind men's superiority

---

73. LaCugna, "The Trinitarian Mystery of God" 149–91.
74. LaCugna, "God in Communion," 87.
75. Ibid., 88.
76. Moltmann, *The Trinity and the Kingdom*, 175.
77. Garcia, "Femininity and the Life of Faith," 125–30. Cf. Werner Neuer, *Man and Woman in Christian Perspective*, 34–41. For a good critique on Neuer's theology of complementarity, see LaCugna, "God in communion with us: The Trinity," 94–99.

over women is the headship of man who has been derived from the Pauline Epistles (1 Cor 11:3; Eph 5:12; Col 3:18; Titus 2:5). Man is the head over woman; man fully images God while woman images God by virtue of her relationship to man.

The religious use of the headship model derives from imperial and monarchical patterns of past political structures.[78] In agreement with Ruether, Anne Carr contends:

> God's relation to human beings and Christ's relation to the church have been dealt as analogous to the feudal religions of husband and wife, male and female, clergy and laity, a relationship of inferiority and subordination for the second term in each pair. This hierarchical scheme embodies the hierarchical dualisms of patristic and medieval thought with their origins in Greek philosophy: spirit over flesh, soul over body, and mind over matter.[79]

It is Thomas Aquinas, according to Ruether, who introduced Aristotelian heritage into Christian language and established the subordination of women as a God-given order. Aquinas speaks of the defective nature of woman in this way:

> For the active power in the seed of the male tends to produce something like itself, perfect in masculinity; but the procreation of a female is the result either of the debility of the active power, of some unsuitability of the material, or of some change effected by external influences, like the south wind, for example, which is damp, as we are told by Aristotle.[80]

According to Aquinas, the soul informs the body; therefore, woman's defective physical state leads to the conclusion that woman's soul is likewise deficient, her mind weak in reasoning, and her will fragile in choosing the good. Her deficiency requires male supervision because "in man the discretion of reason predominates." [81] Given such an assessment of the deficient humanity of women, femaleness is judged to be unsuitable for metaphors when trying to talk about God. Woman as a defective human being cannot represent headship either in society or in the church.[82]

---

78. Ruether, "Women in Medieval Theology," 220.

79. Carr, *Transforming Grace*, 165.

80. *ST* I, q. 92, a. 1, ad. 1. See Ruether, "Misogynism and Virginal Feminism in the Fathers of the Church," 150–83. See also Horowitz, "Aristotle and Women," 183–213.

81. *ST* I, q. 92, a.1, ad.2.

82. Ruether, *To Change the World: Christology and Cultural Criticism*, 45.

According to this complementarity argument, it would be unnatural for a woman to assume a leadership role. Against Thomas Aquinas, LaCugna rightly argues that the subordination of woman to man does not originate from a divinely decreed plan but is a consequence of The Fall.[83] God's providential plan revealed in Christ the restoration of the household of God, in which male and female, Jew and Gentile, free and slave equally live as one family (Gal 3: 28). The church, therefore, is to be the witness of this reign of God in which all false rulers who abuse the weak are exposed and overturned.[84] Another problem of this complementarity argument, according to LaCugna, is that it hinges on the very heresy that the church tried to overcome in its rejection of Arianism, namely the notion that the Son is in any sense subordinate to the Father. Athanasius and the Cappadocians struggled vigorously to eradicate all subordination between Father and Son and asserted their full equality as persons.[85] There is no intrinsic reason why men should be correlated with God the Father and women with God the Son.

The belief that God and maleness are somehow intrinsically related carries with it drastic implications for the roles and positions of men and women. Furthermore, the view that sees the nature of woman as defective and inferior to man has caused the exclusion of women from the Eucharistic acts and the teaching functions of the priesthood. We find this kind of approach in the Vatican declaration of 1976 on the question of women and priesthood. It presents women as unsuitable to act in *persona Christi* during the Eucharist due to their sexual difference to Jesus.[86] This way of thinking is rooted in the belief that Jesus' incarnation as a male is ontologically necessary, as sharing in the maleness of Jesus is the only genuine way to be human.

This ontological connection the Vatican made between the maleness of Jesus and the maleness of God, Elizabeth A. Johnson argues, is at odds with the doctrines of Nicaea and Chalcedon. Thus, Johnson successfully enlists Nicaea and Chalcedon to the feminist side of the argument.[87] Taking seriously the famous patristic dictum made by Gregory of Nazianzus,

---

83. LaCugna, "God in Communion with Us," 98.

84. Ibid.

85. Ibid.

86. Carr, *Transforming Grace*, 164. See also Johnson, "Redeeming the Name of Christ," 119.

87. Johnson, *Consider Jesus*, 153. See also Johnson, *She Who Is*, 152.

"What is not assumed is not redeemed," she asks, "Did God assume the humanity of women?" To answer the question, Johnson closely takes a look at the phrase from the earlier Nicene Confession that "God from God" became a human being (*et homo factus est*), which was further specified by the Council of Chalcedon to mean a genuine human being (*vere homo*).[88] The essential point is that God did not choose to specifically become a male human (*vir factus est*), but fully human in Jesus (*vere homo*).

At the Council of Chalcedon, the controversial Greek word *homoousios*, "one in being", previously used in the Nicene Creed to forge Jesus' identity of nature with God, was further interpreted to forge another identification, namely, that Jesus is also "one in being with us as to his humanity."[89] Thus, "as one in being with us as to his humanity," Jesus was born to a life of creaturely finitude marked by the pleasures and pains of the body, nescience and growth in wisdom, and freedom with the need to risk. Johnson concludes that it is not Jesus' maleness that is doctrinally important but his humanity in solidarity with the whole suffering human race.[90]

Elizabeth A. Johnson, therefore, affirms that God's choice to become a man is not an ontological necessity. Jesus' maleness was but one characteristic that made him human. Jesus' maleness is a historical option. She, therefore, sociologically analyzes the incarnation of the Word in the form of a male human being. Rather than an ontological necessity, she argues, God's choice to be incarnated as a male "is an intentional yet subversive one, that is, certainly a challenge to the patriarchal world. God became a man to break the fetters of sexism by his absolute humility and liberty for others."[91] The male Jesus preached and enacted "the exact opposite of the patriarchal ideal of the powerful man."[92] Elizabeth Johnson argues for this point further by stating:

> For if a woman had preached and enacted compassion and given the gift of self even unto death, the world would have shrugged- is not this what women are supposed to do anyway? But for a man to live and die this way in a world of male privilege is to challenge the patriarchal ideal of the dominating male at its root.[93]

---

88. Johnson, *She Who Is*, 164.
89. Ibid.
90. Ibid., 164–65. See also Johnson, "Redeeming the Name of Christ," 130.
91. Ibid., 161.
92. Ibid.
93. Johnson, *Consider Jesus*, 111.

A Critical Evaluation of Feminist Theologies

In this way Johnson takes Jesus' maleness as a prophecy challenging patriarchy. Instead of capitalizing on his maleness, Jesus practiced compassionate love for women and children in the patriarchal Greco-Roman culture. She also sees the cross as a symbol of the *kenosis* of patriarchy. The death of Jesus on the cross embodies the exact opposite of the patriarchal ideal of the powerful man, and shows "the steep price to be paid in the struggle for liberation."[94]

In agreement with Johnson, I conclude that what the male Jesus taught and practiced in life as well as on the cross is theologically meaningful in a subversive, unsettling way. Bernard Haring rightly emphasizes, "Anyone who wants to overemphasize Christ's maleness in order to establish prerogatives of males ("priests") over females has not understood Jesus as the liberator of all people, men and women, and has not understood the way he liberated us."[95]

I have argued above that to claim that the Father of Jesus is a male God on the basis of Jesus' invocation of God as "Father" or of the incarnation of God as a male human being is to misrepresent the New Testament. Jesus' historical maleness has been used to reinforce an exclusively male image of God and to legalize men's superiority over women, especially in the belief that men are more conformed to the image of Christ than women. However, the Father of Jesus Christ presented in the New Testament does not discriminate based on sex, gender, or social status. In the person of Jesus, God has broken down the barriers, or "the dividing walls" (Eph 2:11-22; Col 1:19-20), and called both men and women, Jews and Gentiles, slaves and freemen to be one in Jesus Christ so that they may live harmoniously in the new household of God.

In this first section, I have looked into various ways in which feminist theologians have dealt with exclusive, patriarchal language in order to renew the idea of God toward greater inclusivity. Now, I will turn to the various ways in which feminist theologians view the cross and how some of them try to retrieve a theology of the cross that serves as a life-giving, liberating symbol of love for humanity including women.

---

94. Johnson, *She Who Is*, 161. See also Ruether, *Sexism and God-talk*, 137.
95. Haring, *Free and Faithful in Christ*, 139.

The Liberative Cross

God's Relation to the Cross

Some feminists have accused the cross as being a symbol of denigration and oppression against women, causing them to ultimately leave Christianity. How far are their charges justified? Can we retrieve a theology of the cross that is a life-giving, liberating symbol of love for humanity including women? We will answer these questions by uncovering neglected strands and revealing countervoices in theological traditions.

Is the Cross a Symbol of Denigration and Oppression?

At the center of Christian faith stands the cross. Yet, some feminists like Valerie Saiving[96] and Judith Plaskow[97] see the cross as a destructive sign for women. They see it as passive victimization. However, Korean Christian women in general do not share their point of view. Two hymns most frequently sung by them are about the cross of Jesus Christ: "Jesus Keep Me near the Cross" written by Francis Jane (Fanny) Crosby (1820-1915), and "Let Us Sing of His Love" written by Francis Bottome (1823-94). Korean Christian women love to sing these hymns with gratitude because they believe that the Lamb of God washed and cleansed them of their sins, winning them perfect deliverance. Through these hymns, they express the joy of the salvation that was given to them through Jesus' substitutionary death on the cross. Instead of taking the cross of Jesus as an offensive symbol of sacrificial victimization, Korean Christian women take it as something to sing about and follow in *imitatio Christi*. Why do those feminists find the cross offensive and regard it as a symbol of denigration and oppression against women? What is it that causes the cross to be seen with negativity?

Those who view the cross as a symbol of denigration and oppression do so in fear of the pernicious impact that it may have on voiceless women and children, forcing them to imitate the silent suffering of Christ and be silenced by patriarchal oppression. The fears of the feminists are caused mainly by how they understand human sin. Valerie Saiving is one among those who view the cross as a symbol of denigration and oppression for women. She argues that in order to see human sin for what it really is

---

96. Saiving, "The Human Situation: A Feminine View," in Christ and Plaskow, *Womanspirit Rising*, 25–42.

97. Plaskow, *Sex, Sin, and Grace: Women's Experience and the Theologies of Reinhold Niebuhr and Paul Tillich*.

theologians must consider the essentially divergent experiences of women and men.[98] Saiving points out that women's sin is not pride or the Niebuhrian understanding of "will-to-power," but underdevelopment or negation of self. To help achieve a firmer understanding of the Niebuhrian conception of sin, we will take a look at how Langdon Gilkey explains it in his *On Niebuhr: A Theological Study*. Gilkey writes:

> Man seeks to overcome his insecurity by a will-to-power to which overreaches the limits of human creatureliness . . . Man is ignorant and involved in the limitations of a finite mind; but he pretends he is not limited. He assumes he can gradually transcend finite limitation until his mind becomes identical with universal mind. All of his intellectual and cultural pursuits, therefore, become infected with the sin of pride. Man's pride and will-to-power disturb the harmony of creation. The Bible defines sin in both religious and moral terms. The religious dimension of sin is man's rebellion against God . . . The moral and social dimension of sin is injustice. The ego which falsely makes itself the center of existence in its pride and will-to-power inevitably subordinates other life to its will and thus does injustice to other life.[99]

In view of the Niebuhrian understanding of sin, Valerie Saiving contends that a danger follows when we apply the understanding of sin as pride or "will-to-power" for women.[100] Totalizing women's experience rather than acknowledging complexity, Saiving defines women's sin as the underdevelopment or negation of the self, which she views as a propensity inherent in the female character. Saiving argues that when women embrace the "selflessness of love" as a cure to the Niebuhrian conception of sin they attempt to strangle any impulse in themselves to achieve a healthy sense of self-differentiation and self-concern.

Judith Plaskow, a Jewish feminist shares Saiving's central claim of women's sin as underdevelopment or negation of self. However, in comparison to Saiving, who tends to see differences in women's experience as rooted in biology, Plaskow takes a social-constructivist approach to sin and sees sin as a product of social experience.[101] Plaskow questions how the underdevelopment or negation of the self, being inherent, can at the same

98. Saiving, "The Human Situation: A Feminine View," 25–42.

99. Gilkey. *On Niebuhr: A Theological Study,* 178–9.

100. Saiving, "The Human Situation: A Feminine View," 25–42.

101. Plaskow, *Sex, Sin, and Grace: Women's Experience and the Theologies of Reinhold Niebuhr and Paul Tillich,* 154.

time be considered sinful. Plaskow also argues how theology should seek to discourage false ideas about what is inherent in the female character.[102] She claims that rather than negation of the self being an inherent characteristic in women, social factors such as race and class work in complex ways to construct female selves as distinct from male selves. According to Plaskow, patriarchal, social, and cultural factors encourage women to live self-sacrificially, and sin originates in cultural and societal structures. The cure, therefore, comes through the transformation of the deformed social and cultural structures that limit women's ability to develop a sense of self. Drawing on the work of Saiving and Plaskow, Daphne Hampson insists that women can experience a transformation through relationships with other persons.[103] In contrast to Luther's emphasis on the personal, social transformation which is dependent on God, Hampson asserts that women have the power to actualize their potential for loving relations.[104] Hampson, therefore, rallies women to claim power in society, urging them to model different systems of interaction in order to transform patriarchal social structures. Diverging from Saiving, Hampson implies that men also possess the inherent potential to be relational, but unhealthy patriarchal structures create obstacles to healthy relationships. She believes that feminists can transform oppressive structures and achieve salvation on their own through right relationship with others.

Unlike Hampson, Rebecca Frey diagnoses female sinfulness by claiming that pride represents an appropriate analysis of women's sin. She contends that societal structures undeniably shape women's expressions of pride but the origin of the sin of women runs deeper than societal structures.[105] Frey insists that instead of magnifying one's own power, righteousness, and knowledge, categorized by Niebuhr as a manifestation of pride, women tend to glorify their sacrifices to others. According to her, women and men may express pride in different ways, but they are guilty of the same sin in terms of disbelief or lack of faith, which is the primary manifestation of pride.

At this point, we cannot help but raise questions: Can and should one speak differently of women and men about sin? Doesn't pride or the

---

102. Ibid., 2.

103. Thompson, *Crossing the Divide: Luther, Feminism, and the Cross*, 106.

104. Hampson, "Luther on the Self: A Feminist Critique," 215

105. Frey, "Why Women Want the Goddess: Experiential and Confessional Reflections," 20.

Niebuhrian understanding of "will-to-power" also represent an appropriate diagnosis of women's sin? Don't women also magnify their power, righteousness, and knowledge like men do? By asserting women's power in society to enact healthy relationships and transform social structures, aren't the feminists only glorifying one half of humanity? Are women so different from men in nature that they need a different savior from men?

I argue that in discussing the nature of sin, we must not totalize women's experience but acknowledge its complexity. We also must acknowledge that the nature of sin is much wider than just *hubris* or pride. From a social Trinitarian view of salvation, I argue, sin is broken relationship, rebellion manifested in a search for autonomy as against perichoretic fellowship with God and others. If we view sin as broken relationship to be healed, we cannot speak differently of women and men about sin. Elizabeth Moltmann-Wendel correctly points out that a theologian of the cross must affirm the reality of trials and temptations in women's lives, acknowledging that "even the power of relationships can break."[106] Women often suffer not only the pain of broken relationships but also the burden of responsibility for healing and mending them. Sally Purvis, a Christian feminist ethicist correctly affirms that women are not immune to temptation to sin through the abuse of power.[107] They undergo the trials of broken and wounded relationships. In fact, all human beings, both men and women, are imperfect and are continuously subjected to the temptation to replicate patterns of domination.

We must locate sin and the accompanying suffering not only in men's lives but also in women's lives; otherwise, women cannot be called to account for their personal sin as well as their participation and perpetuation of sinful structures. Deanna A. Thompson, a Lutheran feminist theologian, therefore, calls women to be freed from "the glory theology assumption that they are capable, in collusion with other women, of healing all broken relationships, sustaining all healthy ones, and nurturing all those who need it."[108] She points to Luther's "freedom from/freedom for" dialectic: Women are freed from scripted roles and patterns of behavior and freed to live for God by "humbly serving God by serving the neighbor."[109]

---

106. Moltmann-Wendel, "A Feminist Theology of the Cross," in Moltmann-Wendel and Moltmann, *God: His and Hers*, 85.

107. Purvis, *The Power of the Cross: Foundations for a Christian Feminist Ethic of Community*, 16.

108. Thompson, *Crossing the Divide*, 111.

109. Ibid.

Feminists such as Saiving, Plaskow, and Hampson have been skeptical of Luther's concept of humility because it seems to advocate the very selflessness they decry. However, Luther's concept of humility is not a self-effacing act which can be easily taken as a personal achievement but it is rather a state of being in which a person allows herself/himself to be defined only by God who created, loves, and sustains her/him.[110] Women, therefore, need to accept in humility our limitation as human creatures and accept the power of God to transform and liberate the lives of women to live for others.

Moltmann, following the *kenosis* passage in Philippians 2, speaks of the incarnation and passion of Jesus Christ as the final and complete self-humiliation of God in the person of Jesus. Moltmann elaborates the meaning of Jesus' death of the cross in this way:

> The suffering in the passion of Jesus is abandonment, rejection by God, his Father. God does not become a religion, so that man participates in him by corresponding religious thoughts and feelings. God does not become a law, so that man participates in him through obedience to a law. God does not become an ideal, so that man achieves community with him through constant striving. He humbles himself and takes upon himself the eternal death of the godless and the godforsaken, so that all the godless and the godforsaken can experience communion with him.[111]

God has made the suffering of the world God's own suffering in the cross of the Son.

Accordingly, a feminist theology of the cross should acknowledge that the death of Jesus on the cross embraces the whole of human existence including women. No women are exempt from the responsibility for perpetrating different forms of oppression.

Decrucifying Jesus

Feminist theologians such as Joanne Carlson Brown, Rebecca Parker, and Rita Nakashima Brock as well as a womanist, Delores Williams repudiate an interpretation of the death of Jesus as required by God in repayment for sin. They reject a theological and Christological symbolic system which stresses

---

110. *LW* 44:27.
111. Moltmann, *The Crucified God*, 276.

A Critical Evaluation of Feminist Theologies

that God sacrificed his Son for our sins. They fear that it may be used to legitimate acts of violence against the powerless, like women and children. Feminist theologians, Rita Nakashima Brock and a womanist, Delores Williams, for example, reject the traditional image of God who allowed the Son to be killed as a "blood-thirsty God," and replace it with an image of God that they believe functions more positively in the lives of women and men.[112] They value Jesus' life over His death. For them, God's relationship to the life-transforming human activities of Jesus is more important than God's relationship to a male savior dying on the cross. For instance, a womanist Delores Williams argues that Jesus conquered sin in life, "during his relentless opposition to oppressive systems of his day rather than through any self-sacrificial experience on the cross."[113]

Brown and Parker also argue that redemption is found in the fullness of life, inspired by Christ's life to remain with faithfulness and integrity in order to refuse the threat of death.[114] Christ's life exemplified justice, radical love and liberation. He chose to live his life in opposition to the unjust and oppressive culture; therefore, redemption is available to all those who, in the same manner Christ did, choose to live in loving relationships with one another. In following Jesus, they are to refuse the threat of death, and choose justice, radical love and liberation to overthrow the power of death. For Brown and Parker, the death of Christ has no redemptive efficacy. Jesus did not choose to die on the cross in order to redeem humanity; rather Jesus' death was an unjust act done by humans who rejected his way of life and chose to silence him through death on the cross. In this way, Brown and Parker insist that Christianity needs to be liberated from abusive theology which glorifies suffering.[115]

Rita Nakashima Brock in her book, *Journeys by Heart*, also promotes the primacy of the life of Jesus. Jesus and those who surrounded him possessed the "erotic power" that brought about the healing of personal and communal relationships. She asserts that Jesus' death was purely a political event, and it neither had to happen nor was it part of a divine plan for salvation.[116] According to Brock, Jesus' acts in the passion narrative are acts

---

112. Brock, "And a Little Child Will Lead Us: Christology and Child Abuse," 43.
113. Williams, "Black Women's Surrogate Experience and the Christian Notion of Redemption," 12.
114. Brown and Bohn, "For God So Loved the World," 2, 27.
115. Ibid., 26.
116. Brock, *Journey by Heart: A Christology for Erotic Power*, 93.

The Liberative Cross

of impassioned commitment to solidarity with those crushed by oppressive powers, even perhaps rage for them, rather than acts of self-sacrifice.[117] She affirms that the death of Jesus is neither salvific nor essential but tragic. It is a testimony to the powers of oppression. The suffering of Jesus, however, compels us not to despair but to remember him and all others who suffer, and to seek erotic power by our own action.

Brock states, even when Jesus cried out on the cross "My God, My God, why have you forsaken me?" Jesus did not die totally abandoned because the women who went with Jesus to Jerusalem were there with him at the cross. The divine erotic power, illuminated through Christa/Community in Galilee and the women at Bethany, is sustained through Jesus' death by those who watched him die and marked his burial site.[118] The women at the cross were afraid, and yet persisted in their care of Jesus' tomb. Even in the midst of broken heartedness they refused to give up on erotic power.

Brock argues that erotic power and the hope of wholeness for the community of Jesus' disciples is restored by those faithful disciples who did not let go of the relationships they had to each other, as well as their refusal to let Jesus' death be the end of their community. The resurrection, according to her, provided a way for Jesus to continue to live in the disciples, and for the disciples to live for and with each other.[119] The disciples' refusal to give up their love for each other and their healing acts of remembrance gave meaning to the resurrection "as a profound affirmation of this life of the lives of those who have gone before and of the right to justice of those who live here and now, who cry out for deliverance and healing."[120]

Elisabeth Wendel-Moltmann argues against this "decrucifying [of] Jesus."[121] She argues that Brock removes God from any involvement in the Cross by saying that Jesus' death was not part of the divine plan for salvation but purely a political event. With regard to Brock, Elisabeth Wendel-Moltmann points out that the New Testament makes a distinction between godforsakenness and being forsaken by human beings. The presence of the women at the cross and the tomb is a proof of their faithful friendship. The godforsakenness Jesus experienced on the cross cannot be done away with by erotic power or by the power of relationship. Wendel-Moltmann

---

117. Ibid., 94.
118. Ibid., 96–100.
119. Ibid., 100.
120. Ibid.
121. Moltmann-Wendel and Moltmann, *God: His and Hers*, 85.

rightly asserts that "we cannot simply reduce experiences of God to human experiences."[122]

Secondly, Brock envisions God not as a person, but as the power of love, the power that energizes life. She affirms that "as the foundation of heart, erotic power compels us toward compassion, collective action, integration, self-acceptance, and self-reflective memory in our critical recollection of the past."[123] I agree with Wendel-Moltmann as she argues that "without the cross, we could turn Christianity into a religion of happiness and *eros*, which makes people blind to the fight for justice."[124] When backing away from the cross we run the risk of diminishing the seriousness of the violence and suffering of Jesus' death, which in turn downplays the reality of sin, suffering, and despair in human life. By promoting the primacy of the life of Jesus and "decrucifying Jesus," feminist theology makes Jesus into the ultimate human example of God's love and justice, thus demoting him from savior to moral exemplar. Consequently, Wendel-Moltmann stresses the danger of this "decrucifying" propensity of feminist theology as she states, "Anyone who crosses out the cross gets lost in illusions and loses reality."[125]

Sölle's Existential Conception of the Cross

Unlike those who attempt to "decrucify Jesus," Dorothee Sölle proposes an existential conception of the cross. She takes the reality of human suffering seriously. Sölle in her book *Suffering* argues that Christianity has been accused of masochism because the cross has been discussed from God's point of view as abandonment rather than through the lens of human suffering. The cross, according to her, has to be discussed from the standpoint of the person who suffers or the person who is sinned against. Sölle, in her existential view of the cross, insists that Jesus continues to die right here in our midst before our eyes as long as the suffering continues in our world. She states, "Jesus' death hasn't ended."[126]

Sölle highlights that God is not an almighty spectator or a tyrant in heaven but a sufferer hanging on the cross. In order to argue this point, she retells a story in *The Night Trilogy: Night, Dawn, the Accident* written by Elie

---

122. Ibid., 83.
123. Brock, *Journey by Heart*, 42.
124. Moltmann-Wendel, *Autobiography*, 180.
125. Ibid.
126. Sölle, *Suffering*, 140.

Wiesel, a survivor of Auschwitz. A key passage in the book is taken from a story taking place in Buma, the camp attached to Auschwitz:

> The SS hung two Jewish men and a boy before the assembled inhabitants of the camp. The men died quickly but the death struggled of the boy lasted half an hour. "Where is God? Where is he?" a man behind me asked. As the boy, after a long time, was still in agony on the rope, I heard the man cry again, "Where is God now?" And I heard a voice within me answer, "Here he is—he is hanging here on this gallows."[127]

Sölle takes this story in parallel to the passion story of Jesus. She observes how in each story a decisive change occurs. She insists, "The way from Gethsemane to Golgotha is a taking leave of (narcissistic) hope." She also insists that in Elie Wiesel's *The Night Trilogy,* "The eye is directed away from the almighty Father to the sufferer himself."[128] Sölle interprets the voice Wiesel hears within himself, "he is hanging here on this gallows . . . .", as an affirmation of her theological position that God is neither executioner nor almighty spectator in heaven. God is on the side of the victim hanging on the cross.[129]

Sölle's interpretation, however, does not coincide with what Wiesel intends in his story. If we read the story carefully, we find that what Wiesel means to portray is a parallel between the death of the possibility of having faith in God and the death of the boy being hanged. Wiesel is actually accusing the God of Israel because God failed to deliver the child. He is sentencing God to death because the holocaust makes theodicy impossible. Wiesel is protesting against God who has permitted the holocaust, consequently causing him to discard his faith in a God of providential justice.[130]

Sölle, in discussing hope and the future, compares Dostoevsky's characters Ivan and Alyosha in *The Brothers Karamazov*. Ivan, who is metaphysically oriented, rebels and accuses God of imposing unjust suffering onto the world. In contrast, Alyosha silently stands in solidarity with the suffering. Although both long for a world free of suffering, their hope is only realized through people like Alyosha, who suffers together in solidarity with the suffering. Sölle's existential approach to interpreting the cross inspires us to actualize justice in the midst of unjust suffering. In fact, she

127. Ibid., 145. Sölle quotes here Wiesel, *Night*, 75.
128. Ibid., 147.
129. Ibid., 148.
130. Bauckham, *The Theology of Jürgen Moltmann*, 78.

A Critical Evaluation of Feminist Theologies

insists, "God has no other hands than ours."[131] Sölle reveals the seriousness of human sin by looking at the cross as "a symbol of reality," where the God of love is consistently driven to an execution by individual, communal, and institutional sin.[132] In her existential understanding of the cross God's relationship to the cross is theologically meaningful for her in so far as it confirms God's intimate, compassionate, life-giving presence in the midst of real suffering. For Sölle, the cross is neither a symbol expressing the relationship between God the Father and God the Son, nor a symbol of a masochistic God who requires suffering, but is a symbol of how reality can be transformed through true followers of the cross. Reality can be changed through those who exemplify Christ in his suffering for the suffering. She restricts the presence of Christ to human involvement. Because Sölle does not view the cross as a Triune event, it seems that she cannot address how inherently sinful and selfish human beings are able to change and become people who are willing to suffer in solidarity with the suffering. In her argument, there is no recognition of the work of the Holy Spirit to change, motivate, and empower people to live in solidarity with sufferers. Consequently, Sölle seems to hand God's salvation over into the hands of people alone.

In this existential approach to the Cross, we miss out on a living sense of God as triune and thus on an operative Trinitarian theology which has been a key part of much of the history of the church. In this approach, the Holy Spirit is easily forgotten. I argue here that power does not arise from human initiative only. It is critical that women recognize they are limited human creatures and acknowledge that the Holy Spirit empowers them to do what is needed for healing. We should therefore draw on Moltmann's theology of the cross where he emphasizes that the Holy Spirit proceeds from the event of the cross between Father and the Son to justify the godless, fill the forsaken with love, and even bring the dead alive. Accordingly, the event of the cross is a Trinitarian event. Moltmann states:

> The Son suffers in his love being forsaken by the Father as he dies. The Father suffers in his love the grief of the death of the Son. In that case, whatever proceeds from the event between the Father and the Son must be understood as the spirit of the surrender of the Father and the Son, as the Spirit which creates love for forsaken men, as the spirit which brings the dead alive. It is the unconditioned and therefore boundless love which proceeds from the grief

---

131. Sölle, *Suffering*, 149.
132. Ibid., 164.

of the Father and the dying of the Son and reaches forsaken men in order to create in them the possibility and the force of new life.[133]

The work of the Spirit must be recognized as it brings forth healing and liberation to damaged people crushed by war and injustice, even when it does so in a partial manner.[134]

In short, I would submit here that we must acknowledge that justice and peace throughout the world are the effects of the Spirit's renewing power coming to fruition through those who willingly live in *imitatio crucis* with those who are weak and helpless.

Elizabeth A. Johnson's Conception of Cross-Resurrection Dialectic

Like Brock, Elizabeth A. Johnson also emphasizes the political nature of Jesus' death. She rejects any understanding of Jesus' death as atonement or sacrifice. Jesus' death is rather the parable that enacts Sophia-God's participation in the suffering of the world. According to Johnson:

> Jesus' death was an act of violence brought about by threatened human men as sin, and therefore against the will of a gracious God. It occurred historically in consequence of Jesus' fidelity to the deepest truth which he knew, expressed in his message and behavior, which showed all twisted relationships to be incompatible with Sophia God's shalom.[135]

For Johnson, the event of the cross is clearly not a divinely decreed passive victimization of Jesus as a penalty for sin. She describes the cross-resurrection dialectic of "disaster and love" as showing God's commitment to solidarity with all those who suffer and are lost."[136] The point she makes by this dialectic is that the crucified one is not abandoned, but resurrected. The resurrection of Christ becomes the promise of a future for all the dead as well as the whole cosmos itself. It also manifests the wisdom God; that "the victory of shalom is won not by the sword of the warrior God but by

---

133. Moltmann, *The Crucified God*, 245.
134. Johnson, *She Who Is*, 135.
135. Ibid., 158.
136. Ibid., 159.

the awesome power of compassionate love, in and through solidarity with those who suffer."[137]

Harold Wells evaluates Johnson as being right in certain respects.[138] According to him, Johnson correctly emphasizes the political reasons for the execution of Jesus and insists that it was the result of human sin. Johnson is also right in that she protests against the widespread understanding of atonement that depicts God as angry Father and judge demanding blood sacrifice before pardoning sinners. Such a theory, Wells affirms, divides the Father from the Son, and destroys the unity of God, encouraging us to fear and distrust the Father while trusting Jesus. However, he correctly points out that a weakness is found in that Johnson's Sophia Christology does not offer an alternative doctrine of atonement.[139]

Anne Carr calls Christian feminists to "reclaim the center," so that feminist perspectives will be incorporated into the whole of theology.[140] According to her, if we want to "claim the center," we cannot simply dismiss the theology of atonement and ignore atonement texts in the New Testament. Feminist theologians cannot simply ignore the very early and persistent teachings of the New Testament which proclaim that salvation is found in the death of Jesus Christ. In fact, the New Testament is full of the texts which witness the coming and dying of Jesus Christ "for us." For instance, the Synoptic words of the Holy Communion contain an implicit theology of atonement: "This is my body . . . This is my blood of the new covenant which is poured out for many" (Mark14:22, 24; Matt. 26:26, 28; Luke 22:19, 20). Jesus came to give his life as a ransom for many (Mark 10:45). God gave His only begotten Son (John 3:16). The Pauline Epistles also testify Jesus' death as atonement: Jesus Christ has made peace through the blood of his cross (Col 1:20); God gave up the son for us all (Rom 8:32); Christ for our sake was made to be sin (2 Cor 5:2); Jesus became a curse for us (Gal 3:13).

As Wells argued, preachers and teachers of the Scriptures, as theologians, must continue to interpret and preach about the texts of atonement. I argue that in order to newly appropriate Jesus' death of atonement, we have to integrate Jesus' death with the whole of his life and resurrection. If we eliminate the atoning aspect of Jesus' death, we can easily reduce Christ's

---

137. Ibid.
138. Wells, "Trinitarian feminism: Elizabeth Johnson's Wisdom Christology," 341.
139. Ibid., 341.
140. Carr, "A New Vision of Feminist Theology: Method," 25.

work to a mere moral example or model for Christian life. Or, if we focus only on the atoning aspect of Jesus' death apart from his life and message, we may present God as so jealous of divine honor that God demands the death of Jesus. Therefore, Jesus' death cannot be separated from his life or resurrection. As Karl Rahner argued, death is the most important moment of any human life. Death sums up a person's life and makes definitive all that happened before death.[141] The death of Jesus is the culmination of his life and message in which he extended God's radically inclusive love to the poor and the social outcasts, the women and the children. The resurrection of Jesus is then the vindication by God of all Jesus did before death. This leads us to revisit and critique Anselm's atonement theory, to examine whether it really, as feminists argue, has promoted an understanding of women as self-sacrificing victims. I will also investigate whether Anselm's atonement theory can be incorporated to reclaim aspects of atonement in the feminist theology of the cross.

Revisiting of Anselm's Atonement Theory in *Cur Deus Homo*

Feminist theologians such as Rita Nakashima Brock, Joanne Carlson Brown, and Rebecca Parker have argued that Anselm's atonement theory is problematic because it is responsible for what has been deemed an "abusive" theology of atonement. They have argued that it promotes an understanding of women as self-sacrificing victims and encourages women to embrace the suffering and oppression in their lives. For example, Rita Nakashima Brock argues that traditional theologies of the cross engender paternalistic dependence and are a form of cosmic child abuse:

> The father allows, or even inflicts, the death of his only perfect son. The emphasis is on the goodness and power of the father and the unworthiness and powerlessness of his children, so that the father's punishment is just and children are to blame.[142]

Joanne Carlson Brown and Rebecca Parker, in their criticism of theologies of the cross, take a close look at Anselm's theology of atonement. They criticize Anselm's approach in this way: "God is portrayed as the one who cannot reconcile himself to the world because 'he' has been royally offended by sin, so offended that no human being can do anything to overcome 'his'

---

141. Rahner, "On the Spirituality of the Easter Faith," 8–15.
142. Brock, *Journeys by Heart*, 56.

sense of offense."¹⁴³ They portray God as bound by God's own system; however, God is a tyrant who is able to do what God wills arbitrarily. God the father demands and carries out the suffering and the death of his own son, and "this image of God," they conclude, "has sustained a culture of abuse and led to the abandonment of victims of abuse."¹⁴⁴

Given the feminist critique of Anselm, I will investigate whether Anselm's God is guilty of child abuse and a tyrannical and arbitrary use of power. In so doing, we will closely look at Anselm's *Cur Deus Homo*, a treatise on the incarnation and redemption, which is one of the most influential texts on the atonement in the western church. Anselm's argument will be viewed by setting it in the socio-religious context of its time. I will then reconsider feminist criticisms of Anselm and finally offer my own criticism of Anselm as a woman pastor searching for a theology of the cross which promotes the dignity and value of Korean-North American immigrant women and calls them to live in mutual, reciprocal relationship in the multicultural context.

The Argument of the *Cur Deus Homo*

The book *Cur Deus Homo* is written in the form of a dialogue between Anselm of Canterbury and his friend Boso who offers possible criticisms and alternatives against Anselm, spurring Anselm to present as tight an argument as possible.¹⁴⁵ In *Cur Deus Homo* Anselm aims to prove the necessity of the incarnation by reasoning alone, apart from any prior knowledge of Christ (*remoto Christo*). This work of Anselm's is composed of two short books. The first book contains the objections of unbelievers who despise the Christian faith because they regard it as contrary to reason. Leaving Christ out of view (*remoto Christo*), it proves by absolute reasons, the impossibility that any man should be saved without him.¹⁴⁶ The second book demonstrates by equally plain reasoning and fact that "human nature was ordained to enjoy happy immortality both in body and soul; and that it was necessary that this design for which man was made should be fulfilled; but

---

143. Brown and Parker, "For God So Loved the World?," 8.
144. Ibid., 9.
145. *St. Anselm: Basic Writings*, "Cur Deus Homo," 191–302.
146. Ibid., 191.

that it could not be fulfilled unless God became man, and unless all things were to take place which we hold with regard to Christ."[147]

The argument of *Cur Deus Homo* could be summarized like this: God created human beings with certain purpose and established a particular order in the universe. God's purpose in creating human beings was that they enjoy perfect blessedness or happiness. This blessedness requires the total and voluntary submission of their will to God's will, for it is God's will upon which the beauty and rational harmony of the universe rests. However, human beings fell through disobedience. Sin according to Anselm is not to render God his due. According to Anselm, "He, who does not render this honor which is due to God, robs God of his own and dishonors him, and this is sin."[148] Human beings caught in a state of sin are no longer able to live as God created them to live. God's order, the way things ought to be according to God's creation, has been disrupted. As a result, human beings are left in a situation of indebtedness to God by not rendering to God what is God's due, and so condemned to death.

This is a dilemma which human beings face: They ought to render to God what is owed to God, but they cannot. Anselm argues God's justice; the order of justice requires that the debt be paid. The offering for redemption ought to be made by human beings; however, they were unable because they already owed everything to God before they sinned and incurred debt on top of that. An obvious solution would be for God to forgive the debt and to show mercy toward sinful humanity by removing the obligation. However, unconditional forgiveness is not an alternative for Anselm, for it would introduce irregularity into God's universe.

The second phase of Anselm's argument proceeds from the dilemma that human beings have no means to pay the debt. Since they cannot pay the debt, it seems that human beings will suffer forever and God's plan for creation will always remain disrupted. God's order and purposes, however, ought to be fulfilled and human beings saved. Only God is able to make the offering human beings are indebted to make. Therefore, the incarnation was necessary so that the God-man, Jesus Christ, would redeem the disrupted order of justice on behalf of humanity. In this respect, the incarnation is God's action on behalf of humanity and for the sake of straightening the disrupted order of justice.

---

147. Ibid.
148. Ibid., 216.

Continuing his argument, Anselm explains that the incarnate Son of God freely offers up his sinless life in honor of God. The Son is sinless, therefore does not have to die. However, death is to be incurred to pay the debt for human beings. Jesus' death is of infinite worth; therefore, it is able to accomplish the redemption of human beings and set right the order of justice.

Critiques of the *Cur Deus Homo*

Is it fair to charge Anselm's God with an abuse of power as feminist theologians like Joanne Carlson Brown and Rebecca Parker have argued? Does Anselm's theology of the atonement lead to what they term "divinely sanctioned child abuse"?[149] Feminist theologians are divided on their opinions. Then in what ways does or does not Anselm's doctrine of atonement contribute to the culture of abuse that some feminists argue has been cultivated in Christianity?

To explore whether Anselm's theology is guilty of a tyrannical and arbitrary use of power, it is necessary to set it in the socio-religious context of his time. Walter Kasper argues effectively that "Anselm's satisfaction theory can be understood only against the background of the Germanic and early medieval feudal system."[150] Within this social system we find a mutual dependence between lord and vassal who promise each other loyalty for loyalty. From the lord, the vassal obtained a fief and protection, and the feudal lord received in return a pledge of allegiance and service. Kasper argues that this system of loyalties not only gives the individual his determined role and rights, but also it secures the social order and peace, unity and coherence of their political structures.[151] Thus, this system regulates and delineates powers and responsibilities for all parties.

We also have to consider another important point about Anselm's concept of God's honor in view of the socio-religious context of his time. Kasper points out that the concept of God's honor which Anselm insists to be upheld is about the moral, rational order of justice established in creation. In the *Cur Deus Homo*, Anselm makes clear that God's personal honor is inviolable: "Nothing can be added to or taken from the honor of

149. Brown and Parker, "For God So Loved the World?," 9.

150. Kasper, *Jesus the Christ*, 220. On this point, Kasper is indebted to Gresake, "Redemption and Freedom," 63.

151. Kasper, *Jesus the Christ*, 220. See also Gresake, "Redemption and Freedom," 63.

God. For this honor, which belongs to him, is in no way subject to injury or change."[152] According to Anselm, God is honored "when the human being chooses what he ought . . . not by bestowing anything upon him, but because he brings himself freely under God's will and disposal, and maintains his own condition in the universe, and the beauty of the universe itself . . . "[153] In other words, when the human wills what he/she ought to will, submitting himself/herself to God's direction, he/she honors God, and when the human does not will what he/she ought, he/she dishonors God. These statements imply that a human's dishonoring of God, according to Anselm, is to be understood as the refusal to recognize God's rightful authority or God's place of rightful honor. Consequently, "the object of offense," Kasper affirms, "is not the lord's personal honor, but his social status by which he is the guarantor of the public peace."[154] Hunter Brown agrees with Kasper's position as he points out that "the focus of *Cur Deus Homo*'s soteriology then is not upon the personal, juridical appeasement of an offended God but upon redressing the abuse of human fiduciary participation in divine power over the world."[155]

Anselm's theory of satisfaction atonement clearly differs from the penal substitutionary image in which God punishes Jesus as a substitute for punishing sinful humankind. According to Anselm, the restoration of harmony, order, and balance requires payment. He understood Jesus' death as the debt payment that satisfied the honor of God, and thus restored balance and order to the universe. In this sense, Anselm's God seems not so much concerned about Godself as about redressing the disorder and disharmony in the universe produced by human sin. The death of Jesus in this view is not about having Jesus bear punishment merited by human beings, but about restoring order and harmony in the universe.

Here is a point at which Anselm's satisfaction atonement differs from Luther's penal substitution. For Anselm, satisfaction is not punishment for sin; rather, it is a substitute for punishment—*aut poena aut satisfaction*. For Luther, satisfaction includes the notion of penal substitution.[156] Jesus' death satisfied the requirement of the divine law that sin be punished. With

---

152. *St. Anselm: Basic Writings*, "Cur Deus Homo," 222.
153. Ibid., 222–23.
154. Kasper, *Jesus the Christ*, 220.
155. Brown, "Anselm's *Cur Deus Homo* Revisited," 194.
156. Tappert, *The Book of Concord*, 414. See also Peters, "The Atonement in Anselm and Luther: Second Thoughts about Gustaf Aulen's *Christus Victor*," 310.

his death, Jesus bore the punishment that was really due to sinners. Jesus was punished in our place. Jesus substituted himself for us, and died a penal, substitutionary death. Luther states: "Christ . . . who offered himself in place of our sinful nature, who took upon himself all the wrath of God merited by ourselves without works . . ."[157]

Both Anselm's satisfaction atonement and Luther's penal substitution attempt to explain why Jesus died for us. For Anselm, satisfaction atonement satisfies God's honor, while penal substitution satisfies the law of God. Both of them, however, require death, whether it is for God's honor or God's law. Without death, the debt to God's honor remains unsatisfied, or the penalty required by God's law remains unpaid. Weaver argues how although Anselm uses different language from penal substitution, his motif of Jesus' death as a payment to God's honor still contains within it the assumption of retributive violence and placation of wrath through the sacrifice of a son.[158]

With regard to the question "Who ultimately killed Jesus?" Weaver explains the dilemma that Anselm's satisfaction theory and Luther's penal substitution theory face like this: With Satan deleted, it is the sinner who offended God. Sinful human beings cannot save themselves by paying their own debt. Therefore, God is the only one left to orchestrate the death of Jesus in order to pay the debt owed to God's honor. In penal substitution, God is the one who arranged to provide Jesus' death as a means to satisfy the divine law. Weaver here points out within the framework of satisfaction atonement or penal substitution we cannot avoid a dilemma:

> The evil powers who oppose the reign of God by killing Jesus, whether the evil powers who oppose the reign of God by killing Jesus, whether the devil, the mob or the Romans, are the ones who are actually doing the will of God, by killing or punishing Jesus to provide the payment that God's honor or God's law demands. The strange implication is that both Jesus and those who kill Jesus would be carrying out the will of God.[159]

In removing the devil from the equation of atonement, Weaver argues, the Father arranges the death of God's Son for the benefit of others. The motif of Jesus as the substitute object of punishment, which assumes the principle of retribution, is the image that feminists have particularly found very

157. *Epistle Sermon, New Year's Day* 50, in *Luther's Works*, ed. Lenker, 7:287.
158. Weaver, "Violence in Christian Theology," 9.
159. Ibid., 5.

offensive. They contend that the Jesus of this motif models passive submission to innocent and unjust suffering for the sake of others.

With the critiques of feminists in mind, we need to look into Anselm's reasoning about why God ought not to put away sins by compassion alone without any payment of debt. Two reasons are given in *Cur Deus Homo*: first, with such forgiveness, "there will be no difference between the guilty and the not guilty . . . and it makes injustice like God. For as God is subject to no law, so is neither injustice."[160] Second, such forgiveness would do nothing to correct the disturbance of the "order and beauty of the universe" caused by sin. The slightest uncorrected disorder argues a deficiency either in God's justice or in His power, which is impossible if we affirm that God is perfect in both ways.[161]

With regard to this problem of mercy and justice, Ted Peters rightly points out that what we have to understand behind Anselm's argument is the neo-platonic structure:[162] God is the final reality for Anselm, and the rational and moral structure of existence issues from the nature of God Himself. The whole universe is an expression of God's intrinsic character and will. Therefore, justice is not reduced to the simple notion of rendering to each person his or her due, but implies doing that which befits the supreme goodness of God.[163] With this background, Peters argues, "mercy cannot finally be seen to work against justice."[164] In the *Proslogium*, Anselm demonstrates that mercy and justice are one insofar as they are expressions of God.[165] Mercy requires that human beings be everlastingly blessed, and justice requires that sin be met on its own terms. The atonement becomes the point at which justice is satisfied and mercy achieves its end. Peters concludes:

> God created man out of love, and it was God's purpose that men find fulfillment in eternal blessedness. And in the final analysis, God's purpose is accomplished. His grace is victorious. But *en route* Anselm wants us to take seriously the gravity of man's sin and the ultimate dimensions of God's historical activity. The legalistic structure of the relationship between God and men is not

160. *St. Anselm: Basic Writings*, "Cur Deus Homo," 216–18.
161. Ibid., 222–24.
162. Peters, "The Atonement in Anselm and Luther," 305.
163. Ibid. See also *St. Anselm: Basic Writings*, "Proslogium," 63.
164. Peters, "The Atonement in Anselm and Luther," 305.
165. *St. Anselm: Basic Writings*, "Proslogium," 60–63.

the last thing to be said about God. It is the means whereby God's mercy is shown to triumph.[166]

Much like Anselm, the demand for the fulfillment and satisfaction of the Law in Luther's penal substitution does not suffocate God's gracious love under a system of divine justice. The work of Christ does not create but presupposes a gracious God. Luther preached:

> There was no remedy except for God's only Son to step into our distress and himself become man, to take upon himself the load of awful and eternal wrath and make his own body and blood a sacrifice for sin. And so he did, out of the immeasurably great mercy and love towards us, giving himself up and bearing the sentence of unending wrath and death.[167]

So, we conclude that God's justice and love are not in conflict with Luther's penal substitution or Anselm's satisfaction atonement. Rather, atonement becomes the point at which justice is satisfied and mercy achieves its end.

Whereas Ted Peters looks into Anselm's satisfaction theory from a perspective of the problem of mercy and justice, Flora A. Keshgegian investigates whether God is guilty of a tyrannical and arbitrary use of power from a perspective of the tensional relation between power and responsibility. She first explains the relation between power and responsibility. In a non-abusive or non-oppressive situation, power and responsibility are always joined whereas in a situation of oppression and abuse, power is divorced from responsibility. She states:

> This dynamic of separation reinforces itself and is institutionalized in such a way that the powerful are not routinely held responsible either for the state of things or even for their own actions. Hierarchies of power are formed and those without poor, those on the 'bottom' of hierarchies, are held responsible not only for their own behavior but also societal conditions. At the same time, they are denied power to effect change in those conditions. Societal thinking then blames the victim, and those who are victimized internalize such standards.[168]

---

166. Peters, "The Atonement in Anselm and Luther," 305.

167. Ibid., 311. *Epistle Sermon, Twenty-fourth Sunday after Trinity* 43–45, in *Luther's Works*, ed. Lenker, 9:376–77.

168. Keshgegian, "The Scandal of the Cross: Revisiting Anselm and His Feminist Critics," 478–79.

The Liberative Cross

To explore whether Anselm's doctrine of atonement includes such a split between power and responsibility, Keshgegian looks into how Anselm made human beings directly responsible to God by deleting the devil from the drama of God's redemption. Citing R.W. Southern, Keshgegian argues that in the ransom version of *Christus Victor* human beings are held less responsible for sin and considered powerless.[169] The souls of humankind are held captive by the devil. In a seemingly contractual agreement, God handed Jesus over to Satan as a ransom payment to secure the release of captive souls. The devil killed Jesus in an apparent victory for the forces of evil. However, the devil is deceived. In raising Jesus from the dead, God triumphed over the devil, and the souls of humanity were freed from his clutches. This victory through resurrection provides the name *Christus Victor*.

Anselm objected the notion of the devil having any right or role in the drama of salvation. Rather than seeing human beings as captive to the devil, Anselm made them directly responsible to God. Human beings sinned against God; sin offended the honor of God, and thus threatened order in the universe. According to Anselm, including the devil into the equation of salvation would mean distorting the issues of power and responsibility. It is human sin which disrupted the order of creation, the right relationship that God intended and to which God is bound. If God uses God's power to forgive humanity, without requiring satisfaction, then human responsibility will be compromised. The God-human, Jesus Christ exercises power and responsibility. Keshgegian concludes that God's power is not arbitrary or absolute in the sense that God takes responsibility for the order of the universe and uses power for the sake of that order.

Denny Weaver disagrees with her. According to Weaver, even though Anselm's motif of Jesus' death represented payment to God's honor, it has the same assumption of retributive violence and the same implication of God's killing of Jesus, just as in the penal substitution version of atonement. He states,

> The atonement formulas, and in particular the satisfaction motif, encompasses the violent imagery of retribution. And asking who authors and who requires or receives the violence of retribution exposes the fact that Anselm's deletion of the devil leaves God as the only one who can direct the death of Jesus and who needs the death in satisfaction of offended honor. Eliminating Satan from

---

169. Ibid., 483. See also Southern, *The Making of the Middle Ages*, 235.

the equation and subsequently making sinful human beings responsible directly to God exposes the way that God both arranges the retribution and is the recipient of Jesus' death thus produced.[170]

In the logic of atonement, Weaver insists, God is made the chief avenger or the chief punisher, or in its worst case a child abuser.[171]

Weaver argues how Jesus, in this theory of satisfaction atonement, is a model of voluntary submission to innocent suffering:

> If the Father needs the death of Jesus to satisfy the divine honor, Jesus as innocent victim voluntarily agrees to submit to that violence needed by the honor of God. Or as innocent victim Jesus voluntarily agrees to undergo the punishment deserved by sinful humankind in order that the demand of divine justice be met. Because Jesus' death is needed, Jesus models being a voluntary, passive and innocent victim, who suffers for the good of another.[172]

Weaver argues further that this model of Jesus as an innocent and passive victim poses a particular concern. He insists, "It is an unhealthy model for a woman abused by her husband or a child violated by her father, and constitutes double jeopardy when attached to hierarchical theology that asserts male headship."[173]

I will argue against Weaver's contention that in this satisfaction motif of Anselm "Jesus is the innocent victim who voluntarily agrees to submit to that violence needed by the honor of God."[174] According to Weaver's definition, a victim is one who is "controlled by forces and circumstances beyond himself or herself."[175] He contends that Jesus, in satisfaction and substitutionary atonement, represents victimization. Here I pose a question to Weaver: "Is there such a thing as 'voluntary victim' unless one is a sadist?" God is not a tyrant or cruel father who abuses his absolute power. As argued above, God's power is not arbitrary or absolute because God takes responsibility for the order of the universe and uses power for the sake of that order. What Weaver misses here is that Anselm in the *Cur Deus Homo*

---

170. Weaver, "Violence in Christian Theology," 12.

171. Ibid., 13.

172. Ibid.

173. Ibid. See Brown and Parker, "For God So Loved the World?" See also Brock, *Journeys by Heart*, 55–57; and Heyward, *Saving Jesus from Those Who Are Right: Rethinking What It Means to Be Christian*, 151.

174. Weaver, "Violence in Christian Theology," 13.

175. Ibid., 14.

THE LIBERATIVE CROSS

does not see Jesus' death as a necessary action. Jesus' death is the only way that Anselm can see out of the dilemma posed by sin; however, Jesus does have freedom and choice. He wills to be obedient, to meet the requirements of the Father's order and justice. It was on his own accord that Jesus endured death for the salvation of humanity. The Father did not compel the Son to suffer death, or even allow the Son to be slain against his will.[176]

I have looked into the *Cur Deus Homo* and argued against the accusations feminist theologians have made of Anselm's idea of God as being an abusive tyrant who demands the death of an innocent son. Anselm's God, as Keshgegian argued, is acting not only out of power but also out of the responsibility to restore the relation and order that was disrupted by sin. Thus, Anselm's God does not abuse God's power arbitrarily. Anselm's theology of atonement does not lead to what feminists term "divinely sanctioned child abuse."[177]

Having refuted the charge of feminists that Anselm's God is an abusive tyrant, we now turn to the question of whether Anselm's theology of atonement is empowering for today's Korean-North American women. How does Anselm's theology empower Korean-North American women, and in what respect is it limited and inadequate for Korean-North American women living in the multicultural world?

Contributions and Inadequacy of Anselm's Theory of Atonement in Relation to the Contemporary Theological and Ecclesiological Concerns in the Korean-North American Christian Women's Context

The spirituality of Korean-North American women is greatly influenced by Anselm's theology of atonement. They confess through prayers and songs that Jesus Christ gave himself up to satisfy the demands of justice which they could not satisfy with their human spiritual disciplines.[178] Anselm portrays Jesus' crucifixion as self-giving: No person can give himself more fully to God than Jesus does when he surrenders himself to death for God's

---

176. In chapter 3, I will discuss Moltmann's conception of Jesus' death as *passio activa* in the sense that Jesus the Son delivers himself up to death on the cross (Gal 2:20). See Moltmann, *The Crucified God*, 243.

177. Brown and Parker, "For God So Loved the World?," 9.

178. Anselm, *Cur Deus Homo*, 239–42.

honor.[179] Jesus Christ as sinless did not owe anything to God, but Jesus gave himself up for us as pure self-offering. This Anselm's view of the cross gives first generation Korean-North American Christian women a strong sense of spiritual devotion to pay the debt that they individually owe to Jesus. Salvation, for the majority of these women, is defined and accepted in inherently individual terms. The sinner owes a debt and the debt is personal. Because of this view of individualistic heavenly salvation, the social component is logically an afterthought, something to consider after one has dealt with the prior fundamental and individualistic problem of personal guilt and penalty. This Anselm's view of atonement also leads to an overemphasis on personal sin and grace and the separation of the spiritual life of an individual from his/her daily concrete conditions.

Consequently, salvation becomes a transformation of an individual's relationship with God, from an unredeemed and oppressive position into some mystic communion with God. According to Simon S. Maimela:

> In itself this emphasis may very well be correct, but the problem lies in its anthropological limitation: it sees the problem of man [and woman] largely in spiritual terms, and proposes to offer us a theory of atonement which hardly affects the situation of oppression in which man [woman] concretely lives.[180]

This Anselm's view of atonement overlooks the broader view of the work of Christ, which aims at the transformation of a person, not only in his spiritual aspect but also in his total physical context. By positing a transaction outside of history and involving only the death of Jesus, It excludes the life and ministry of Jesus. Consequently, it offers very little theological ground upon which one can challenge injustice in the social order. Salvation according to Anselm envisions a change in an individual's status outside of or beyond this life. This a-historical orientation has caused in Christian believers an a-ethical orientation throughout history. With this a-historical, a-ethical approach to the cross, Christian churches have accommodated violent exercises and social injustices like slavery, racism, classism, and etc. instead of challenging them. For example, James Cone, founder of the black theology movement, criticized this a-ethical orientation of the churches. He argues that Anselm's theory de-historicizes the work of Christ, separating God's liberating act from history, defining atonement in a way which

---

179. Ibid., 269–74.
180. Maimela, "The Atonement in the Context of Liberation Theology," 48.

favors the powerful and excludes the interests of the poor.[181] Cone affirms that this abstract, a-historical character has caused ironies, such as the situation in which slave owners have preached salvation to slaves.

This Anselm's view of atonement, which focuses primarily on personal regeneration, fails to deal adequately with the complexity of human suffering as well as explain what God's involvement in these sufferings entails for human oppression in the situation of injustice. *Cur Deus Homo* was written for the purpose of demonstrating why the incarnation was necessary. Anselm, therefore, mentioned nothing about the life or person of Jesus except that he was obedient and chose freely. It was not important to Anselm that Jesus had a life history, except that Jesus exercised his will freely and chose to offer his life. Anselm, in fact, clearly stated in the Preface to the *Cur Deus Homo* that he was "leaving Christ out of view" and proceeding "as if nothing were known of Christ."[182] There is no narrative of Jesus' personhood and actions.

Even though it was not important to Anselm that Jesus had a life history, the lack of Jesus' personhood in his atonement theory limits its ability to empower. By reducing the entire work of Christ on the cross to the forgiveness of sins and guilt, it tends to overlook the liberating and transforming power of Christ's work in sociopolitical conditions. It fails to comprehend the extent of divine involvement in human suffering on behalf of the oppressed, the weak, and the helpless. In this respect, it is very important to include in the theology of the cross the person and work of Jesus Christ in order to construct a comprehensive view of salvation, not merely as the salvation of an individual soul but also as the total liberation of humanity from its physical suffering.

To sum up chapter 2, I have critiqued the theological works of feminist theologians centered on two main issues: first, the male-centered language and symbolism of God, and second, God's relation to the cross. Exclusive, literal patriarchal speech about God has played a role in justifying social structures of dominance, such as the androcentric world view. Therefore, I have looked into different approaches feminist theologians take toward exclusive, patriarchal language in order to renew the idea of God in more inclusive way. In so doing, I have argued that God needs to be spoken of as both male and female in order to relativize undue emphasis on any one image. In addition, in respect to the richness of God, it is necessary to utilize

---

181. Cone, *God of the Oppressed*, 230–32.
182. Anselm, *Cur Deus Homo*, 191.

a full complement of God images, both masculine and feminine as well as both personal and impersonal. However, none of the symbols for God, either mother or father, grasps the transcendent. Consequently, I have argued that in worship and prayer God should be spoken of in various symbols and images both masculine and feminine as wells as both personal and impersonal.

For the purpose of renewing the idea of God in more inclusive way, I have assessed various attempts that feminist theologians made to expose oppressive theological patterns within theology and tradition. First, I have looked into how they argue against the notion of maleness of God under the categories of the incarnation of the Word in the male Jesus, God understood as a Father, and the Father-the Son-the Holy Spirit language of the Trinity. The incarnation of the Word in the male Jesus has been used to legitimize men's superiority over women. Following Elizabeth Johnson I have argued that it is not Jesus' maleness that is doctrinally important but his humanity in solidarity with the whole suffering human race. In fact, as Johnson argued, God's choice to welcome women and children while incarnated as a man is an intentional and subversive choice that challenges the patriarchal systems of the world. Various attempts to use female images of God and to call God "mother" have been made; however, these attempts suggest reversal of patterns of domination rather than genuine transformation. To bypass the masculinity of Trinitarian images, feminist theologians have also designated the Holy Spirit as feminine, or replaced the Father-Son-Holy Spirit understanding of the Trinity with other triads that are neither masculine nor feminine. As LaCugna and Johnson pointed out, there is a danger in designating the Holy Spirit as feminine while the Father and Son remain masculine. LaCugna and Johnson point out how, according to a subordinationist Trinitarian theology, the Spirit is third in rank in the Trinity. Thus associating feminine imagery solely with the Spirit would only reinforce the subordination of women in the church and in society. Replacing Father-Son-Holy Spirit triad with other triads neither masculine nor feminine, like Creator, Liberator, and Advocate, may also be dangerous. It emphasizes the individuality and separateness of the divine persons and their respective responsibility for different aspects of redemption; however, such functional or modalistic language is not in every case an exact equivalent of the unique personal name, Father, Son, and the Spirit. In order to approach the Trinity holistically, Fiorenza and Johnson turn to the Sophialogical tradition to reject exclusively male metaphors for God language. Johnson especially uses the concept of Sophia to develop her social Trinity. The concept of Sophia Trinity, Spirit-Sophia, Jesus-Sophia and Mother-Sophia as a threefold *koinonia*, she believes, resonates with the feminist values of mutuality, relation, and community in diversity. It is a great attempt to overcome the weakness of traditional descriptions of God, which have underwritten male domination and the dehumanization of women. However, the question as to whether we could view the Trinity, God the Father, God the Son, and the Holy Spirit apart from God's sexuality still remains to be answered.

I also looked into why feminist theologians have rejected the cross as a symbol of denigration and oppression against women. They selectively read Anselm's theory of atonement, leading them to make attenuated critiques of said theory. I revisited Anselm's atonement theory in his *Cur Deus Homo* to argue against the feminist accusation that Anselm's God is an abusive tyrant who demands the death of an innocent victim son. Anselm's theology of atonement does not lead to what feminists term "divinely sanctioned child abuse. However, in terms of whether Anselm's theology of atonement empowers Korean-North American women today, I argued that its effect is limited and inadequate for a few reasons. Since Anselm wrote within the worldview of medieval feudal patterns and neo-platonic philosophies of relationship, his theory of atonement carries with it hierarchical forms of social ordering as well as a hierarchical understanding of God. His commitment to a static and hierarchical view of the created order may not empower Korean-North American women to reject their traditional views of women as inferior to men. An appropriate view of social relations for Korean-North American women in today's multicultural world would reject commitments to static and hierarchical views of the created order. Instead, it would have to create free, dynamic human relations characterized by mutual, reciprocal concerns. In addition, the Anselm's view of empowerment lacks a socio-political dimension because it is primarily concerned with personal regeneration. Lacking emphasis on Jesus' personhood or actions, it is a-historical and a-ethical.

In the following chapter, I will mainly explore Moltmann's social Trinitarian understanding of the Cross in order to present it as a resource for a feminist theology of the cross, and to prepare Korean-North American women for the Trinitarian praxis in their multicultural North-American context. In so doing, I will need to first discuss Luther's theology of the cross, what common factors Luther and Moltmann share, and how Moltmann tries to overcome Luther's theology of the cross.

3

Toward a Social Trinitarian Theology of the Cross

Moltmann's Social Trinitarian Theology of the Cross as a Contributing Resource for a Feminist Theology of the Cross

FEMINIST THEOLOGIANS APPROACH THE cross of Jesus in various ways. Some reject the notion that God sent his Son to die as payment for the penalty of sin. Their objection is that this image of the cross speaks of a Father God who murders or allows the murder of his Son.[1] Others depart from the traditional feminist criticism of the cross as sado-masochistic, redirecting the focus of the cross to life-giving images of healing and solidarity.[2] The outcry of these feminist theologians is for the cross to encompass a call to suffer in solidarity with the suffering.

Concurring with those feminist theologians who contest that the cross must encompass a call to suffer in solidarity, I will, in this chapter, explore Moltmann's social trinitarian theology to propose it as a contributing

---

1. Sölle, *Suffering*, 27.

2. For instance, Grey claims that the death of Jesus Christ is to be seen not as the wrath of God against a guilty world for which Jesus was punished. Rather she interprets it "as the culmination of the great refusal and blockage of the dynamic of mutuality in relation, which was the outstanding feature of the way Jesus related to the world. See Grey, *Redeeming the Dream: Feminism, Redemption and Christian Tradition*, 125. Carr, in her *Transforming Grace*, also argues that a proper understanding of the cross necessarily concludes that God did not send Jesus to the cross, but rather humanity in its sinfulness did. See *Transforming Grace*, 188. Johnson also rejects the teaching that Jesus' death was demanded by God, and sees it instead that it was demanded by a humanity which refused the will of a God of life and love. See Johnson, "*Redeeming the Name*," 124–25.

resource for a feminist theology of the cross which constitutes Trinitarian praxis for Korean women in the multicultural North American context. The image of God the Father as a suffering God identifies the crucified Jesus with the oppressed, the poor, and the socially rejected. This view of the cross as a symbol of God's suffering love for God's creation is possible when we view it as a triune event. By adhering to the social Trinitarian concept of God as *perichoretic* community, I will argue how feminist theologians of the cross can deal with the social, ethical issues which involve relationships between women and men and their mutuality and reciprocity.

Contemporary theologians of the cross, including Moltmann, share with Luther the understanding of God as suffering in solidarity with those who suffer. Luther's understanding of *commucatio idiomatum* made it possible to conceive of God in the godforsakenness of Christ and to ascribe suffering and death on the cross to the divine-human person of Christ. Luther by affirming a communication of attributes describes the mutual interpenetration of the divine and human natures of Christ. Luther does not specifically use the term *perichoresis*, but employs the Cappadocian image of iron/fire to express the mutual penetration of the divine and human properties in Christ: "Whoever touches the heat in the heated iron touches the iron, and whoever has touched the skin of Christ has actually touched God."[3] Moltmann uses the concept of *perichoresis* in his theology of the cross, but not exactly in same way that Luther does. Moltmann uses the concept of *perichoresis* to describe the reciprocal indwelling and dynamic interpenetration of the three divine persons of the Trinity. By presenting the cross as a Trinitarian event, Moltmann tries to overcome Luther's theology of the cross which is based on two different natures, the divine and the human, in the God-human being Christ. Therefore, it is necessary to look into Luther's *theologia crucis* first and investigate how Moltmann tries to overcome Luther's theology of the Cross.

Luther's *theologia crucis*

Although the term, *theologia crucis* was not coined until Luther first used it in the Heidelberg Disputation in 1518, we see currents of a theology of the cross running throughout the Apostle Paul's epistles.[4] We must note

3. *LW* 26:267.
4. Dunn, *The Theology of Paul the Apostle*, 212. See also Moltmann, *The Crucified God*, 69.

that in the Pauline epistles, different aspects of the cross are emphasized in different contexts. Calvin Roetzel rightly points out that "if the cross is at the core of Paul's theology, as many argue, it is simply inadequate to say the cross is foundational without noting the way the interpretation of the cross is changed by its context and then bends back onto the context to shape that as well."[5] Likewise, we cannot properly understand the nature of Luther's theology of the cross without understanding the social and theological environment in which it was developed.

In *the Resolutions*, Luther uses the expression *theologia crucis* in the context of a long discussion of Thesis 58 which concerns indulgences and the merits of the saints and of Christ.[6] He develops his theology of the cross in Thesis 58 as a polemical tool against the scholastic theologians who he identified with *theologia gloriae*. A theologian of glory does not recognize the crucified and hidden God. A theologian of glory sees and knows only a glorious God. He sees in creation a God who is present everywhere and is omnipotent.[7] On the contrary, the theologian of the cross knows of a crucified and hidden God. God is concealed not only because God Godself is crucified but also hidden under all the crosses and sufferings of true Christians. McGrath insists that Luther's God of the *theologia crucis* is an answer to the question, "Who is this God who deals with humanity?"[8] The God who deals with sinful humanity in this astonishing way is none other than the crucified and hidden God, the God of the *theologia crucis*. Thesis 58 has become the basis upon which Luther constructs his *theologia crucis* in the Heidelberg Disputation. [9]

Analysis of the Heidelberg Disputation and Some Important Treatises of Luther

In the Heidelberg Disputation, Luther provides us with his profound theology of the cross. I will analyze the Heidelberg Disputation from a

---

5. Roetzel, "The Grammar of Election in Four Pauline Letters," 228. See also Madsen, *The Theology of the Cross in Historical Perspective*, 33–63. Through her thorough overview of Paul's theology of the cross, Madsen demonstrates how Paul interpreted the cross to be suitable for the cultural and religious contexts of the recipients of his epistles.

6. LW 31:212–28.

7. Loewenich, *Luther's Theology of the Cross*, 23

8. McGrath, *Luther's Theology of the Cross*, 146–47

9. Rupp, "Luther's Ninety-five Theses and the Theology of the Cross," 76.

soteriological, epistemological, and ethical perspective. First of all, soteriologically viewing the Disputation, we find "justification by faith and grace alone" in its central position. In the first two theses Luther states his understanding of *iustitia Dei*: righteousness has been manifested without the law, and apart from human works. In theses 3-12 Luther lay out his attack on human reason, insisting that the sinner surrenders every claim to self-righteousness or self-justification. Luther rejects every kind of personal preparation for grace by free will. He calls theologians of the cross to abandon the Bielian theology of *"faciendo quod in se est"* (by doing their best). God deals with us through God's *opus alienum* (alien work).

Luther insists that after the Fall free will exists in name only, and this is evident because the fallen will is captive and subject to sin. The fallen will is "not free except to do evil." There is indeed a will but the problem is that it is not free but bound. Forde clarifies that we are not dealing with determinism or fate.[10] Rather, the will is captive thus bound to sin. The will is bound to will what it wills. Only in its passive capacity, as thesis 15 states, the will can do "good" only when it is rescued and acted upon from without. For Luther, justification, therefore, must be *aliena*, foreign to us, and is imputed to us in our relationship *coram Deo*, by faith in Christ.

The theologian of the cross, for Luther, knows that we can do nothing but throw ourselves at the mercy of God in Christ. Thus, in thesis 16, Christ is spoken of as the bringer of salvation, hope, and resurrection. Luther in theses 17 and 18 insists that grace is not acquired by "doing what is in us," or by "doing our best" but it is acquired "when we are so completely humbled by God's alien work in law and wrath that we see how completely we are caught in the web of sin and turn to Christ as the only hope."[11] By the "utter despair of our own ability" we are prepared to receive the grace of Christ.

Secondly, to view the Disputation epistemologically, we need to focus on theses 19-21 where Luther deals with the way theologians operate. Luther contrasts theologians of *crucis* with theologians of *gloriae*. Theologians of glory operate on the assumption that they can see the "invisible things of God" through creation and history. They assume that creation yields clues, if not directly at least by analogy, to the invisible characteristics of God, such as "virtue, godliness, wisdom, justice, goodness and so forth."[12]

---

10. Forde, *On Being a Theologian of the Cross*, 53.
11. Ibid., 61.
12. *LW* 31:52.

Referring to Romans 1:20, Luther asserts that the one who attempts to see the "invisible things of God" through insight into what can be seen in creation does not deserve to be called a theologian.[13] For Luther, knowledge of God gained in this way is not true knowledge because it arises out of human speculation.

Thesis 20 presents the paradoxical nature of the cross as a reality of revelation. Luther furthers in thesis 21 the point that a true theologian recognizes God in the crucified Christ.[14] The theologian of glory, on the contrary, expects God to be revealed in glory, majesty, and strength and deduces that God cannot be present in the cross of Christ. Luther refers to the theologian of glory as an "enemy of the cross" who refuses to accept reality as it is. A theologian of the cross calls a thing what it is, declaring that it is God incarnate who suffers death, even death on the cross for the sake of humanity's salvation. Only in the shame and humility of the cross can we find the true and gracious God; therefore, "*Crux sola est nostra theologia*" (Cross alone is our theology).[15] In contrast to a speculative knowledge of God gained by reason, true knowledge of God in the *theologia crucis* is available only through faith in God's suffering and weakness on the cross.

Thirdly, to view the Disputation ethically, we must not forget that the epistemology of God is to be embodied in "practical suffering." In thesis 20, Luther mentions, "It is not sufficient for anyone and it does him no good to recognize God in his glory and majesty unless he recognizes God in the humility and shame of his cross."[16] A number of theologians of the cross have followed Luther in affirming the suffering of God as fundamental to their theologies. Bonheoffer once said, "Only suffering God can help."[17] Hall also states, "It is God who, 'with trembling' endured abandonment, hopelessness and the absurd, has become the test of theological authenticity in our time."[18] Moltmann also suggests that God continues to suffer in and with the world's suffering. God specifically identifies with the oppressed, the poor, and the socially rejected through the crucified Jesus. Likewise, the suffering God has become a kind of theological condition today.

---

13. *LW* 31:40. See also Madsen, *The Theology of the Cross in Historical Perspective*, 76.
14. *LW* 31:52–53.
15. McGrath, *Luther's Theology*, 149–51. See also Loewenich, *Luther's Theology*, 20.
16. *LW* 31:52–53.
17. Bonheoffer, *Letters and Papers from Prison*, 360.
18. Hall, *Lighten Our Darkness*, 211.

The Liberative Cross

In the last section of the Heidelberg Disputation from thesis 25 to 28, Luther contends that a theologian of the cross understands that it is not works that make sinners righteous, but it is righteousness that creates works. In thesis 27 Luther insists that Christians live as imitators of God not because it is a requirement for righteousness but because they have been motivated by the "operative power" to love in this world.

As demonstrated above, Luther clearly expresses through his theology that God is on the cross, in the suffering of human existence, rather than with the powers of medieval Christendom. However, Moltmann argues that because Luther's main focus was on the cross and the forgiveness of sin, he forgot the political implications of the cross as was evidenced in Luther's stance in the Peasant Wars.[19] Is this critique fair to Luther? To answer the question we need to see whether Luther remained faithful to his theology of the cross after the Heidelberg Disputation. For this purpose, we will examine some of the important treatises which Luther produced after the Heidelberg Disputation.

First of all, in his *Appeal to the Christian Nobility*, Luther singles out the pope, highlighting his operative stance as a theologian of glory. He insists that the pope is not the vicar of Christ in heaven, but only in the form of a servant as he walked on earth, working, preaching, suffering and dying.[20] Luther appeals to the princes to protect the German people from "these rapacious wolves in sheep's clothing" who thieve and rob by selling indulgences, letters of confession, and other tactics that fill their coffers. Luther, in *Babylonian Captivity of the Church*, attempts to dismantle the tyrannical ecclesial powers. As a theologian of the cross, Luther incites Christians to embrace their role as priests and live in confident conformity to Christ's life, death, and resurrection.[21] Lastly in the third Reformation Treatise, *On the Freedom of the Christian*, Luther makes the paradoxical claim that "a Christian is perfectly free lord of all, subject to none. A Christian is a perfectly dutiful servant of all, subject to all."[22] We stand *coram Deo*, where the "inner person" has been pronounced righteous through Christ's joyous exchange through faith and set free to live for God. However, Christian freedom *coram Deo* does not alter our necessary obedience to temporal authorities. Christians are to be subject not just to rulers but

---

19. Moltmann, *The Crucified God*, 72.
20. *LW* 44:165.
21. Thompson, *Crossing the Divide*, 41.
22. *LW* 31:344.

Toward a Social Trinitarian Theology of the Cross

also to all others "in works of freest service, cheerfully and lovingly done without hope of reward." [23]

In these three treatises, we see that Luther was remaining faithful to the theology of the cross he had elucidated in the Heidelberg Disputation. However, dispute had erupted on whether Luther' position on the Peasants' War was compatible to his theology of the cross. In his treatise, *On Temporal Authority*, which Luther published in 1523, he developed the theology of the two kingdom and two governments. Here he makes heavy use of Romans 13:1: "Everyone must submit himself to the governing authorities, for there is no authority except that which God has established. The authorities that exist have been established by God."[24] The two kingdoms, according to Luther, refer to the two overlapping spheres of Christian existence, the life of the Christian before God and the life of the Christian in society. The two governments, on the other hand, refer to the two ways in which God governs the world.[25] God governs the Church through the gospel, from which all modes of coercion are excluded. On the other hand, God governs the world through law and coercion. God stands as ruler of both the Church and the world. Therefore, according to Luther, there is no sphere of life beyond God's purview.[26] God governs the earthly realm with the left hand, which constitutes God's alien work. Since the earthly realm stands under God's governance, Christians freely live out their response to God's mercy and forgiveness given through the cross.

Nevertheless, Luther's doctrine of two kingdoms has often been criticized for leading to political passivity. In fact, in his *Admonition to Peace: A Reply to the Twelve Articles of the Peasants in Swabia*, Luther implores peasants to passively endure the suffering and injustice thrust upon them by the authorities.[27] Also in the pamphlet, *Against the Robbing and Murdering Hordes of Peasants*, which Luther wrote in the late spring of 1520, he insists the peasants to conform to the crucified Christ in passivity. Because the peasants committed violence in the name of Christ Luther accuses them of "blaspheming God." Luther also says, "A pious Christian ought to suffer a hundred deaths rather than give a hairs-breadth of consent to the peasants'

---

23. *LW* 31:365.
24. *LW* 45:85–129.
25. Steinmetz, *Luther in Context*, 114.
26. Thompson, *Crossing the Divide*, 50.
27. *LW* 46:17–43.

cause."²⁸ What is worse is that Luther encourages the rulers to take up the sword when necessary as the punishment for the Peasants' War.

It seems that Luther stands with the authorities instead of the suffering peasants in these writings he produced on the Peasants' War. Is this position of Luther on the Peasants' War faithful to his theology of the cross? Moltmann points out that Luther believed that the reformation of life necessarily follows from the reformation of faith. In other words, he believed that social reformation follows quite naturally from the "recognition of divine vocation for every Christian" in the earthly realm.[29]

Harold Wells, however, has a different understanding from Moltmann. He wisely warns us not to read Luther from the twenty-first century democratic socialist's perspective. We have to consider Luther's context and remember that "his original motivation was to challenge the practice of indulgences and therefore the whole operative theology of sin and grace was in large measure a defense of the poor who were deceived and cheated by ecclesiastical oppression."[30] In the medieval world, Wells argues, the religious world is so tightly tied with the socio-political world that the religious reformation cannot be contemplated separately from the socio-political reformation and *vice-versa*.[31]

Thompson reminds us of Luther's change of attitude toward imperial authorities in the aftermath of Augsburg. She argues that it certainly shows Luther's uncompromising spirit to defend the gospel.[32] Here, Luther sternly calls for an active, subversive disobedience to imperial authorities. Luther's consistent refusal to submit to ecclesial abuses, Thompson insists, ultimately overflowed to imperial abuses as well. According to Luther, when the gospel is at stake, a believer must actively resist any and all efforts which thwart its proclamation. Luther declares that all Germans are duty-bound to resist and defend against repression of the gospel, even when resistance means sanctioning armed protests against threatening imperial powers.[33]

---

28. *LW* 46:54.

29. Moltmann, "Reformation and Revolution," 186. See also Thompson, *Crossing the Divide*, 57.

30. Wells, "The Theology of the Cross and the Theologies of Liberation,"152.

31. Ibid.

32. Thompson, *Crossing the Divide*, 74–78. The Diet of Augsburg was convened in 1530 by Emperor Charles V in hopes of achieving a compromise among Germany's fracturing religious groups.

33. *LW* 47:35.

So far I have argued that Luther's theology of the cross was not merely a theology for the eternal salvation of individuals, but also a profound challenge to the ecclesiastical systems, as well as political systems, of the medieval world which deprived the poor of social, political, and religious rights. Could Luther's theology of the cross become a contributing resource in contemporary contexts? If so, we need to discuss in what respect Luther's theology of the cross can make a contribution to contemporary contexts.

A Contribution Luther's Theology of the Cross Makes to Contemporary Contexts

The first feature of Luther's theology of the cross which can contribute to contemporary contexts is the concept of divine solidarity. For Luther, it is "the most joyous of all doctrines" that God in Christ reached out to sinful humanity and took the consequence of human sin so that condemnation need not fall upon them.[34] The incarnate God identifies with the suffering of those whom God loves. Luther's theology of the cross was motivated by his indignation on behalf of the poor and underprivileged people who were oppressed by the powerful ecclesiastical authorities.

Uniquely, Luther's God is a suffering God. Ngien contends that "Luther's *theologia crucis* opens up an attack upon the understanding that only the humanity of Christ suffers on the cross while Christ's divine nature is untouched."[35] In contrast to the Christian tradition of understanding God as omnipotent and immutability as impassible, Luther insisted that, given the unity of Jesus Christ in his two natures as divine and human, we must " . . . ascribe to the divinity because of this personal union, all that happens to humanity and *vice versa*."[36]

---

34. *LW* 26:280. See also Wells, "The Theology of the Cross and the Theologies of Liberation," 151.

35. Ngien, *The Suffering of God*, 71. In keeping with the Chalcedonian orthodoxy, Luther stresses the unity of Christ's person in his repudiation of Zwingli, who in his attempt to secure the transcendence of God advocates that the Son of God does not suffer and die, and that Christ suffers and dies only insofar as he is a man. See *LW* 23:101–3. *LW* 41:100. Luther refuted Nestorius's understanding of the *communicatio idiomatum* in his work, *On the Councils and the Church* (1599). Luther argues, "Nestorius' error was not that he believed Christ to be a pure man or that he made two persons of him; on the contrary, he confesses two natures, the divine and human, in one person –but he will not admit a *communicatio idiomatum*" between the two natures.

36. *LW* 37:210. See also Wells, "The Theology of the Cross and the Theologies of Liberation," 150.

The Liberative Cross

We need to understand the two-nature Christology and Luther's use of the doctrine of *communicatio idiomatum* to understand in what way he attributed the suffering of Christ to God. According to Luther what is attributed to one aspect of a person is attributed to the whole person. Luther insists that if it is true that only the human nature of Jesus suffers while his divine nature has no part in the suffering, then Christ is of no more use to us than any other saint because His death is merely that of a human being's. Christ's sacrifice would merely act as an exemplar for the faithful, a model of proper Christian virtue. For Luther, it is a theological axiom that Christ must be affected by suffering, even according to his divine nature[37] When Christ's human nature suffers, his divine nature suffers along with His human nature *via communicatio idiomatum*.

Luther transcends the Alexandrian Christology[38] by asserting the idea of a real communication that moves not only from divine nature to human nature but also from human nature to divine nature. The mutual penetration of the divine and human properties in Christ is well expressed in Luther's use of the Cappadocian image of iron and fire: "Whoever touches the heat in the heated iron touches the iron and whoever has touched the skin of Christ has actually touched God."[39] Ngien points out that Luther's use of the doctrine of the *communicatio idiomatum* breaks with the Hellenistic doctrine of divine *apatheia*. The absolute unity of Christ's person means for Luther that "no suffering, no work can apply to him without our saying that it touches his entire person."[40] *Theologia gloriae* fails to define the nature of God in terms of God's self-identification with the crucified Christ. It

---

37. Ngien, *The Suffering of God*, 75.

38. Ibid., 68–86. The Alexandrian theologians (Cyril, John of Damascus) conceived of the communication principally only in one direction, that is in terms of the action of the divine nature with respect to the human nature. Their motive was to establish the "one sole agent of what happens in Christ." On the other hand, the Antiocheans thought of the communication as the communication of the attributes of each of the two natures to the person. The motive of Antioch's formulation was to establish "two agents of what happens in Christ": the divine Logos or Son is divine and is impassible whereas the human Jesus is temporal and is passible. Luther, however, went further than the communication of attributes from nature to person. Luther conceived in the person of Christ the idea of a real communication of attributes between the two natures themselves.

39 *LW* 26:266. On the origin of this image, see the note 95 in *LW* 23:123–24: "From its source in Origen and in Basil this analogy of the glowing iron came into John of Damascus. See *Exposition of the Orthodox Faith* 3.17 (Concerning the Deification of the Nature of our Lord's Flesh and of His Will), *NPNF* 9/2:65–66.

40. *LW* 28:267.

Toward a Social Trinitarian Theology of the Cross

subjugates the cross to a preconceived metaphysical idea of divine apathy. Luther therefore rejects *theologia gloriae*. For Luther, if God is denied suffering, then the cross cannot be a revelation of God. Jesus, the crucified One, is the substantial content, the revelation of the true identity of God. Therefore, Christian faith must speak of no other God than the incarnate God, the human God, or the crucified God. The concrete unity of the two natures in the one Person of Jesus Christ requires the passibility of God. In the incarnation, God suffers not only in the humanity of the Son but also as God the eternal Son because "God's Son and Mary's Son is only one Person" or "one Son."[41] For Luther, "suffering is, therefore, ontologically constitutive of the being of God or the eternal Son of God."[42]

As argued above, through the doctrine of the *communicatio idiomatum*, Luther established that the suffering of Christ is God's own suffering in the totality of God's being (God-man in *toto*). Thus, Luther discards the conception of *apatheia*. For Luther, Christ suffers in the totality of His being, and God's Son is of one being (*homoousios*) with the Father. In this manner, the Father, though He does not suffer dying as the Son, suffers through divine unity with the Son.[43]

Luther's Christology of the crucified God certainly developed the doctrine of the *communicatio idiomatum* in an important way. However, Moltmann insists that Luther never arrived at a developed Christological doctrine of the Trinity. He explicates the weakness in Luther's Christology in this way:

> Luther used the name "God" generically and promiscuously for a) the nature of God, b) the person of the Son of God, c) the persons of the Father and the Spirit. Because he spoke emphatically of God and man, of the incarnate God and the man Jesus who became divine, he arrived at paradoxical distinctions between God and God: between the God who crucifies and the crucified God; the God who is dead and yet is not dead; between the manifest God in Christ and the hidden God above and beyond Christ.[44]

In the following section, I will look into how Moltmann overcomes Luther by his theology of the cross.

---

41. *LW* 24:97. See also *LW* 15:341.
42. Ngien, *The Suffering of God*, 86
43. *LW* 24:98
44. Moltmann, *The Crucified God*, 235

Moltmann's Theology of the Cross

Moltmann's theology of the cross has been developed from his life experiences. He testifies how his experience of surviving the bombing of his hometown of Hamburg as a teenager by the RAF's "Operation Gomorrah," which annihilated the city and killed his friend (1943), as well as his experience as a prisoner of war for three years (1944-6) during World War II, influenced his theology: "Ever since then, the question about God for me has been identical with the cry of the victims for justice and the hunger of the perpetrators for a way back from the path of death"[45]

However, it is not only these wartime experiences that affected Moltmann's theology. He attributes the development of his theology to the multivalent influences of history. He writes:

> My theological methods ... grew up as I came to have a perception of the objects of theological thought. The road emerged only as I walked it. And my attempts to walk it are of course determined by my personal biography, and by the political context and historical *kairos* in which I live.[46]

Moltmann keeps himself open to the socio-political changes in the world in order to reflect them in his theology. Moltmann turned to the theology of the cross as a critique to the false optimism of his society which, he felt, refused to acknowledge suffering.[47] Christian hope and love, according to him, can only be sustained from the crucified and risen Jesus who maintains solidarity with the suffering.

In the context of the suffering of the world, Moltmann insists that a god who sits enthroned in heaven in detached bliss is not acceptable.[48] Thus, we must ask what the real meaning of Christ's suffering is and how God's being is to be seen in terms of Christ's forsakenness by God. Moltmann insists that to answer these questions we must look at the question of Christ's suffering before looking at the suffering of the world because only when we are clear as to what happened on the cross between Jesus and God can it be clear who this God is for us and for our experience.[49]

45. Ibid., xi.
46. Moltmann, *Experiences in Theology*, xv.
47. Ibid., 13–14.
48. Moltmann, *The Crucified God*, 274.
49. Ibid., 235. Moltmann explains what happened on the cross between Christ and the God whom he called Father by the word, "*paradidonai*" which is used in Mark and the Pauline Epistles. See Moltmann, *The Way of Jesus Christ*, 172–78.

The Cross of Christ as the Foundation and Criticism of Christian Theology

For Moltmann, the cross is the "inner criterion of all theology" and "the key signature of all Christian theology."[50] He insists that "the crisis of the church today is the crisis of its own existence as the church of the crucified Christ."[51] Therefore, we must not forget that it is the crucified Christ himself that is "the criterion of truth for churches, theologians and forms of belief."[52] Moltmann explains: "If they are to be Christian, then they are appealing to the one who judges them most severely and liberates them most radically from lies and vanity, from the struggle for power and from fear."[53] Their faith, church, and theology, which dare to call themselves by the name of the crucified Christ, must demonstrate what they really believe about the crucified Christ and what practical consequences they wish to draw from their belief.[54]

In his monograph, *The Crucified God*, Moltmann struggles with this fundamental question: "What kind of theology of the cross does justice to the man from Nazareth who was crucified under Pontius Pilate, and is necessary today?" He insists that in order to answer the question, we must go back to the history of Jesus and, eventually, the cross. Moltmann emphasizes that "not from the cross in isolation but from the cross understood in its context both of Jesus' earthly life and of his resurrection can Jesus be recognized not just another condemned criminal or another innocent victim but as one who in love became their brother."[55] Jesus' message of God's justifying grace for the godless and his life of fellowship with sinners incited the world against himself. Therefore, the death of Jesus was the result of a life of proclaiming God to be on the side of the godless. However, Jesus' life and death, Moltmann affirms, must be viewed in the light of his resurrection because "Only in the light of his resurrection from the dead does his death gain that special, unique saving significance which it cannot achieve otherwise, even in the light of the life he lived."[56] Only in light of the

---

50. Moltmann, *The Crucified God*, 2, 72.
51. Ibid., 2.
52. Ibid.
53. Ibid.
54. Ibid., 3.
55. Ibid., 51.
56. Ibid., 182.

resurrection is the death of Jesus understood to be the death of the Christ, the Son of God.

The dialectical Christology of Moltmann contrasts the death of the resurrected Jesus with the resurrection of the crucified Christ. Crucified Jesus in his death is identified with all the negative qualities of the present reality, such as godlessness, godforsakenness, and transitoriness. However, this same Jesus is raised from the dead to affirm God's promise of new creation for this godforsaken reality. Jesus, who was raised into the glory of the coming God, is in his cross the incarnate God who identifies with godless and godforsaken people so as to bring the new life of the resurrection to them in their situation. The resurrection of the crucified Christ is God's promise and awakening of hope for a different future.[57] God, who raised the crucified Christ, creates anticipation for the future kingdom of God within history and thus becomes the source of hope for transformation. Authentic Christian hope allows people to resist and work to redeem the brokenness of the world.[58]

In his dialectical Christology Moltmann stresses other aspects of the revelation of God in the cross: In the cross God is revealed as contrary to the false gods of the law, political religion, and theistic religion.[59] Moltmann explains:

> The history of Jesus which led to his crucifixion was rather a *theological history* in itself, and was dominated by the conflict between God and the gods; that is between the God whom Jesus preached as his Father, and the God of the law as he was understood by the guardians of the law, together with the political gods of the Roman occupying power.[60]

The crucified Christ liberates humanity from enslavement to the false gods of the law, political religion, and theistic religions.

First of all, Jesus was crucified as a blasphemer against the law by the guardians of the law. Following Ernst Käsemann, Moltmann sees Jesus' teaching as characterized by the tendency to place himself above the authority of Moses and the Torah.[61] In his ministry, Jesus placed himself with sovereign authority above the limits of the contemporary understanding

---

57. Moltmann, *Theology of Hope*, 30.
58. Ibid., 22.
59. Moltmann, *The Crucified God*, 68–69.
60. Ibid., 127.
61. Käsemann, *Essays on New Testament Themes*, 37.

Toward a Social Trinitarian Theology of the Cross

of the law. He also demonstrated God's eschatological law of grace towards those without the law and the transgressors of the law through his forgiveness of sins. In so doing, Jesus sets himself against the law by introducing a new basis of righteousness that abolishes the legal distinctions between the religious and the secular, the righteous and the unrighteous, the devout and the sinful. Jesus also preached the imminence of the kingdom of God, not as judgment but as the gospel of the justification of sinners by grace. For Jesus, the kingdom comes as the unconditional and free grace of God by which the lost are sought out and the unrighteous are accepted. From this point of view, the life and ministry of Jesus was a theological clash between him and the prevailing understandings of the law. That is why the gospel Luke describes Jesus as dying by the law as one who was reckoned with transgressors (Luke 22:37). The Apostle Paul also interprets the death of the crucified Jesus in relation to the law: Since the law had brought Jesus to his death upon the cross, so the risen and exalted Jesus becomes "the end of the law" that everyone who has faith may be justified (Rom 10:4). The crucified God, therefore, liberates us from the idols of legalism. Here, we see Moltmann concur with Luther as he emphasizes that if we want to justify ourselves by works we idolize our own achievements and become slaves to the idol of justification by works.[62]

Secondly, the crucifixion of Jesus was also caused by the conflict between God and the political gods of the Roman occupying power. According to Moltmann, Jesus was crucified by the Romans not merely for the immediate political reasons of peace and good order in Jerusalem, but also for the glorification of Roman state gods who assured the *Pax Romana*.[63] This is proven by the fact that the Christians of the early church openly rejected emperor worship, and consequently faced martyrdom, which was both a religious and political act.

Moltmann adds a political dimension to the theology of the cross from the fact that Jesus was crucified as a political criminal, who in some respect threatened the *Pax Romana* and yet was raised up and vindicated by God. Accordingly, the theology of the cross is not "pure theology" in a modern non-political sense or in the sense of private religion.[64] The theology of the cross bears a public testimony to the freedom of Christ and the law of grace in the face of the political religions of nations, empires, races, and classes.

---

62. Moltmann, *The Crucified God*, 128–35.
63. Ibid., 136.
64. Ibid., 144–45.

Political religions emerge whenever religion serves to integrate society and to sanctify the existing political and social systems. In other words, religion becomes a kind of political idolatry when it absolutizes rulers or ruling systems, consequently leading to a pattern of domination and enslavement.[65]

Moltmann calls for a new critical political theology. He insists, "Christianity did not arise as a national or a class religion . . . The crucified God is in fact a stateless and classless God. But that does not mean that he is an unpolitical God. God is the God of the poor, the oppressed and the humiliated." [66] For him, "the rule of the Christ who was crucified for political reasons can only be extended through liberation from forms of rule which make men [and women] servile and apathetic, and from the political religions which give them stability."[67]

Thirdly, Moltmann maintains that the cross contradicts and liberates people from the false god of theistic religion. He uses 'theism' in the sense of the traditional metaphysical concept of God which defines God's infinity over and against humanity's finiteness. God, according to theism, is indivisible, immutable, impassible, immortal, and omnipotent whereas humanity is finite, mortal, weak, and suffering. In the model of theistic religions, humanity finds support from suffering and the nothingness of death in a divine being that is completely free from suffering and death.[68] According to him, the crucified God contradicts the false god of theistic religion in that while the idolatry of theism seeks freedom from suffering and death through "its projection of childish needs for authoritarian protection in a god who cannot suffer and die,"[69] the crucified God represents liberation from suffering and death through loving solidarity.

The Cross of Christ in the Context of Atheism and Theism

While making the assertion that God is revealed as suffering God through the cross, Moltmann sets his discussion of the cross of Jesus in the context of atheism and theism.[70] The cross of Christ contradicts traditional theism which is based upon natural theology, particularly the cosmological

65. Ibid., 328.
66. Ibid.
67. Ibid., 329.
68. Ibid., 214.
69. Ibid., 216–19.
70. Ibid., 207–27.

Toward a Social Trinitarian Theology of the Cross

argument for the existence of God. Moltmann rejects any kind of natural theology which finds God evident in or deducible from the natural world. He argues that the present state of the world, full of evil and suffering, not only fails to prove God but also provides grounds for rejecting God.

The fundamental problem of theism for Moltmann is the problem of theodicy: "How can an all-powerful, invulnerable creator and ruler of the world be justified in the face of suffering?" To discuss the problem of theodicy, Moltmann cites Dostoevsky's famous presentation of Ivan Karamazov's rejection of God.[71] Ivan represents protest atheism, an atheism which emerges from struggling with the injustice of the world. While discussing with his brother Aloysha, Ivan Karamazov argues against any eschatological theodicy that justifies suffering as the price to be paid for the achievement of some eschatological purpose of God in the future. To make his point, Ivan tells the story of an eight-year-old serf-boy who accidentally injured his landowner's favorite dog. The landowner had him hunted like an animal and torn into pieces by the master's hounds before his mother's eyes. By this story, Ivan insists that it is not only incomprehensible but also morally unacceptable to try and justify this kind of unjust and senseless suffering as part of some ultimate divine purpose for the world. Even if it were to become comprehensible to him at the *eschaton*, Ivan would not accept an eternal harmony built upon the sufferings of the innocent. Ivan therefore concludes that the idea of God is morally unacceptable and rejects the idea that God can be justified by justifying the sufferings of the innocent.

In discussing the problem of protest atheism, Moltmann points out that the crucified Christ is a protesting God. In agreement with him, Bauckham, an expert on Moltmann's theology, points out an important principle of theodicy: Innocent and senseless suffering must not be justified as necessary to God's purpose or explained as necessary for some higher human purpose.[72] Such justifications suppress the sense of moral outrage against evil, thereby removing the motive to relieve and overcome suffering. At worst, such justifications justify the infliction of innocent suffering by totalitarian regimes, either theocratic or atheistic. Therefore, Bauckham affirms that an adequate theological response to the problem of suffering must contain an initiative for overcoming suffering. It must help to maintain the protest against suffering and convert it into an initiative for overcoming suffering.[73]

---

71. Ibid., 220. Moltmann cites Dostoevsky, *The Brothers Karamazov*, 292.
72. Bauckham, *The Theology of Jürgen Moltmann*, 81–82.
73. Ibid., 81–82.

At this point, we are led to ask how we can maintain the protest against innocent and senseless suffering and yet avoid lapsing into the tyranny of the revolutionary regime. By protesting against God, humanity has claimed control over human destiny. Upon the pretext of establishing a world of justice, the revolutionary elites have inflicted innocent suffering and effectively silenced revolts by means necessary. Bauckham rightly points out that in this way the modern age has substituted an eschatological theodicy with an eschatological anthropodicy which also justifies suffering.[74]

Moltmann, taking protest theism seriously, rejects any possible justification for suffering.[75] Whereas Sölle looks into Elie Wiesel's *Night* to insist that we take off our eyes from the almighty God and perceive the cross existentially from below,[76] Moltmann reflects on it to insist that the Christian God is a protesting God who suffers under the history of injustice. A key passage in the book is taken from a story that took place in a camp attached to Auschwitz called Buma. The SS hanged two Jewish men and a boy in front of the whole camp. The men died quickly, but the child, being light, was still alive:

> For more than half an hour he stayed there, struggling between life and death, dying in slow agony under our eyes . . . He was still alive when I passed in front of him. His tongue was still red, his eyes were not yet glazed. Behind me, I heard the same man asking: "Where is God now?" And I heard a voice within me answer him: "Where is He? Here he is- He is hanging here on this gallows.[77]

As I have already mentioned in the case of Sölle, this story marks the final, crucial step in Wiesel's loss of faith in God. The possibility of faith in God for Wiesel dies with the dying child.[78] Wiesel, like Ivan Karamazov, protests against God, the God who permits Auschwitz. He loses his faith in the god of providential justice.[79] However, Moltmann reflects on the story

74. Ibid., 76.
75. Moltmann, *The Crucified God*, 165, 278.
76. Sölle, *Suffering*, 145, quoting Wiesel, *Night*, 75.
77. Moltmann, *The Crucified God*, 46, quoting Wiesel, *Night*, 75.
78. Bauckham, *Theology of Jürgen Moltmann*, 78.
79. Ibid., 80. However, in the midst of his struggle for sheer survival, Wiesel sees the dehumanizing effect of extreme suffering and finds himself praying for strength not to desert his father what rabbi Eliahou's son has done. Bauckham points out that Wiesel here recognizes the idea of God in a dialectical relationship to the problem of suffering. God is not only the authority over history to whom the rebel directs his accusation; he also represents and so sustains human values which alone keep human beings human

Toward a Social Trinitarian Theology of the Cross

and answers the question "Where is God now?" in a sense different from Wiesel. Wiesel sentences faith to death as he watches the boy dying on the gallows because God is no longer able to answer the question of theodicy. Moltmann, however, sees God who suffers with the boy dying on the gallows. Moltmann states his point like this:

> There cannot be any other Christian answer to the question of this torment. To speak here of a God who could not suffer would make God a demon. To speak here of an absolute God would make God an annihilating nothingness.[80]

For Moltmann, God is a protesting God. The incarnate God identifies with the suffering of those whom God loves. God takes up and expresses their protest against innocent and senseless suffering. According to Moltmann, in Jesus' cry of dereliction, "*Eloi, Eloi, Lama Sabachthani?*" the crucified Christ protests on behalf of all innocent sufferers. Jesus does not cry in fatalistic acceptance of suffering, but in his voluntary, loving identification with the godless and the god-forsaken. Thus, protest against suffering is not suppressed but sustained by the cross, and becomes an essential element for Jesus' followers to practice in loving solidarity.

Having said all the above, we may still ask if it is really good enough for God to suffer with us and to be involved with us in the struggle against suffering, unless we know that God is doing all God can to overcome suffering. Moltmann insists that the crucified God's solidarity does not abolish suffering, but it does overcome "suffering in suffering," which he claims is the lack of love. He states,

> The suffering in suffering is the lack of love, and the wounds in wounds are the abandonment, and the powerlessness in pain is unbelief. And therefore the suffering of abandonment is overcome by the suffering of love, which is not afraid of what is sick and ugly, but accepts it and takes it to itself in order to heal it.[81]

Essential to Moltmann's argument is the intrinsic connection in this world between suffering and love. The one who cannot suffer cannot love either. God suffers not because of any deficiency in God's being but because of

---

in the face of unacceptable suffering. God lives in the affirmation of human dignity and human solidarity which prevent the rebel's lapse from protest into nihilism.

80. Moltmann, *The Crucified God*, 274.
81. Ibid., 46.

love.[82] The God of theism who cannot suffer cannot love, and so is poorer than men and women who suffer because they love.[83] The cross, for Moltmann, is the event of God's suffering love by which it embraces the world.

Moltmann argues that only when it becomes clear what happened at the cross between Jesus and His Father do the soteriological implications and the political dimensions of the cross become unfolded in a substantial way. Moltmann, therefore, puts much emphasis on Jesus' cry of forsakenness on the cross (Mark 15:34) and claims that "all Christian theology and all Christian life is basically an answer to the question which Jesus asked as he died."[84]

Who is this man who has been utterly 'godforsaken'? What happened at the cross between Jesus and His Father? To answer these questions, Moltmann compares Christ's cry on the cross (Mark 15: 34), "My God, my God, why have you forsaken me?" with that of a pious Jew in Psalm 22. In so doing, Moltmann distinguishes the death of Jesus from that of a pious Jew in Psalm 22. He says, "Even when the two use the same words, they do not necessarily mean the same thing."[85] Originally the words of the psalmist are uttered to the covenant God of Israel for God's faithfulness, but on the lips of Jesus the cry is addressed to the God of grace whom Jesus calls "My Father."[86] The psalmist is making a claim upon the faithfulness of the God of Israel to God's covenant while Jesus is laying claim upon the faithfulness of the Father to the Son. Moltmann sees in the cry of Jesus not only Jesus himself in agony but also the Father for whom he lived and spoke.[87] Thus, he argues that we can change the cry of Jesus from "My God, why have thou forsaken me?" to "My God why have thou forsaken thyself?"[88]

Accordingly, Jesus' use of the Psalm 22 is not to be understood as an expression of his doubt and reassurance of the faithfulness of the covenantal God. If Jesus' cry is understood as an expression of his doubt and reassurance of the faithfulness of the covenantal God, his death merely becomes that of a martyr's. Jesus, the Son, however, claims unity with the Father, and acts on behalf of the Father. Jesus lays claim to his being in this

---

82. Ibid., 230.
83. Ibid., 222–23, 253.
84. Ibid., 4.
85. Ibid., 150.
86. Ibid.
87. Moltmann, *The Crucified God*, 152.
88. Ibid., 151.

special relationship with the Father, in which he is the Son. For Moltmann, the death of Jesus is not merely that of a martyr's, but it is the event of God's suffering love. By presenting the death of Jesus as a divine event between Jesus and his Father, Moltmann challenges the traditional concept of the theistic God to the extent of shattering the idea of divine impassibility.

The Cross of Christ as Divine Passibility

What does Moltmann's understanding of the cross as a divine event of the Trinity say to the traditional theistic idea of an apathetic, impassible God who is subject neither to change nor to suffering? What does the event of the cross really tell us of the character of God's presence in the cross of Jesus? In order to answer these questions, Moltmann analyzes the apathetic theology of Greek antiquity and the pathetic theology of later Jewish philosophy of religion derived from a new Jewish exegesis of the history of God in the Old Testament and in the present suffering of the Jewish people.[89]

Traditional Christian theology stressed divine impassibility, but many theologians today have argued for divine passibility. Paul Fiddes gives four factors which illustrate this change in contemporary theology.[90] First, God's love includes God's vulnerability. Love ordinarily means we are open to being affected by someone else. Second, the renewed emphasis on Luther's theology of the cross prompted interest in divine suffering. Third, divine suffering provides consolation to humans who are suffering. Fiddes notes, "At the most basic level it is a consolation to those who suffer to know that God suffers too, and understands their situation from within."[91] Fourth, we tend to see the world now in an organic model which highlights interdependence of all the parts of reality rather than in a mechanical or hierarchical model. Many of these factors are illustrated also in Moltmann's theology of the cross.

In his critique on Luther's Christology of the crucified God, Moltmann affirms that Luther's doctrine of *communicatio idiomatum* made it possible to conceive of God in the godforsakenness of Christ and to ascribe suffering and death on the cross to the divine-human person of Christ.[92] For Luther,

89. Ibid., 267.
90. Fiddes, *The Creative Suffering of God*, 16–45. For a shorter statement, see Fiddes, "Suffering Divine," 634.
91. Ibid., 31.
92. Moltmann, *The Crucified God*, 234–35.

The Liberative Cross

the absolute unity of Christ's person means that "no suffering, no work can apply to Christ without our saying that it touches His entire Person."[93] In this way, Luther breaks with the Hellenistic doctrine of divine *apatheia*. Luther's doctrine of *communicatio idiomatum*, therefore, provided complete reciprocity between the divine and human natures of Christ and the mutual sharing of those attributes. The suffering of Jesus as God's own suffering lies in the unity of the personal identity, Jesus as the God-man *in toto*. Christ suffers in the totality of His being, and this person (*hypostasis*), God's Son, is of one being (*homoousios*) with the Father.[94] However, Moltmann points out that Luther, remaining within the framework of the early church's doctrine of two natures, never arrived at a developed Christological doctrine of the Trinity.[95] Moltmann, therefore, suggests that in order to understand what happened on the cross between Jesus and his Father, we must see the suffering and death of Jesus on the cross as an event in the Trinity.

Moltmann is critical of the notion of divine impassibility which traditional Christian theology stressed in order to protect God's self-sufficiency and perfection.[96] Since Plato and Aristotle the metaphysical and ethical perfection of God has been described as *apatheia*. The term *apatheia* has been used to designate the metaphysical and ethical perfection of God, and a freedom from the imbalance of the finite life that is marked by needs and desires. Thus, the moral ideal of the wise person is to become similar to the divinity and lead a life free of trouble and fear, anger and love in *apatheia*.

In early Christianity the notion of *apatheia* was taken up to designate God's essential incapacity for suffering. It distinguished God from human beings and other non-divine beings subject to suffering, transience, and death. Consequently, salvation confers immortality, non-transience, and impassibility.[97] In contrast, Moltmann insists that to perceive God as either essentially incapable of suffering or as fatefully subject to suffering lacks the notion of the suffering of God's passionate love. According to him, God does not suffer in the exact same way humans suffer. God suffers not because of any deficiency in God's being but because of love.[98] God can go toward suffering and accept it because God is interested in

---

93. *LW* 26:266. See also the note 95 in *LW* 23:123–24.
94. *LW* 24:98.
95. Moltmann, *The Crucified God*, 234–35.
96. Ibid., 228–29.
97. Moltmann, *The Trinity and the Kingdom*, 23.
98. Moltmann, *The Crucified God*, 230.

God's creation and people. Therefore, God of love is affected by human actions and suffering.[99]

Recently, appropriation of God's pathos in theology has become recognized first in Jewish thought and then in Christian thought. The Jewish philosophy of religion, influenced by Philo, strongly believed that God, being free from passions, is moved neither by feelings of joy or grief. In contrast, Abraham Heschel, a pioneer in the area of pathetic theology, insists by pointing to biblical evidence in the Old Testament that the religion of the prophets was marked by the pathos of God.[100] Heschel points out that if we start from the pathos of God, we do not think of God in God's absoluteness and freedom, but understand God's passion and interest in terms of the history of the covenant.[101] The pathetic theology of Judaism begins from the covenant of God with the people of God. God has opened God's heart in the covenant, but God is injured by their disobedience and suffers in them. In this respect, the wrath of God in the Old Testament is a consequence of the divine pathos.

Moltmann differentiates the prophet's pathetic theology of Heschel from his theology of the cross. While the prophet's pathetic theology proceeds along bipolar lines between the pathos of God and the sympathy of people within the covenant of God, the Christian experience begins with the crucified Christ who makes this an open relationship extended to all people.[102] In other words, "while for Israel the immediacy of God exists in the covenant, for Christians there is Christ, who mediates the Fatherhood of God and the power of the Spirit."[103] Through the Crucified One, God creates a new covenant for the Godless and Godforsaken.

The Cross of Christ as a Trinitarian Event

If the cross of Jesus is understood as a divine event between Jesus and his God and Father, Moltmann insists, "It is necessary to speak in trinitarian terms of the Son and the Father and the Spirit."[104] According to him, the abandonment of Jesus is God's divine act of solidarity with all people in

99. Ibid., 270.
100. Moltmann, *The Crucified God*, 270. See also Heschel, *The Prophets*, 4.
101. Heschel, *The Prophets*, 2–10.
102. Moltmann, *The Crucified God*, 275.
103. Moltmann, *Experiment Hope*, 78.
104. Moltmann, *The Crucified God*, 246.

pain who cry out to God in their abandonment. For him, it is not only Jesus the Son of God who suffers, but also the Father who suffers as the Father of the Son. Moltmann explains this mutual act of surrendering between the Father and the Son by looking at the use of the Greek word "*paradidonai*", which means "delivered up." In this process, he also discusses how the event of God-forsakenness on the cross is *passio activa*, the active surrender of the Son as the love of God.[105]

First of all, Moltmann points out that the word *paradidonai* was used in the passion narratives with a negative connotation to mean "hand over," "give up," "deliver," "betray," "cast out," and "kill." It also appears in Pauline theology as an expression of the wrath and judgment of God for the lost state of humanity. In the first chapter of Romans, the apostle Paul uses the word to express God's wrath over the godlessness of humanity. God abandons the heathens to their unrighteousness (Rom 1:23, 25, 28) and idolatry, the Jews up to their legalism, and thus all people to their self-willed compulsion to die.[106] However, in light of the resurrection of Jesus Christ, the apostle Paul completely turns around the sense of the word *paradidonai* to mean how the Father's forsaking the Son was "for us." The God who raised Jesus from the dead is the same God who "gave him up" to death on the cross. In the forsakenness of the cross itself, out of which Jesus cries "Why?," the apostle Paul already sees the answer to that cry: "He who did not spare his own Son but gave him up for us all, will he not also give all things with Him? (Rom 8:32). Moltmann insists, "The Father 'gave up' the Son so that through Him God may become the Father of all those who are 'given up' (Rom 1:18ff)."[107] God himself abandoned God's own Son to evil people and to the abyss of destruction. The Son is surrendered to death in order to become the brother and Savior of all men and women who are condemned (2 Cor 5:21) and accursed (Gal 3:13).[108]

---

105. Moltmann, *The Way of Jesus Christ*, 173.

106. Ibid., 172–78.

107. Ibid., 173.

108. Ibid. Moltmann has provoked considerable feminist critique and concern with respect to his claim that the Father "abandons" the Son in the event of the crucifixion. Sölle's accusation in her *Suffering* is given significant attention in Moltmann-Wendel's *Autobiography* (see 177–80) as well as in Moltmann's *Autobiography* (see 198–200). I discuss on this topic more in depth as I am dealing with Jowers' critique of "Moltmann's staurocentric Trinitarianism," where he joins with feminist theologians who accuse Moltmann of presenting the Father as the "divine executioner." See Jowers, "The Theology of the Cross as Theology of the Trinity," 246–66.

Toward a Social Trinitarian Theology of the Cross

In the historical event of the cross, the apostle Paul sees eschatologically the Son surrendered by the Father for the godless and god-forsaken. He stresses that it is God's own Son whom God gives up. Moltmann emphasizes that this act of not sparing the Son affects the Father. When the Father abandons the Son, the Father also abandons Himself. When the Father sacrifices the Son, the Father sacrifices Himself. However, Moltmann claims that this act is not *patripassionism*.[109] It is not the Father who was crucified, dead, and buried. The suffering of the Father, he insists, was different from that of the Son's. Jesus experiences what it is to die abandoned, but the Father experiences the death of the Son in the infinite suffering of the Father's love. If the Father does not spare the Son but gives Him up, then the Father suffers His separation from the Son.

Having said that, Moltmann also warns against understanding the Father's suffering in *theopaschitic* terms. The cross is not the death of God. God did not die. God did not cease to exist or cease to function. We must speak of the death of God in Trinitarian terms: "The Son suffers dying, the Father suffers the death of the Son of the Father . . . The Fatherlessness of the Son is matched by the Sonlessness of the Father."[110] Each person of the Trinity suffers, although in different manners. Moltmann insists that though they are most deeply separated in forsakenness, they are most inwardly one in surrendering.

Secondly, the suffering and death of Jesus on the cross is a *passio activa*. In the passage of *kenosis* in Philippians 2, we see how Jesus deliberately chose the path of suffering, and by dying on the cross affirmed His passion for the Father. In Galatians 2:20, we find the *paradoken* formula again, but with Christ as the subject: "The Son of God, who loved me and gave himself for me." It is not only that the Father gives up Jesus, but the Son also gives Himself. This corresponds to the presentation of the passion of Christ in which Jesus consciously and willingly set out on the road of suffering to Calvary.[111]

With regards to the role of the Spirit in this mutual act of surrendering between the Father and the Son, Moltmann insists that the suffering and death of the Son was an act of "*passio activa*" for us through the eternal Spirit (Heb 9:14). The offering of the Son takes place through the Spirit, who is the link joining the bond between the Father and the Son in their

---

109. Moltmann, *The Way of Jesus Christ*, 243.
110. Ibid.
111. Ibid., 173.

The Liberative Cross

separation at the cross.¹¹² In his *The Crucified God*, Moltmann describes the Spirit as creative love proceeding out of the Father's pain and the Son's self-surrender to justify the ungodly, rescue the forsaken, and raise the dead.¹¹³

These Trinitarian aspects of Moltmann's theology of the cross have received much criticism. I will look into the criticisms he receives in these three categories: 1) Moltmann is a binitarian lacking the Holy Spirit in his theology of the cross.¹¹⁴ 2) Moltmann lacks a robust doctrine of sin.¹¹⁵ 3) Moltmann is a sado-masochistic theologian of the cross.¹¹⁶ How true are these critiques? What has been overlooked by these critiques?

First of all, Carl E. Braaten critiques how the cross as an event between the Father and the Son, in *The Crucified God*, appears only as a binitarian event.¹¹⁷ Moltmann does mention the work of the Spirit in *The Crucified God*, although he identifies the Spirit with the love which unites the Son and the Father on the cross.¹¹⁸ This definition suggests that Moltmann has in mind the Augustinian and Barthian view of the Spirit as a bond of love between the Father and the Son.¹¹⁹ In his later work in *The Trinity and the Kingdom*, however, Moltmann argues for the Holy Spirit's distinct existence as a Person in the Trinity. He points out a problem in Barth's pneumatology in this way:

---

112. Moltmann, *The Trinity and the Kingdom*, 82.

113. Moltmann, *The Crucified God*, 244.

114. Braaten, "A Trinitarian Theology of the Cross," 118. Braaten remarks here, "Whereas the relations between the Father and the Son are spelled out in the event of the cross, the Spirit goes along for a free ride. Would not a binitarian concept of God work as well?" See also, Jowers, "The Theology of the Cross as Theology of the Trinity," 263. Even though he wrote the article after Moltmann published *The Trinity and the Kingdom*, Jowers mistakenly states, "Moltmann ascribes to the Holy Spirit no role in the cross/resurrection event which requires the act of a distinct subject."

115. Kelsey, "Whatever Happened to the Doctrine of Sin?," 169–78. Kelsey offers one of the few critical discussions of the doctrine of sin in Moltmann's theology. He included Moltmann within his typology of modern theologies of sin under the liberationist paradigm as an analysis of oppression of "unjust societal self-contradiction" (see 173). He takes into account neither Moltmann's interpretation of sin in *The Crucified God* nor the development of his doctrine in *The Spirit of Life*.

116. Jowers, "The Theology of the Cross as Theology of the Trinity, 246–66.

117. Braaten, "A Trinitarian Theology of the Cross," 118.

118. Moltmann, *The Crucified God*, 245.

119. Barth, *CD* I/1:480. Barth states, "The Holy Spirit is the love which is the essence of the revelation between these two modes [the Father and the Son] of being of God."

Toward a Social Trinitarian Theology of the Cross

> [For Barth] The Spirit is merely the common bond of love linking the Father with the Son . . . But this bond is already given with the relationship of the Father to his beloved Son and *vice versa*. The Father and the Son are already one in their relationship to one another, the relationship of eternal generation and eternal self-giving. In order to think of their mutual relationship as love, there is no need for a third person in the Trinity. If the Spirit is only termed the unity of what is separated, then he loses every center of activity. He is then an energy but not a Person. He is then a relationship but not a subject . . . It is only when the Holy Spirit is understood as the unity of the difference, and the unity of the Father and the Son, that a personal and active function in the Trinitarian relationship can be ascribed to him. Barth then only formally secures the divine person of the Holy Spirit through the common "*proskynesis*" (object of worship) of the Spirit with the Father and the Son.[120]

Ever since Augustine, the Spirit has often been termed the *vinculum amoris* (bond of love) between the Father and the Son. This third 'mode of being' does not add anything special and individual to the Revealer and his Revelation. This approach, according to Moltmann, provides no justification for the Holy Spirit's distinct existence as a person in the Trinity. In his *The Trinity and the Kingdom*, Moltmann insists that the conception of the Spirit as the love in which the Father eternally generates the Son and the Son eternally obeys the Father contradicts the tradition which acknowledges the Holy Spirit as the third person of the Trinity, and not merely a correlation of the two other persons.[121]

In his works, *God in Creation* and *In the Way of Jesus,* Moltmann describes the Holy Spirit as the Spirit of life who identifies with the godless, fills the forsaken with love, and even brings the dead to life.[122] Finally, in his *The Spirit of Life: A Universal Affirmation*, Moltmann develops fully his pneumatology, arguing that "the operations of God's life-giving and life-affirming spirit are universal and can be recognized in everything which ministers to life and resists its destruction. The efficacy of the Spirit does not replace Christ's efficacy, but makes it universally relevant."[123] With all

---

120. Moltmann, *The Trinity and the Kingdom*, 142–43. Cf. Barth, *CD* I/1:480 and 488.

121. Ibid., 143.

122. Moltmann, *God in Creation*, 98–103. See also Moltmann, *The Way of Jesus*, 73–111.

123. Moltmann, *The Spirit of Life*, xi.

The Liberative Cross

the evidences mentioned above, I conclude that Moltmann has fully developed his pneumatology in his books following his *The Crucified God*, in which the event of the cross seemingly appears a binitarian event.

Secondly, Moltmann is criticized for lacking a robust doctrine of sin. Eckardt remarks that "Moltmann rejects the language of atonement, and prefers to think of Jesus' death primarily as an event in which Jesus was abandoned by God."[124] Although Moltmann emphasizes how we must go beyond the ideas of expiatory sacrifice, he clearly recognizes that Christ's death is representative suffering 'for us' in that he "died for our sins."[125] Moltmann writes, "The phrase 'died for our sins' means that the cause of his suffering was our sins, the purpose of his suffering is expiation for us, the ground of his suffering is the love of God for us."[126] Moltmann is worried that the idea of expiatory offerings, however, has a retrospective character, and how its future concern is "the *retitutio in integrum*" (restoration to original condition), not the beginning of new life.[127] Nevertheless, Moltmann affirms that the idea of expiation is important for three reasons:

> 1) How little unrighteous man can achieve his own righteousness, how there can be no new future for him without the acceptance of guilt and liberation from it, at least through good intentions by which he only denies himself; 2) that as the Christ of God, Jesus took the place of helpless man as his representative and in so doing made it possible for man to enter into communion before God in which he otherwise could not stand and survive; 3) that in the death of Christ God himself has acted in favor of this man.[128]

Moltmann recognizes "the unique and unrepeatable nature"[129] of the course taken by Christ when he went to the cross. He also recognizes the eternal significance of the cross; "the divine value of the self-sacrifice of Christ for the relationship of God to man and of man to God."[130]

In order for the death of Christ to be understood as atonement for the sins of the world, Moltmann insists, we must see God in Christ.[131]

---

124. Eckardt, "Luther and Moltmann: The Theology of the Cross," 22.
125. Moltmann, *The Crucified God*, 183.
126. Ibid.
127. Ibid.
128. Ibid.
129. Ibid., 63.
130. Ibid., 43.
131. Moltmann, *The Spirit of Life*, 135.

Toward a Social Trinitarian Theology of the Cross

According to Moltmann, the atoning Christ is the revelation of the compassionate God. The nature of God revealed by the atoning Christ is love: The Father loves the world through the Son with the very same love which the Triune God *is* in eternity. Accordingly, to say "God so loved the world that he gave his only begotten Son . . ." (John 3:16) presupposes that "God is love" (1 John 4:16).[132] In this sense, Moltmann contends that "notions like a God of retribution or a divine judge presiding over a criminal court are foreign to 'the Father of Jesus Christ.'"[133] By seeing the cross as the revelation of the compassionate God, Moltmann affirms that "Christ's suffering on the cross is human sin transmuted into the atoning suffering of God."[134] The Son experienced the God-forsakenness on the cross. Moltmann contends that the Son experiences the pain of the divine love for sinners and takes it on himself on the basis of the statements the Apostle Paul made: "For our sake he [God] made him [Jesus] to be sin who knew no sin" (2 Cor 5:21), and Christ "became a curse for us" (Gal 3:13).

In saying all the above about the death of Christ, Moltmann sees in the death of Christ more than just Christ's solidarity with the accursed of the earth. Moltmann emphasizes the aspect of atonement in the death of Jesus by saying that in the death of Christ is "the divine atonement for sin for injustice and violence on earth. This divine atonement reveals God's pain. But God's pain reveals God's faithfulness to those he has created, and his indestructible love which endures a world in opposition to him and overcomes it."[135]

If we understand atonement in this way, it is certainly wrong to assume that God sadistically crucified his own Son. However, in his critique of "Moltmann's staurocentric Trinitarianism," Dennis W. Jowers joins with feminist theologians who accuse Moltmann of presenting the Father as the "divine

---

132. Ibid., 137.

133. Ibid., 135. See also Moltmann, *Sun of Righteousness, Arise!*, 133–34.

134. Moltmann, *The Spirit of Life*, 136.

135. Ibid. See Ansell, *The Annihilation of Hell*, chap. 4, section 2. See also Ansell, "Annihilation of Hell and the Perfection of Freedom: Universal Salvation in the Theology of Jürgen Moltmann (1926–)," 436–38. In this essay Ansell discusses the centrality of the Son in Moltmann's conception of universal salvation. Ansell points out that for Moltmann, the justification of sinners is "more than merely the forgiveness of sins," because in Moltmann's understanding, the cross addresses and overcomes the conditions that make sin possible. Ansell gives a good discussion on how the conditions of possibility will be transformed in the eschatological perfection of creation and sin will no longer be an "option."

The Liberative Cross

executioner."[136] He insists that regardless of how the Father suffers the death of the Son, the fact that he has delivered him up and abandoned him to this death makes him guilty of the death of his Son. Similarly, Paul Fiddes contends that Moltmann depicts the Father as directly causing the Son to suffer and die on the cross, thus producing his own bereavement.[137] Both Jowers and Fiddes mainly focus on the Father's willingness to deliver up the Son and of his abandoning the Son, but they downplay the significance of Moltmann's recognition that the Son is united with his Father and the Father with the Son in these actions. They downplay the death of Jesus as *passio activa* in the sense that the Son also delivers himself up to death on the cross.

Moltmann-Wendel in her *Autobiography* argues that the abhorrence of Moltmann's theology of the cross among feminist theologians was instigated by Sölle. According to her, Sölle in her book *Suffering* quotes from Popkes and deals with the quotation as if it was Moltmann's original statement. At the end of the quotation, Sölle states "The author is fascinated by his God's brutality."[138] Moltmann-Wendel defends her husband by saying, "The author really should be Popkes, but somehow [feminist theologians] have now assumed that she means Moltmann and . . . this false attribution has spread and has caused further misunderstanding."[139] In Popkes' statement, God becomes the one who acts, who has "cast out his Son" into "the powers of destruction."[140] Moltmann-Wendel argues that Moltmann uses the verb *paradidonai* to mean something like "hand over, betray, abandon"; however, for Sölle the verbs take on another emphasis and come to mean "deliver up, toss out, disown and slay."[141] Accordingly, God of the theology of the cross appears in the role of an active sadist. Moltmann-Wendel argues, "The tormenting hiddenness of God which lies in the 'giving up' (*paradidonai*) is simply dissolved, and the hostile picture of a sado-masochistic theologian of the cross is created."[142] In short, Sölle, on the basis of Popkes' statement, accuses Moltmann of developing a theology where "one of the persons of the Trinity underwent suffering while another person of

---

136. Jowers, "The Theology of the Cross as Theology of the Trinity," 246–66.

137. Fiddes, *Past and Present Salvation: The Christian Idea of Atonement*, 193.

138. Sölle, *Suffering*, 27.

139. Moltmann-Wendel, *Autobiography*, 178.

140. Sölle, *Suffering*, 27, citing Popkes, *Christus Traditus*, 286. Cf. Moltmann, *The Crucified God*, 241.

141. Sölle, *Suffering*, 27.

142. Moltmann-Wendel, *Autobiography*, 178.

Toward a Social Trinitarian Theology of the Cross

the Trinity was the very one who caused it."[143] She further argues, "The story of Abraham did not reach this height of brutality; it was the Father of Jesus Christ who first acted intentionally, 'deliberately' slaying his Son."[144]

For Moltmann, the Father is neither the active subject, nor the Son the passive object. Refuting the substitutionary theory of atonement, Moltmann insists that the surrender of Jesus on the cross must not be understood as a sacrifice made to appease the Father's wrath, for in the surrender of the Son the Father also surrenders himself, though not in the same way. The Father who abandons the Son and delivers him up suffers the death of the Son in the infinite grief of love. Therefore, the Father is not in confrontation with Jesus as a "dominating almighty Father" or as "a God who feeling no pain himself causes pain."[145] Moltmann also notes a "deep conformity between the will of the Father and the will of the Son in the event of the cross, as the Gethsemane narrative also records."[146] Accordingly, for Moltmann, the Father is not the active subject and perpetrator of the crucifixion of Christ while the Son is the passive object and victim.

The problem caused by Moltmann's potentially problematic language of "abandonment" is notably addressed in his recent work, *Ethics of Hope*. Moltmann writes, "If God goes wherever Jesus goes, he brings God to the victims.... He himself [i.e., Jesus] entered into Godforsakenness on the cross to bring God to the Godforsaken."[147] Ansell explains that according to Moltmann's understanding, in freely going to the cross, the Son actually takes the lead within the Trinity, and leads the Father into the Godforsaken space that had been opened up within God prior to creation. This is done so that God might become all in all. The fact that the Son freely goes beyond the (post-creation/pre-cross) limits of the divine presence has as its 'flipside' the Father's "surrendering" or "yielding up" the Son. In other words, the letting go of the Son is not a demand for but an acceptance of the Son's free going beyond the Father, an acceptance of the Son's leadership/freedom that entails the Father's own free embrace of suffering also. This is a suffering that is embraced by Father and Son, each in his own way, so that all suffering including the conditions and limits of possibility that make

---

143. Sölle, *Suffering*, 27.
144. Ibid., 27. See Moltmann, *The Crucified God*, 191.
145. Moltmann, *The Way of Jesus Christ*, 176.
146. Moltmann, *The Crucified God*, 243.
147. Moltmann, *Ethics of Hope*, 181.

The Liberative Cross

suffering possible may be overcome.[148] In other words, Ansell continues, rather than simply and freely accepting and following the Father's will, it is Jesus who leads the Father into the *nihil* such that the Father follows. Accordingly, because Sölle did not see the Son's free leading of the Father in *The Crucified God* but saw only the Father's letting go (abandonment) of the Son, she like many other feminist theologians saw abuse.

So far I have looked into the criticisms Moltmann's theology of the cross, and argued that Moltmann is not a binitarian lacking the Holy Spirit in his theology of the cross. Moltmann is neither lacking a robust doctrine of sin, nor a sado-masochistic theologian of the cross. Now I will turn to Moltmann's social doctrine of Trinity and critique how Moltmann explains the unity of the Trinity. For him, the unity in the triune God is not rooted in its homogeneity of substance *(una substantia)* but the loving perichoretic relationship which binds the divine persons of the Trinity together.[149]

Moltmann's Social Doctrine of Trinity

One of Moltmann's signature emphases is his social doctrine of the Trinity.[150] In contrast to Augustine who tends to highlight the unity of God and uses psychological analogies for the Trinity, Moltmann argues that the Bible reveals three persons at work, not one. Therefore, an understanding of the Trinity must begin with the fellowship of a plurality of persons understood as three centers of conscious activity, and only then progress to the question of their unity.[151] For Moltmann, the basis of the Trinity lies in the separation-in-unity that God experienced within God's divine life in the event of the cross. He explains it this way: "What happened on the cross was an event between God and God. It was a deep division in God himself, in so far as God abandoned God and contradicted himself, and at the same time a unity in God, in so far as God was at one with God and corresponded to himself."[152]

---

148. Ansell, *The Annihilation of Hell*, 152n38.

149. LaCugna also points out that the concept *perichoresis* by emphasizing "a true communion of persons" avoids the pitfall of locating the divine unity in the divine substance, as the Latin fathers did. See LaCugna, *God for Us,* 271.

150. For good introduction to this trend, see Gresham Jr., "The Social Model of the Trinity and Its Critics," 325–43.

151. Moltmann, *The Trinity and the Kingdom*, 16–20, 150, 174–76.

152. Moltmann, *The Crucified God*, 244.

Toward a Social Trinitarian Theology of the Cross

The unity of the divine tri-unity, for Moltmann, does not lie in the identity of a single subject but in the fellowship of the divine persons of the Trinity. He argues the point by exegeting John 10:30: Here, Jesus says, "I and the Father are one (*en*). He does not say "I and the Father are one and the same (*eis*)."[153] Therefore, Moltmann insists that "the unity of Jesus the Son with the Father is a unity which preserves their separate character, indeed actually conditions it."[154]

In contrast, to secure oneness in God, Barth emphasizes the unity of essence between Father, Son, and Spirit, which the church fathers confessed via the *homoousion*. Barth states: "The God who reveals himself according to Scripture is one in three distinctive modes of being subsisting in their mutual relations: Father, Son and Holy Spirit."[155] The trinitarian "persons" or *Seinsweisen* (the modes of being), Barth insists, do not have their own distinct subjects of inherence. Rather, they are modes of existence of one common divine subject. They are thus not just "of one substance" with one another, but "of one subject" as well.[156] Barth renders *persona* as "modes of being" for theological reasons. Barth argues that the rendering of *hypostasis, prosopon*, or *persona* in terms proper to modern concepts of human personhood or personality commits a fundamental category mistake. Barth insists that this is not at all what the fathers intended in their formula "one *ousia* and three *hypostases (personae)*." He asserts that the patristic use of *hypostasis* had little to do with what we would call today the "personality." He explicates that the term *hypostasis* had been used in philosophical tradition to designate the incommunicable aspects of a concrete particular. On the other hand, *prosopon* carried with it the overtone of relationality; the role of a thing that looks outwards to others and is viewed by others. These two terms were fused in Christian theology, and the fusion resulted in a concept which we might describe as "the incommunicable ontological subject in relation." The subject, however, is used here strictly in the grammatical sense, and not in the sense of consciousness or mind. On this basis, Barth challenges an automatic shift from speaking of three persons to thinking in terms of three rational agents or three centers of conscious-

---

153. Moltmann, *The Trinity and the Kingdom*, 95.

154. Ibid.

155. Barth, *CD* I/1:348.

156. Hart, "Person and Prerogative in Perichoretic Perspective," 48. Hart explains that Rahner also makes the point that there are not three consciousnesses; rather the one consciousness subsists in a threefold way.

ness in Trinitarian theology."[157] In this challenge, Barth is prepared to speak of three relations in God (Fatherhood, Sonship and Holy Spirit) whereas he is not prepared to tolerate that which the patristic confession of three *hypostases* entails, namely "the presence of three unique incommunicable ontological subjects in one *ousia*, one concrete reality."[158]

Barth thus replaces the term "person" with "mode of being" because the modern notion of person refers to "an independent, free, self-disposing center of action in knowledge, freedom, different from others."[159] Barth refuses to accept three such persons in God. Barth is insistent that we do not have to accept three distinct selves in God or three separate self-conscious agents.[160] Rather we must approach the Trinity as one divine subject who exists in three distinct ways or "modes", both in relation to creation and in relation to Godself.[161]

This position of Barth, however, has caused theological controversies. First, Barth has been accused of lapsing into a tacit Sabellian modalism. Hart points out how Barth actually attempts at avoiding the lapse into tacit Sabellian modalism as Barth affirms "three simultaneous and not consecutive modes or ways of subsisting in God."[162] Hart contends that "Barth's relegation of divine threeness to the level of modes of being", however, compels him to repeatedly refer to the Trinity as "a divine self or subject who is strictly speaking identical with none of the three named above (Father, Son, and Holy Spirit), since these are relative ways in which this one divine "I" is God."[163] Another problem caused by Barth's denial of multiple subjects in God is that it "makes the traditional language of, for example, inter-personal communion or love between Father and Son, or of the obedience of the Son to the Father, difficult to take altogether seriously."[164] Thus, as Hart affirms, the love between the Father and Son is reduced to self-love and the obedience of the Son to the Father to self-obedience. In this way, the love

---

157. Hart, "Person and Prerogative in Perichoretic Perspective," 58.

158. Ibid., 50.

159. Moltmann, *The Trinity and the Kingdom*, 145.

160. Barth, *CD* I/1:351.

161. Rahner also concurs with Barth as he writes, "There are not three consciousnesses; rather the one consciousness subsists in a threefold way... The distinctness of the persons is not constituted by a distinctness of conscious subjectivities, nor does it include the latter." See Rahner, *Trinity*, 107

162. Hart, "Person and Prerogative in Perichoretic Perspective," 48.

163. Ibid.

164. Ibid., 50.

Toward a Social Trinitarian Theology of the Cross

for the other, and obedience to the other are absent "except in the relations of the one divine subject *ad extra*."[165] Consequently, to think of trinitarian persons as modes of being is dangerous because it robs both the Son and the Spirit of any genuine personhood, as the divine "I" is tacitly identified with the person of the Father.

Over against Barth's conception of God as "One in three distinctive modes of being subsisting in their mutual relations: Father, Son and Holy Spirit," Moltmann resists any reduction of the concept of "person" to the concept of "relation" and stresses the absolute hypostatic diversity of the Father, Son, and Spirit. For Moltmann, there are three unique and irreducible subjects in God. In this respect, as Hart points out, Moltmann emphasizes "the diversity of hypostatic prerogatives, rather than viewing all divine prerogatives (both immanent and economic) as ultimately predicated of one subject who exists as Father, Son and Holy Spirit."[166] Father, Son, and Spirit are ultimately distinct both in their relationship to creation and in relation to one another in the eternal life of God.

As we recognize three distinct and unique persons in the Trinity, we face the problem of determining in what sense it is still possible to speak of a genuine unity between the three persons. Moltmann insists that this question is raised by the economy of the Trinity itself. According to him, the unity of the Trinity is not rooted in its homogeneity of substance. Rather, the unity of the Trinity is a perichoretic unity in which the persons "indwell" one another.[167] As Hart affirms, "perichoretic unity is a unity which presupposes rather than conflicts with absolute hypostatic diversity, since it is only unique persons who can be at one in fellowship with each other."[168] Perichoretic unity is a unity in which the distinctive personal prerogatives, far from being compromised or relativized, are actually fulfilled. Moltmann states: "Precisely through the personal characteristics that distinguish them

---

165. Ibid.

166 Ibid., 52. Hart points out that Moltmann here follows Lossky and others with the eastern tradition in his emphasis on the absolute hypostatic diversity of Father, Son, and Spirit. Lossky states, "The relations only serve to express the hypostatic diversity of the Three; they are not the basis of it. It is the absolute diversity of the three hypostases which determines their differing relations to one another, not vice-versa." See Lossky, *In the Image and Likeness of God*, 79.

167. Moltmann, *The Trinity and the Kingdom*, 150.

168. Hart, "Person and Prerogative in Perichoretic Perspective," 53.

from one another, the Father, the Son and the Spirit dwell in one another and communicate eternal life to one another."[169]

In the next section, I will observe how Moltmann explains "the trinitarian unity," specifically how the three distinct and unique subjects are truly one. Moltmann borrows from the Eastern Church Fathers the ancient image of *"perichoresis,"* which provides us with an invaluable tool to avoid both Sabellian modalism and tritheism. This image of *perichoresis* points to a genuine unity which yet presupposes an absolute hypostatic diversity. For Moltmann, the unity of God is expressed through the concept of *perichoresis*.

Perichoresis (περιχωρησις)

From Joas Adiprasetya's studies, we can briefly summarize how the term *perichoresis* has been used since the term *perichoresis* was first introduced by Gregory of Nazianzus (329-390 CE).[170] Gregory of Nazianzus used it to explain the relationship between the humanity and divinity of Christ. Gregory of Nazianzus in his *Epistle* used the term *perichoresis* for the first time in the sense of interpenetration of Christ's divine and human natures.[171] Pseudo-Cyril of Alexandria employs the idea of *perichoresis* to explain how the divine and human natures of Christ are united hypostatically and do not change into one composite nature. In the section 24 of *De Sacrosancta Trinitate*, Pseudo-Cyril explains how the penetration of the divine and human nature of Christ does not occur mutually but in a causal relation:

> This penetration springs not from the flesh but from the divinity, since it is impossible for the flesh to penetrate through (διά) the divinity; still the divine nature, having once penetrated through (διά) the flesh, bestows on the flesh an ineffable penetration with (πρός) itself, which in particular we call union.[172]

Joas Adiprasetya contends that Pseudo-Cyril added nothing new to the Christological use of *perichoresis*. However, Adiprasetya insists that

---

169. Moltmann, *The Trinity and the Kingdom*, 175.

170. Adiprasetya, "Toward a Perchorietic Theology of Religions," 154.

171. Harrison, *"Perichoresis* in the Greek Father," 55, quoting Gregory of Nazianzus, *Epistle* 101. 5.

172. Wolfson, *The Philosophy of the Church Fathers*, 423, quoting Pseudo-Cyril, *De Sacrosancta Trinitate* 24.

Toward a Social Trinitarian Theology of the Cross

Pseudo-Cyril made a great contribution in that he developed the concept *perichoresis* in trinitarian discourses.[173] According to Pseudo-Cyril, the three persons of the Trinity possess coinherence in each other, though without confusion or division.[174] Thus, the term *perichoresis*, which Gregory of Nazianzus used to explain the interpenetration of Christ in Christ's two natures, Pseudo-Cyril employed to refer to the mutual indwelling of the Triune persons.

John of Damascus (676-749 AD) further developed the concept of trinitarian *perichoresis* from Pseudo-Cyril and wrote in his *De Fide Orthodoxa*:

> The substances dwell and are established firmly in one another. For they are inseparable and cannot part from one another, but keep to their separate courses within one another, without coalescing or mingling, but cleaving to each other. For the Son is in the Father and the Spirit, and the Spirit in the Father and the Son, and the Father in the Son and the Spirit, but there is no coalescence or commingling or confusion. And there is one and the same motion: for there is one impulse and one motion of the three subsistences, which is not to be observed in any created nature.[175]

From this statement by John of Damascus we can draw a fundamental notion of *perichoresis*, that even though the Trinity exists as three distinct persons, the Father, the Son, and the Spirit completely indwell one another and act as one unity. Here, the term *perichoresis* describes a kind of unity in which plurality is preserved rather than erased. The term suggests that every divine person is indwelled by the other divine persons while all the persons interpenetrate each other. The interpenetration of the three persons of the Trinity presupposes their distinctiveness because the action of interpenetration demonstrates how the subject of interpenetration is not inherently interior to its object. Every divine person is and acts in itself and yet the two other persons are present and act in that person.

As observed above, the term *perichoresis* has been used first to describe the mutual interpenetration of the divine and the human natures of Christ, and then to describe the reciprocal indwelling and the interpenetration

---

173. Adiprasetya, "Toward a Perichoretic Theology of Religions", 154.

174. Harrison, "*Perichoresis* in the Greek Father," 59, quoting Pseudo–Cyril, *De Sacrosancta Trinitate* 10.

175. Adiprasetya, "Toward a Perichoretic Theology of Religions", 158, quoting John of Damascus, *De fide Orthodoxa* 1.14.

of the three distinct divine persons. Moltmann explains the unity in the triune God through this notion of *perichoresis* instead of the idea of one substance (*una substantia*). For Moltmann, the unity in the Trinity is not a substantial unity but a relational unity. The unity of the divine persons is found in the mutual fullness of their indwelling of each other. It is their loving perichoretic relationship that binds them together as one. Moltmann explains:

> This concept grasps the circulatory character of the eternal divine life. An eternal life process takes place in the triune God through the exchange of energies. The Father exists in the Son, the Son in the Father, and both of them in the Spirit, just as the Spirit exists in both the Father and the Son. By virtue of their eternal love they live in one another to such an extent, and dwell in one another to such an extent, that they are one.[176]

The concept of *perichoresis*, according to Moltmann, links together the threeness and the unity of the Trinity without reducing the threeness to the unity, or dissolving the unity into the threeness. The concept of *perichoresis* does not understand the trinitarian persons as three modes of being or three repetitions of the One God, as modalistic interpretations suggest. The unity does not lie in the one lordship of God, but it is to be found in the eternal *perichoresis* of the trinitarian persons who form their own unity through the circulation of the divine life.[177] Thus, according to Moltmann, the concept of *perichoresis* averts the danger of modalism because the three persons of the Trinity cannot be reduced to each other. It also averts the danger of tritheism because they cannot fully be persons apart from their shared nature.

Moltmann explains two different Latin translations of *perichoresis*: *circumincessio* (from *circum-incedere*, to move around) and *circuminsessio* (from *circum-insedere*, to sit around). Moltmann insists that the Latin words *circumincessio* and *circuminsessio* express a double sense of the trinitarian unity: movement and rest. Moltmann explains that the word *circumincessio* is understood in the sense that "the trinitarian persons offer one another reciprocally the inviting space for movement in which they can develop their eternal livingness . . . They move with one another, and round one another, and in another, and change 'from glory to glory' without leaving what is transient behind . . . "[178] Moltmann insists that in their eternal mo-

---

176. Moltmann, *The Trinity and the Kingdom*, 175.
177. Ibid., 174–75.
178. Moltmann, *Sun of Righteousness Arise!*, 155.

Toward a Social Trinitarian Theology of the Cross

bility (*circumincessio*), "the trinitarian persons are at once persons and the space."[179] Moltmann also explains the meaning of *circuminsessio* in terms of both three trinitarian persons and three trinitarian spaces in which they mutually exist. He states that "In the *perichoresis* each person makes itself 'dwellable' for the two others, and prepares the wide space and the dwelling for the two others."[180]

This concept *perichoresis*, which portrays the tri-unity as the community and fellowship among three equal persons, necessarily leads to a doctrine of God that is characterized by mutuality and reciprocity. Therefore, Moltmann claims that the *perichoretic* trinitarian fellowship not only describes divine community but also prescribes the true nature of human community. Moltmann envisions the relation of the Father, the Son, and the Holy Spirit as a kind of fellowship (*koinonia*), which he describes as an "open Trinity."[181] The unity of the Son with the Father is not a closed unity; it is an open union as expressed in the High Priestly prayer (John 17:21). The fellowship of the disciples with God and with one another in God presupposes that "the tri-unity is open in such a way that the whole creation can be united with it and can be one within it."[182] God invites God's creation to enter into the trinitarian fellowship; therefore, Moltmann affirms, "the unity of the Trinity is not merely a theological term; at heart it is a soteriological one as well."[183] In other words, for him, the triune God is not "a closed circle" of perfect beings in heaven; rather, the triune God is "the open Trinity," God who is "open to humanity, open to the world and open to time."[184] We are called to participate in the trinitarian process of God's history by participating actively and passively in the sufferings and joys of God by loving, praying, and hoping.[185] In this way, Moltmann argues through the notion of *perichoresis* that in God's relationship with the world it is not so much lordship as loving fellowship which God seeks, and in

---

179. Ibid.

180. Ibid.

181. Moltmann, *God in Creation*, 242. See also Moltmann, *The Crucified God*, 255; and *The Trinity and the Kingdom*, 96.

182. Moltmann, *The Trinity and the Kingdom*, 96. See also Moltmann, *Experiences in Theology*, 322.

183. Moltmann, *The Trinity and the Kingdom*, 96.

184. Moltmann, *The Crucified God*, 255. See also Moltmann, *God in Creation*, 242.

185. Moltmann, *The Crucified God*, 255.

God's kingdom it is relationships of free friendship which most adequately reflect and participate in the trinitarian life.[186]

Moltmann emphasizes the role of *perichoresis* for his trinitarian theology in his book, *Experiences in Theology*.[187] In this book, we are invited to participate in the life of God. Ideally, the fellowship of Father, Son, and Holy Spirit will be reflected in the Christian community.[188] The community within the Trinity can be "a social program."[189] Is it possible for human beings to reflect and apply what happens in the inner life of the Trinity in this world, marred by sin and evil? I will discuss the question in the next chapter and refer back to the notion of *perichoresis* to discuss social trinitarian praxis for Korean-North American women.

To make the point that Father, Son, and Holy Spirit are interrelated in mutuality, reciprocity, and equality, Moltmann draws attention to two other traditional trinitarian issues: 1) the relation of the economic Trinity and the immanent Trinity and 2) the *filioque* controversy.

"The Economic Trinity Is the Immanent Trinity, and the Immanent Trinity Is the Economic Trinity"

Karl Rahner explains that the early church understood God as triune by specifically reflecting on the salvation history of Jesus Christ and the lively power of the Holy Spirit. In so doing, he insists that as trinitarian reflection ventured into platonic and neo-platonic speculation, the Trinity doctrine as a whole was developed without reference to the revelation of the three persons in the salvation history. This type of speculation has brought about the separation of God-in-eternity from the salvation history, and consequently eliminated true self-communication or revelation of God to humans within history.[190] Rahner then suggests how "the economic Trinity is the immanent Trinity, and the immanent Trinity is the economic Trinity."[191] He insists that

---

186. Bauckham, *The Theology of Jürgen Moltmann*, 17.

187. Moltmann, *Experiences in Theology*, 84–87.

188. Ibid., 328.

189. Ibid., 332–33. This I will discuss in details social Trinitarian praxis in our Christian life in chapter 4.

190. Rahner, *The Trinity*, 99–101.

191. Rahner, *The Trinity*, 22. See also Moltmann, *The Crucified God*, 240. Volf makes an interesting point that this rule, "the economic Trinity is the immanent Trinity" and *vice versa* makes sense on the one hand because "if the immanent and the economic

Toward a Social Trinitarian Theology of the Cross

God cannot be known in a way other than how God is presented in the economy of salvation. Moltmann follows Karl Rahner's suggestion that we should abandon in our theology the traditional distinction between what God eternally is in Godself and how God acts outside Godself in the world.[192] According to Moltmann, if we perceive the cross as an event of divine suffering, we are obliged to speak of God's experience of the world, and if we perceive the cross as an event of suffering between the divine persons of the Trinity, we are obliged to speak of a trinitarian experience in which God experiences Godself in the act of experiencing the world. In other words, what God is for us, God is also for Godself in God's trinitarian self-relation.

Moltmann treats the New Testament as an account of the three divine persons' activities and ever changing relationships to one another in the economy of salvation. He maintains that Jesus Christ is "the revealer of the Trinity" in agreement with Rahner who argued for the epistemological link between the economic Trinity and the immanent Trinity through this axiom: "The economic Trinity is the immanent Trinity, and the immanent Trinity is the economic Trinity." [193]

LaCugna clarifies some misunderstandings of Rahner's axiom. Some theologians have objected that no strict identity can be posited between the immanent Trinity and the economic Trinity. She corrects them by explaining that Rahner's axiom has to be seen as providing a methodological, rather than an ontological insight. LaCugna insists that "the order of theological knowledge must adhere to the historical form of God's self-communication

---

Trinity were not one and the same Trinity, we would have two gods in the six persons rather than one God in three persons." And yet, he argues, there is always a surplus in the immanent Trinity that the economic Trinity does not express. And the other way around: something new is introduced into the life of the Trinity with creation and redemption–the encounter of the self-giving love of God with the world of enmity, injustice, and deception. Thus, he insists, "A strict identity between the economic and immanent Trinity is untenable." See Volf, "The Trinity is Our Social Program," 407. Volf accepts both the unity and the distinction between the immanent and the economic Trinity. He presupposes the immanent Trinity as the ultimate horizon, and builds his egalitarian view of the Trinity on the narrative of the triune God's engagement with the world. See also Congar, *I Believe in the Holy Spirit*, 3:13–15. He argues in this book that the rule, "the economic Trinity is the immanent Trinity" applies only if it is not reversible–only if it does not imply the rule "the immanent Trinity is the economic Trinity."

192. Moltmann, *The Crucified God*, 239–40.
193. Rahner, *The Trinity*, 72.

in Christ and the Spirit. Knowledge of God takes place through Christ and the Holy Spirit, according to the order of the divine missions."[194]

Moltmann explains why he has affirmed and taken up Rahner's thesis in this way:

> If the central foundation of our knowledge of the Trinity is the cross, on which the Father delivered up the Son for us through the Spirit, then it is impossible to conceive of any Trinity of substance in the transcendent primal ground to this event, in which cross and self-giving are not present . . . The economic Trinity ascribes unity to God outwards and "threeness" inwardly. But the event of the cross (which is an "outward" event) can only be understood in Trinitarian terms—i.e., terms that are "divided" (*divisa*) and differentiated. Conversely, the surrender of the Son for us on the cross has a retroactive effect on the Father and causes infinite pain. On the cross God creates salvation outwardly for his whole creation and at the same time suffers this disaster of the whole world inwardly in himself. From the foundation of the world, the *opera trinitatis ad extra* corresponds to the *passiones trinitatis ad intra*. God as love would otherwise not be comprehensible at all.[195]

Moltmann reformulates Rahner's axiom by emphasizing the identity between the loving relationships of the trinitarian persons with the world and the essence of the divine life. He affirms that "the history of salvation is the history of the eternally living, triune God who draws us into and includes us in his eternal triune life with all the fullness of its relationships . . . God loves the world with the very same love which he is in himself."[196] He also insists that the infinite self-giving in the relationship of the Father, Son, and the Holy Spirit emerges vividly from the incarnation of Jesus Christ, reaches its depths in the event of the cross, and culminates with the glorification of all creation in the eternal Trinitarian life.[197]

The *Filioque* Controversy

Motlmann insists that the social doctrine of the Trinity must retain a non-hierarchical relationship among the Father, Son, and Holy Spirit.

194. LaCugna, *God for Us*, xv.
195. Moltmann, *The Trinity and the Kingdom*, 160.
196. Ibid., 157.
197. Ibid., 61–96.

Toward a Social Trinitarian Theology of the Cross

Consequently, in order to maintain a non-hierarchical relationship in the Trinity, the subordinating of the Holy Spirit, implied by *filioque*, needs to be abolished.[198] This Latin term, *filioque*, meaning "from the Son", was added to the Western version of the Niceno-Constantinopolitan Creed of 381[199] at a local council in Toledo in 589. The original text said the Holy Spirit proceeded from the Father, but the addition of *filioque* specified that the Holy Spirit proceeded from both the Father and the Son. This term gained acceptance in the West and was officially endorsed in the Mass in 1014.[200] Denounced by the Eastern Church in general, *filioque* became a major doctrinal issue in the schism of the East and West in 1054.

Barth and Moltmann, both coming from the Reformed tradition, take opposite positions on the legitimacy of *filioque*. Karl Barth affirms the *filioque* through his understanding of the immanent and economic trinities.[201] Barth asserts that Eastern theologians took texts such as John 15:26 in isolation, overlooking other texts that clearly point to the relationship of the Spirit to the Son. Barth argues that since the biblical witnesses supported *filioque*, *filioque* must also be true of the immanent Trinity. When *filioque* is affirmed in the immanent Trinity, then the relationship of God to humanity has an eternal basis. Barth explains that "the *filioque* expresses recognition of the communion between the Father and the Son . . . And recognition of this communion is no other than recognition of the basis and confirmation of the communion between God and man as a divine, eternal truth, created in revelation by the Holy Spirit."[202] Barth, favoring a double procession of the Spirit, argues that the presence of the Spirit in Christian experience is always tied to the presence of the living Christ. For him, to reject *filioque* would open the door to an affirmation of the possibility of a meaningful relationship to God apart from the special revelation in Jesus.

198. McWilliams, "Why All the Fuss about *Filioque*? Karl Barth and Jürgen Moltmann on the Procession of the Spirit," 167–81.

199. There is no indication of the *Filioque* in the original text of the Niceno-Constantinopolitan Creed. With regards to the Holy Spirit, it states: "And we believe in the Holy Spirit, the Lord, and Giver of Life, Who proceeds from the Father, Who with the Father and the Son together is worshipped and glorified, Who spoke by the Prophets." Cf. Heron, who gives an excellent summing up of the dogmatic history and makes a good dogmatic suggestion in "Who Proceedeth from the Father and the Son: The Problem of the *Filioque*," 149–66.

200. For a fuller history, see Ritschl, "Historical Development and Implications of the *Filioque* Controversy," 46–65.

201. Moltmann, *The Spirit of Life*, 305.

202. Barth, *CD* I/1:480.

The Liberative Cross

In contrast, Moltmann views *filioque* as not only superfluous but also pernicious to the doctrine of the Trinity. He goes back to the original form of the Niceno-Constantinopolitan Creed of 381. He suggests that one way to recover the original insight of the creed would be to say that the "Holy Spirit proceeds from the Father of the Son."[203] The creed tells us that the Holy Spirit "proceeds from the Father." Moltmann insists that the first Person of the Trinity is the Father, but only in respect to the Son, that is to say, in the eternal generation of the Son. Therefore, he suggests that one way to recover the original insight of the creed would be to say that the "Holy Spirit proceeds from the Father of the Son."[204] Such a construction, according to Moltmann, reminds us that the Father is Father only because of his relation to the Son. The first Person of the Trinity is the Father not because he is the "Sole Cause" upon whom all things are dependent, but because of his relation to the Son. God shows Godself as the Father solely and exclusively in the eternal generation of the eternal Son. The Father is in all eternity solely the Father of the Son. He is not the Father of the Spirit. The procession of the Spirit from the Father therefore has as its premise the generation of the Son through the Father in eternity, because it is only in this relationship that the Father manifests himself as the Father.[205]

Moltmann, therefore, concludes that the Spirit's procession from the Father of the Son presupposes firstly the generation of the Son, secondly the existence of the Son, and thirdly the mutual relationship of the Father and the Son. The Son is the logical presupposition and the actual condition for the procession of the Spirit from the Father; but the Son is not the Spirit's origin, as the Father is. The procession of the Spirit from the Father must, therefore, be essentially distinguished from the generation of the Son through the Father, and yet the procession must stay connected with that generation relationally. The Son is eternally with and in the Father. The Father is never without the Son and nowhere acts without him, just as the Father is never without, and never acts without, the Spirit.[206]

As argued above, Moltmann raises his theological objection to the *filioque* because if he were to affirm it he would subordinate the Spirit to

203. Moltmann, *The Trinity and the Kingdom*, 182–85.

204. Ibid., 185.

205. Ibid., 183–84.

206. Ibid., 184. In his later book, *The Spirit of Life*, Moltmann returns to the *filioque* issue. Here again, he insists that affirmation of *filioque* implies subordination of the Spirit to the Son and limits the doctrine of the Spirit to a christological Pneumatology. For details, see *The Spirit of Life*, 289–308.

the Son, thereby negating the reciprocal relationship between the Son and Spirit. Therefore, Moltmann suggests that the unity and interrelationship of the Father, Son, and Spirit is best presented through a social Trinity. According to him, the essential nature of the triune God is community. The unity of God appears as the community of the three Persons who exist with one another, for one another, and in one another.

In conclusion, the social trinitarian theology reveals that the very essence of God is to be in relation, mutuality, and community in diversity. The social trinitarian approach to the cross embraces Jesus' passion from his birth to his resurrection, and it reveals God as a passionate loving God who suffers in solidarity with the marginalized, the victimized, and the dehumanized. Therefore, the social trinitarian approach to the cross invalidates the traditional descriptions of God which have endorsed binary oppositions between men and women, and promotes mutuality and reciprocity between them. What challenge does this social trinitarian approach to the theology of the Cross give to Korean-North American women living in multicultural, multiracial contexts?

In the following chapter, I will discuss what constitutes social trinitarian praxis for Korean-North American women in multicultural, multiracial contexts from the perspective of a Korean-North American immigrant woman pastor. First, I will explore how the social trinitarian praxis can be applied in their personal social relations even though it is not free of criticism. Second, I will demonstrate how the social trinitarian perspective of the cross can bring about change within the structure of the church and the leadership in relation to gender. Third, I will show how the social trinitarian perspective challenges Korean-North American women to have a new understanding of the mission. Fourth, I will discuss from a social trinitarian perspective the attitude required from Korean North-American Christian women to live in harmony with people of different faiths and cultures.

4

Social Trinitarian Understanding of the Cross and Its Praxis for Korean-North American Women in the Multicultural, Multiracial, Pluralistic Context

IN CHAPTER 3, I have looked into the concept of *perichoresis* which Moltmann employs to explain that the mutual interpenetration and indwelling of the Father, Son and Holy Spirit arise from the three persons' eternal acts of self-donation.[1] Yet, this triune God is not a closed circle but an "open Trinity," yearning for fellowship with God's own creation.[2] Human beings as *imago Dei* are called to participate in the trinitarian fellowship through emulating the *perichoretic* love of the Trinity in their relationships with others. Therefore, in view of this trinitarian fellowship, I will explore various ways in which a social trinitarian understanding of the cross directs its praxis for Korean-North American women at both personal and corporate levels. The social trinitarian praxis, as an inclusive approach, recognizes their interconnectedness and embraces the need of their interdependence regardless of gender, ethnicity and race. It promotes their dignity and self-worth because there is no hint of hierarchy but mutuality and reciprocity in the triune God. The Crucified God as the passionate loving God stands in solidarity with them as they suffer.

1. McDougall, "The Return of Trinitarian Praxis?," 186. See also Moltmann, *The Spirit of Life*, 217–21.

2. Moltmann, *The Crucified God*, 255. See also Moltmann, *God in Creation*, 242.

Social Trinitarian Understanding of the Cross

In this chapter, I will argue that Korean-North American women will be restored to self-respect and self-worth as they participate in trinitarian fellowship and seek to be *imago Dei* through true human fellowship in the service of God's kingdom. They will be empowered to protest against the intolerance of difference and oppression in the form of injustice like sexism, classism or racism. The social trinitarian praxis calls them to build a human society mirroring the divine communion of the Trinity who exists in the reciprocity of love and service.

Moltmann's Claim of Trinitarian Fellowship as "Prescription of the Nature of True Human Community" Faces Criticism

Moltmann claims that the *perichoretic* trinitarian fellowship not only describes divine community but also prescribes the nature of true human community. He contends, "True human fellowship is to correspond to the triune God and be *imago Dei* on earth. True human fellowship will participate in the inner life of the triune God."[3] Social trinitarian theologians such as John Zizioulas, Miroslav Volf, Leonardo Boff, and Catherine LaCugna have also proposed a social doctrine of the Trinity as a model for a particular kind of human community, that is, egalitarian, reciprocal, and inclusive.[4]

However, Moltmann's claim of trinitarian fellowship as "prescription of the nature of true human community" has not been exempt from criticism. I will, therefore, look into two main criticisms before I explore various ways in which the social trinitarian theology of the cross directs its praxis for Korean-North American women. Karen Kilby, for example, criticizes Moltmann's social trinitarian program as projectionism.[5] She accuses Moltmann of projecting onto the divine life his own preferred political ideals and ethical values for human society.[6] The other criticism Moltmann faces

---

3. Moltmann, *History and the Triune God*, 60. See also Moltmann, *God in Creation*, 242–43.

4. Zizioulas is an orthodox theologian and the author of the remarkably influential *Being as Communion: Studies in Personhood and the Church*; Boff, *Trinity and Society*; Volf, *After Our Likeness*; LaCugna, *God for Us*; Moltmann, *The Trinity and the Kingdom*.

5. Kilby, "*Perichoresis* and Projection," 432–45.

6. Ibid.

has to do with the practicality of his social doctrines of the Trinity.[7] Those who criticize him ask, "Could the picture of the relationships between the Father, Son and Holy Spirit function as something of a blue print for human society?"[8] In view of these criticisms, I will first discuss whether Moltmann, as Kilby argues, projects his preferred social and political agenda into immanent Trinitarian life. And then, I will discuss how Kathryn Tanner suggests Christology instead of social trinitarianism as a better rationale for proper human relationships.[9] I will finally explore Moltmann's understanding of *Imago Dei* as an *analogia relationis*, and argue that the social trinitarian praxis can be applied to mold the interpersonal, social relations of Korean-North American women living as *imago Dei*. I recognize that it is very difficult to transmute the *perichoretic* love of the Trinity in the world which is permeated and marred by sin and evil. Nevertheless, the social trinitarian theology of the cross, I will argue, provides a vision which calls Korean-North American women to live with a sense of mission to live in mutual, reciprocal, life-giving relationships in the multicultural context. It motivates them to envision not only an ecclesial reform in the leadership and structure of the church but also a new approach to mission and interreligious dialogue.

Is Moltmann's Social Trinitarian Theology a Projection of His Own Social Values and Political Ideals?

In his essay "The Social Doctrine of the Trinity," Moltmann summarizes his understanding of the Trinity as a model of both church and society as follows:

> Father, Son and Spirit . . . do not exist with each other, but rather empty themselves on to each other and live in each other by virtue of love . . . When the church is such "an icon of the Trinity," she can also become a life-principle of human society" a society without privileges—a society without poverty and need—a society of free and equal persons. Then the Trinity will become our "social

---

7. Cunningham, *These Three Are One*, 42–43. Cunningham criticizes the "high level of abstraction" of Moltmann's social Trinitarian program. In his view, its practical recommendations are too unspecific to engage the challenging issues facing Christian communities today.

8. Chapman, "The Social Doctrines of the Trinity: Some Problems," 239–54.

9. Tanner, *Christ the Key*, 207–46.

Social Trinitarian Understanding of the Cross

programme," the programme of social personalism, or of personal socialism. We would overcome the possessive individualism of the West as well as the depersonalizing collectivism of the East. We would be able to integrate a human "culture of sharing" symbiotically into the *perichoretic* texture of nature and to live and become blessed together with the fellowship of the entire creation in the fellowship of the triune God.[10]

In this statement, Moltmann draws connections between the Trinity, church and society by claiming the Trinity as our "social programme." In a similar way, a politically progressive trinitarian theologian, Leonardo Boff also argues that the Trinity means more than just our entry into the divine life in the next life but the model in this life for society in general, and our church in particular.[11] Boff insists that the divine communion of the Trinity who exists in the reciprocity of love serves as inspiration for social structures and relationships. It motivates and indeed demands structures which are characterized by participation, inclusion, equality, reciprocity, and respect for individual differences.[12] The Trinity thus effectively constitutes a social project to be accomplished in this life. The social, interpersonal, and non-hierarchical model of the Trinity underpins Boff's critique of society and of the church. Thus, for him, "the Trinity is our social program."[13]

Karen Kilby criticizes this social understanding of the Trinity. She argues, "This line of thought has been gaining momentum especially since the publication of Jürgen Moltmann's *The Trinity and the Kingdom*, and by now . . . it has become the new orthodoxy."[14] She charges that Moltmann oversteps epistemological limits by describing the immanent trinitarian life in passion-filled terms such as interrelatedness, love, empathy, mutual accord, mutual giving and so on.[15] In Kilby's view, such terms are projections of his preferred social and political agenda. She, therefore, questions

---

10. Moltmann, "The Social Doctrine of the Trinity," 110–11.

11. Boff is an ex-Franciscan priest, educated in his native Brazil and München, Germany. A professor of theology in Petropolis, Brazil, Boff also served as advisor to the Brazilian Conference of Bishops and the Latin American Conference of Religions.

12. Boff, "Trinity," 78.

13. Volf notes that it was Nicholas Fedorov, "an erudite friend of such great Russian intellectuals as Leo Tolstoy, Vladimir Solovyov, and Fyodor Dostoyevsky," who first formulated this expression. See Volf, "The Trinity is Our Social Program," 403.

14. Kilby, "*Perichoresis* and Projection: Problems with Social Doctrines of the Trinity," 433.

15. Ibid., 432–42.

whether such projections can be used prescriptively to guide human relationships. Kilby sums up her argument in this way:

> First, a concept, *perichoresis*, is used to name what is not understood, to name whatever it is that makes the three Persons one. Secondly, the concept is filled out rather suggestively with notions borrowed from our own experience of relationships and relatedness. And then, finally, it is presented as an exciting resource Christian theology has to offer the wider world in its reflections upon relationships and relatedness.[16]

Kilby argues here that Moltmann and other social trinitarian theologians indulge in using highly anthropomorphic language to create social analogies for the divine life and then reverse the direction of these analogies and propose them as norms for human relationships. She further criticizes that Moltmann uses the term *perichoresis* which was meant to refer exclusively to the immanent Trinity to norm human relations. Kilby calls on theologians to renounce the notion that the concept of *perichoresis* gives insight into God.[17] She also contends that instead of proposing the Trinity as "social program", it should be taken simply as a grammatical rule for how to read the biblical stories, how to think and talk about the experience of prayer and how to structure Christian discourse in an appropriate way.[18]

In response to Kilby's criticism, we will raise the questions as follow: First, does Moltmann project his preferred social and political agenda into immanent trinitarian life as she argues? Or, does he glean attributes of immanent trinitarian life from reading of the Scriptures and develop his social trinitarian theology from the biblical witness? If Moltmann does not project his ideals into the nature of God, for what reasons is he often charged with projectionism?

Before investigating whether or not Kilby's criticism is valid, I will first discuss why Moltmann is often charged with projectionism even though Moltmann himself insists that his doctrinal reconstruction and the Trinity are true and necessary interpretations of the New Testament. Joy Ann McDougall takes up the question and argues that Moltmann's univocal predication of terms to the divine and human life without qualifications causes the misunderstanding.[19] McDougall points out, "Moltmann neither

16. Ibid., 442.
17. Ibid.
18. Ibid., 443.
19. McDougall, "The Return of Trinitarian Praxis?," 189. Cf. Kilby, "Perichoresis and

Social Trinitarian Understanding of the Cross

develops a theory of divine predication that helps distinguish between his literal and figurative or metaphorical use of terms, nor does he often introduce distinctions, such as *apophatic* or *cataphatic* predication to help qualify how such imagery applies to God."[20] For instance, McDougall insists, in applying the term *perichoresis* Moltmann does not qualify the ways in which it applies in a primary sense to the divine life and only metaphorically to our own.[21] I concur with McDougall that "In absence of such qualifications Moltmann remains open to the charge of projectionism that Kilby among others levels against him."[22]

Nevertheless, I disagree with Kilby as she contends that the term *perichoresis* was meant to refer exclusively to the immanent Trinity; therefore, not to be used to norm human relations.[23] From Adiprasetya's works on the concept of *perichoresis*, we learn that the concept of *perichoresis* has been used in various ways in response to the new challenges arising from their contexts.[24] For instance, this term, *perichoresis* was first developed by Gregory of Nazianzus (329-390 AD) to explain the relationship between the humanity and divinity of Christ. Maximus the Confessor (580-662 AD) employed this term, which had been Christologically understood, to express further a soteriological interpenetration of believers and Christ. Here, the idea of interpenetration was applied to the unification of human beings and Christ in terms of *theosis*. Then, the notion of *perichoresis* was further developed to explain the inner relationship of the Trinity especially in the writings of Pseudo-Cyril as he argued against the tritheistic understanding of God in the sixth century.[25] John of Damascus (676-754 AD) borrowed the concept of trinitarian *perichoresis* from Pseudo-Cyril and used it to argue further that the unity of indwelling of the divine persons in each other is in totality and fullness, and yet the totality of this *perichoresis* does not

---

Projection: Problems with Social Doctrines of the Trinity," 435-37. For similar criticisms, see Otto, "The Use and Abuse of *Perichoresis* in Recent Theology," 366-84.

20. McDougall, "The Return of Trinitarian Praxis?," 189.

21. Ibid.

22. Kilby, "*Perichoresis* and Projection: Problems with Social Doctrines of the Trinity," 435-37. See also McDougall, "The Return of Trinitarian Praxis?," 189.

23. Kilby, "*Perichoresis* and Projection: Problems with Social Doctrines of the Trinity," 433.

24. Adiprasetya, "Toward a Perichoretic Theology of Religions," 158.

25. Harrison, "*Perichoresis* in the Greek Fathers," 59, quoting Pseudo-Cyril, *De Sacrosancta Trinitate* 10.

The Liberative Cross

disturb the integrity of each person at all.[26] Moltmann takes up this notion of *perichoresis* from John of Damascus and uses to describe both the inner life of the Trinity and his ideal of human relationships. These various ways in which the term *perichoresis* has been used show that theological language is fundamentally of an analogical and metaphorical nature. Besides, theologians as "beings-in-the-world" are influenced by their historical reality, and they use theological concepts in various ways in order to respond to the new challenges arising from their contexts.[27]

The very issue which we need to discuss is then whether Moltmann draws such anthropomorphic terms like interrelatedness, love, empathy, mutual giving, and so on from the biblical witness, or he simply projects his preferred social and political agenda into the triune God. According to McDougall, Kilby's critique overlooks that Moltmann remains true to his own methodological intent. For Moltmann, McDougall affirms, the biblical witness has been his governing source and *norma normans* for his doctrinal reconstruction and the Trinity as a true and necessary interpretation of the New Testament witness.[28] Although she does not argue the point in detail, I find that it is necessary to explore Moltmann's trinitarian hermeneutics, which he deals with in depth in his *Trinity and Kingdom*. He argues that the seeds of the development of the doctrine of the Trinity are already found in the New Testament.[29] In arguing the point, Moltmann looks into different hermeneutical positions in comparison to his own position. He first critiques Harnack's position: Harnack views the acknowledgment of Jesus, "the Son of God" as a later *apotheosis* of Jesus by Paul and the disciples who worshiped him.[30] Moltmann argues that Harnack's position arises out of a preliminary hermeneutical decision which is highly questionable. The apostle Paul, according to Harnack, proclaimed Jesus as the Christ, and the apostles of Jesus falsified his orthopraxy, turning it into the orthodoxy of faith in Christ.[31]

---

26. Adiprasetya, "Toward a Perichoretic Theology of Religions," 158.
27. Gadamer, *Truth and Method*, 276–77.
28. McDougall, "The Return of Trinitarian Praxis?," 189.
29. Moltmann, *The Trinity and the Kingdom*, 60–65.
30. Ibid., 62. See also Harnack, *What is Christianity?*, 124–44.
31. Moltmann, *The Trinity and the Kingdom*, 62.

Social Trinitarian Understanding of the Cross

Moltmann points out that Harnack's preliminary hermeneutical decision is that "history means human history, and human history is the sphere of morals."[32] Moltmann affirms:

> For Harnack, Jesus has to be understood as a human person, and is only authoritative as a human person to the extent in which he is able to be a pattern for our own moral actions. All theological statements which the Christian faith makes about God therefore have to be understood and interpreted as the expressions of Christian moral existence. If they cannot be understood as the expression of moral existence, then we have to reject them as dogmatic.[33]

Moltmann points out that Kant and Schleiermacher have exerted an influence on this moralistic understanding of Jesus. Ever since Kant, people have held that "nothing can be gathered for practical purposes from the doctrine of the Trinity."[34] Ever since Schleiermacher, people have been told that "the doctrine of the Trinity cannot count as being the direct statement of the devout personal consciousness."[35] Thus, the doctrine of the Trinity has been criticized as speculative and superfluous for faith, and even harmful for morals. Moltmann affirms that this position can be traced back to the preliminary decision which led to the moral interpretation of the Bible: "Faith means being man in the true sense morally."[36]

What is Moltmann's trinitarian hermeneutics? Moltmann follows Barth's hermeneutical lead to defend the argument that the Trinity is a true and necessary interpretation of the New Testament witness. However, Moltmann diverges himself from Barth's monotheistic conception of the doctrine of the Trinity.[37] As I have already discussed in chapter 3, Barth insists that God reveals Godself as Lord in three distinctive modes of being subsisting in their mutual relations: Father, Son and Holy Spirit. He secures God's sovereignty through his doctrine of the Trinity by stating that God is one in three modes of being.[38] For Barth, the trinitarian "persons" or *Seinsweisen* are modes of existence of one common divine subject, rather than

---

32. Ibid.
33. Ibid.
34. Ibid. Cf. Kant, *Der Streit der Fakultäten,* A 50, 57.
35. Moltmann, *The Trinity and the Kingdom,* 62. Cf. Schleiermacher, *The Christian Faith,* section 170.
36. Moltmann, *The Trinity and the Kingdom,* 62.
37. Ibid., 63–65.
38. Barth, *CD* I/1:295.

The Liberative Cross

three separate self-conscious agents.[39] Moltmann argues that there is the ever-present danger in this position.[40] If we see the trinitarian "persons" as "modes of existence of one common divine subject," we rob both the Son and the Spirit of any genuine personhood as God. Also, it makes the traditional language of interpersonal communion or love between Father and Son, or of the obedience of the Son to the Father, difficult to take altogether seriously. Moltmann, therefore, finds the unity of God in the *perichoresis* itself, the interpenetration of the three distinct divine persons, instead of seeing the unity of God in "one substance" subsisting in three distinct modes.[41] In accordance with Moltmann's conception of *perichoresis*, Trevor Hart precisely states, "To be God is to be Father, Son, and Holy Spirit in eternal perichoretic *koinonia*."[42]

Moltmann also argues that Barth's monotheistic conception of the doctrine of the Trinity arises out of a preliminary hermeneutical decision which is in itself questionable, and thus needs to be tested against the testimony of the New Testament.[43] He insists that according to the testimony of the New Testament, it is not God who reveals Godself; rather, it is the Son who reveals the Father (Matt 11:27) and the Father who reveals the Son (Gal 1:16). In addition, Barth's Christian monotheism has to talk about "God's giving of himself"; however, the New Testament witness, according to Moltmann, tells us that it is "God who has given up God's own Son for us" (Rom 8:32) and "the Son who gave himself for me" (Gal 2:20). Moltmann, therefore, concludes that the Christian monotheism which reduces the interpretation of Christ' history in a monotheistic sense to the one divine subject does not do justice to the history of Christ.[44]

---

39. Barth chooses the term *Seinsweisen* (modes of being) in place of the traditional term, "person," to refer to the "three" in God. LaCugna contends that Barth's concept of *Seinsweisen* leads him into a form of modalism, though she carefully qualifies, "whether this modalism is Sabellian could be debated." See LaCugna, *God for Us*, 252. Moltmann views Barth's use of *Seinsweisen* as a late triumph for the Sabellian modalism, which the early church condemned. See Moltmann, *The Trinity and the Kingdom*, 139.

40. The Trinitarian "persons" or *Seinsweisen* according to Barth and also Rahner are modes of existence of one common divine subject. Rahner writes: "There are not three consciousnesses; rather the one consciousness subsists in a threefold way . . . The distinctness of the persons is not constituted by a distinctness of conscious subjectivities, nor does it include the latter." See Rahner, *The Trinity*, 107.

41. Moltmann, *The Trinity and the Kingdom*, 150.

42. Hart, "Person & Prerogative in Perichoretic Perspective," 54.

43. Moltmann, *The Trinity and the Kingdom*, 63.

44. Ibid., 63–64.

Social Trinitarian Understanding of the Cross

Moltmann, in this way, distinguishes himself from Barth who interprets the doctrine's biblical root in terms of divine lordship.[45] Moltmann argues that Jesus the Son is the "revealer of the Trinity," and treats the New Testament as an account of three divine persons' activities and ever-changing relationships to one another in the economy of salvation. Thus, the New Testament as the trinitarian history of the Father, the Son, and the Spirit narrates the salvation history.[46] He states:

> The history of salvation is the history of the eternally living, triune God who draws us into and includes us in his eternal triune life with all the fullness of its relationships . . . God loves the world with the very same love which he is in himself.[47]

Because the Son is "the revealer of the Trinity," Moltmann argues, we must look into the history of Jesus, the Son, in order to grasp the Social Trinity.[48] According to him, the history of Jesus through his birth, life, death, and resurrection discloses the dynamic relationships among the divine persons in a unique and definitive manner. It reveals the fellowship of the divine persons characterized by an infinite self-giving and reciprocal sacrifice of love. Moltmann depicts the sending of the Son as an event of free self-giving that involves all three persons of the Trinity.[49] This trinitarian self-giving is both an outward movement toward the world and a reciprocal inward movement among the divine relations. McDougall sums it up clearly as follows:

> On the side of creation, the Father's self-giving of the Son involves a communication of the Father's eternal essence, his infinite goodness, into the world. Through the power of the Holy Spirit, the Father opens the exclusive fellowship that he shares with the Son to all human beings. On the divine side, this outward movement involves an inward self-donation among the divine persons where "in the sending of the Son, God . . . yields himself up." Here the Son responds to the Father's yielding himself up by taking up his own mission into the world. The Holy Spirit participates equally in this reciprocal self-giving of the Son and the Father as the mediator of their fellowship. The Spirit's self-giving inspires Jesus'

---

45. Ibid.
46. Moltmann, "The Inviting Unity of the Triune God," 83.
47. Moltmann, *The Trinity and the Kingdom*, 157.
48. Ibid., 65.
49. Ibid., 75.

proclamation, empowers his ministry, and accompanies him unto the cross.[50]

This divine self-giving in the Trinity culminates at the event of the cross. The cross event, according to Moltmann, reveals not only a reciprocal inward movement among the divine relations but also the infinite depths of the trinitarian self-giving for humankind. At the cross, we discover the utter boundlessness of divine mercy, a "love which does everything, gives everything, and suffers everything for lost men and women."[51]

As discussed so far, Moltmann's trinitarian hermeneutics, "Jesus as the Revealer of the Trinity" is rooted in the history of the trinitarian self-giving toward the world, which at the same time involves a reciprocal inward movement among the divine relations as disclosed in the Scriptures. Through the event of Jesus Christ at his birth, life, death, and resurrection, the triune God demonstrates the divine nature such as infinite self-giving love and generosity. Thus, I conclude that the terms such as interrelatedness, love, empathy, and mutual giving describe the divine nature which is revealed through the event of Jesus Christ and drawn from the biblical witness. In this respect, I concur with McDougall that those terms used by Moltmann to describe the nature of the triune God should not be regarded as projections of his preferred ideals as Kilby argued, but rather be taken as anthropomorphic descriptions of the divine life which are witnessed throughout the Scriptures.[52]

This attempt to establish how human societies should be organized on the basis of trinitarianism is also criticized by Kathryn Tanner because of its complex nature and the possible variety of political purposes which different theories of the Trinity might serve. Tanner asks this critical question: "How is one to draw out the implications of the Trinity for human society with any specificity, given how little one really understands about the Trinity?"[53] She also points out a problem that much of what is said about the Trinity simply does not seem directly applicable to humans because of their essential finitude. Consequently, Tanner views it as "a fraught task" to figure out the socio-political lessons of the Trinity. She, therefore, tries to steer our attention away from trinitarian relations and turns to Christology

---

50. McDougall, "The Return of Trinitarian Praxis?," 184.
51. Moltmann, *The Trinity and the Kingdom*, 83.
52. McDougall, "The Return of Trinitarian Praxis?," 188.
53. Tanner, *Christ the Key*, 224.

as a "better" rationale.[54] She insists that we need to make judgments about the proper character of human relations on the basis of the character of Jesus' relationships with others instead of trinitarian relations. According to Tanner, it is Jesus, not the Trinity, who provides direction for our social relations. She argues that if we replace the idea of "modeling" human relations on the Trinity with the idea of "sharing" in the life of the Trinity by joining Jesus, we do not need to fathom more fully and comprehend the Trinity in order to draw inferences about human community from it. Instead, we can look to the character of Jesus' human relationships to understand its implications for human life more directly.

According to Tanner, Christ is what unifies us in our relations with the Father, as both a gift to us and as an example for us. Following the example of Jesus, human beings are to worship the Father, carry out the will of the Father as they are filled up with and empowered by the Holy Spirit, and work for the wellbeing of others. Through union with Christ, we are to participate in the Father's mission to the world, mediating the life-giving Spirit of Christ.

As observed above, Tanner points out two critical problems with this theological attempt to figure out the socio-political lessons of the Trinity: 1) Discussion of the Trinity is not very comprehensible and 2) The essential finitude of human beings makes it impossible to apply the very character of the Trinity in their relations.[55] Volf also points out a similar problem in his monograph, *After Our Likeness*. According to him, there can be no correspondence to the interiority of the divine persons of the Trinity at the human level, and because of the essential finitude of human beings in both ontic and noetic levels, human beings correspond to the uncreated God only in a creaturely way.[56] However, Tanner and Volf have different approaches to the question whether the Trinity should serve as a model for human community. Tanner looks to what is happening in the life of Jesus to find implications of the Trinity for our lives. She insists, "Human beings are not left to their own devices in figuring out what the Trinity means for human relations. Instead, the Trinity itself enters our world in Christ to show us how human relations are to be reformed in its image."[57] According

---

54. Ibid., 208.

55. Ibid., 224.

56. Volf, *After Our Likeness*, 198–200. See also Volf, "The Trinity is our Social Program," 405.

57. Tanner, *Christ the Key*, 234.

to Tanner, it is the Trinity in the economy that closes the gap by incorporating the human into its very own life through the incarnation. By way of the incarnation we are brought to participate in the Trinity.

Whereas Tanner looks to the life of Jesus to find the implications of the Trinity for our lives, Volf looks to the cross of Jesus through which the triune God painstakingly engages with the world. Consequently, for Volf, *imitatio crucis* is orthopraxy to be practiced in relationships. Volf does not dismiss theological efforts to draw implications of the Trinity for human life and argues that human community should be modeled on the Trinity. Therefore, it is a matter of human responsibility whether we "copy God" or "not copy God at all." The question for him is in which respects and to what extent we should do so. While I appreciate Tanner's additional dimension of "participation in the Trinity" by focusing on Jesus' incarnation and life, I choose to follow Volf's approach to find out how the picture of the relationships between the Father, Son, and Holy Spirit is able to function as a model for human society.

Is the Picture of the Relationships between the Father, Son, and Holy Spirit Able to Function as a Model for Human Society?

In his article "The Trinity is Our Social Program," Volf deals with the question, "Can we copy God?"[58] Here, he argues against Ted Peters who insists that it is impossible for us to copy God because "God alone is God and that we as creatures cannot copy God in all respects."[59] By posing a few rhetorical questions, Volf argues that the Trinity should serve as a model for the ecclesial community:

> And would it not be anomalous to insist that human beings, created for communion with the Triune God and renewed through faith and baptism into the Triune Name "according to the likeness of God" (Ephesians 4:24), should not seek to be like God in their mutual relations? If the idea of an image that is not supposed to reflect the reality of which it is an image does not strike us as odd, Jesus' injunction in the Sermon on the Mount should set us straight: "Be perfect" he commands his disciples, "as your heavenly Father is perfect" (Matthew 5:48; cf. I Peter 1:16). The earthly

---

58. Volf, "The Trinity is Our Social Program," 403–23.
59. Peters, *God as Trinity*, 186.

Social Trinitarian Understanding of the Cross

children should be like their heavenly parent, he states (v. 45); the character of God should shape the character and behavior of those who worship, he implies.[60]

Volf, however, admits that there can be no correspondence to the interiority of the divine persons of the Trinity at the human level. In his monograph, *After Our Likeness*, he points out that because of the essential finitude of human beings in both ontic and noetic levels, human beings correspond to the uncreated God only in a creaturely way.[61] Since ontically human beings are not divine and since noetically human notions of the triune God do not correspond exactly to who the triune God is, the trinitarian concepts of "person", "relation", or "*perichoresis*" can only be applied to our understanding of human existence and community in a strictly analogical, and not a univocal, sense.[62] Human relationships are marred by sin, evil and transitoriness (Isa 40:6ff; 1 Pet 1:24), and consequently, the human society is full of suffering, conflict, and tension. Thus, according to Volf, human beings can appropriate the peaceful and perfectly loving mutuality of the Trinity only in a creaturely way within the conditions of history.[63]

Volf rightly points out that there is a gap between the Trinity and sinful finite human beings. In light of this observation, a question comes to mind: How should we understand the command of Jesus Christ to his disciples, "Be perfect as your heavenly Father is perfect" (Matt 5:48)? According to Volf, in this world full of broken relationships and enmity, we cannot simply emulate the internal reciprocal love of the Trinity that gives and receives in love's freedom and trust. Those whom we love do not necessarily respond to us with love and trust. Consequently, the kind of love we are to emulate is the suffering love that risks the result. Jesus commanded the disciples to imitate a divine kind of love which makes "the sun rise on the evil and on the good, and sends rain on the righteous and on the unrighteous" (Matt 5:45) by loving "enemies" and praying "for those who persecute" them (Matt 5:44). We, as Jesus' disciples, must imitate the divine suffering love. The love that suffers is the internal love of the Trinity engaged in the transformation of the deeply flawed world of sin. Volf affirms that this love's engagement with the world of sin entails a process of complex and

---

60. Volf, "The Trinity is our Social Program," 404.

61. Volf, *After Our Likeness*, 198–200. See also Volf, "The Trinity is our Social Program," 405.

62. Volf, *After Our Likeness*, 199.

63. Ibid., 200.

difficult translation: "Sent by God in the power of the Spirit, the Word became the Lamb of God who takes away the sin of the world (John 1:29) . . . In the labor of taking away the sin, the delight of love is transmuted in the agony of love . . . hence, the cross of the Christ."[64] The cross, according to Volf, is the triune God's painstaking engagement with the world in order to transform the unjust, deceitful, and violent kingdoms of this world into the just, truthful, and peaceful "kingdom of our Lord and of his Messiah" (Rev 11:15). Volf affirms that our social vision and praxis image the triune God as "coming down in self-emptying passion" in order to take "human beings caught in the snares of non-love and seduced by injustice, deceit, and violence"[65] into the trinitarian perfect fellowship of reciprocal self-giving and receiving in love.[66] In this respect, Volf emphasizes that we should hold true *imitatio crucis* not only for social knowledge but also for social practices. Since *imitatio crucis* as orthopraxy is practiced in relationships, I will describe Moltmann's understanding of *imago Dei* as *analogia relationis* in the following section. In so doing, I will also explore the potential of Moltmann's notion of trinitarian fellowship in guiding Korean-North American women into orthopraxy in their life situation today.

Moltmann's Understanding of *imago Dei* as *analogia relationis*

Before we relate Moltmann's notion of trinitarian fellowship in the life situation of today's Korean-North American women, I will first explore his understanding of *imago Dei* as *analogia relationis* because human beings, according to Moltmann, mirror the trinitarian life in their relationships. Moltmann neither sees *imago Dei* in terms of "analogy of substance," which focuses on a singular attribute inherent in human beings such as the rational soul or the will. Nor does he see it as "analogy of form," which focuses on the human being's peculiar upright posture. Moltmann defines *imago Dei* as an *analogia relationis* in terms of relationships that mirror the trinitarian life instead of God's general lordship over the earth.[67] As *imago*

---

64. Volf, "The Trinity is our Social Program," 414.
65. Ibid., 415.
66. Ibid., 419.
67. Moltmann, *God in Creation*, 219–20. See also, Bonhoeffer's earlier discussion of this analogy of relation in Bonhoeffer, *Creation and Fall: A Theological Interpretation of Genesis 1–3*, 36–37.

Dei, human beings not only respond to God's gift of fellowship in love, but are also blessed with the possibility of expressing ecstatic and passionate fellowship toward one another. The regenerated, according to Moltmann, experience the reciprocal *perichoresis* of God through the Holy Spirit who pours out the love of God in their hearts.[68] Consequently, they are able to participate in God's unconditional love of all living things and discover "a passion for life" and "a new delight in living in the joy of God."[69]

Since *imago Dei*, according to Moltmann, is not an innate capacity of human beings but a gift of grace that God offers freely, human beings receive it in gratitude ever anew. The human being's relationship to God is subsequent to God's relationship to human beings. Accordingly, whatever likeness or correspondences to the trinitarian fellowship become manifest in and among human beings come as a response to God's initiating a relationship with them by God's prior self-giving.[70] God's relationship to human beings can never be abrogated or withdrawn except by Godself. It means that human sin may certainly pervert human beings' relationship to God, but not God's relationship to human beings.[71] Consequently, human beings are God's image and sinners at the same time.[72] In other words, they are, subjectively speaking, wholly and entirely a sinner and godless, but remain at the same time wholly and entirely God's image because God remains faithful to them. Thus, the human being's relationship to God may be perverted by sin but never lost. It means that human beings never cease to be an *imago*; but from being *imago Dei* they turn into an *imago satanae* or an *imago mammonis*.[73]

Moltmann, in his understanding of *imago Dei* as *analogia relationis*, stresses that human beings as *imago Dei* are social beings who mirror the Trinitarian life in relationships. Just as the divine persons only exist in and through their ecstatic relationships of self-giving communion with one another, so analogously, human beings only become who they are called to be in and through their fellowship with others.[74] Moltmann affirms:

---

68. Moltmann, *The Spirit of Life*, 195.
69. Ibid., 178.
70. Moltmann, *God in Creation*, 220.
71. Ibid., 233.
72. Ibid.
73. Ibid., 234.
74. McDougall, "The Return of Trinitarian Praxis?," 192.

> From the very outset, human beings are social beings. They are aligned towards human society and essentially in need of help (Gen 2:18). They are gregarious beings and only develop their personalities in fellowship with other people. Consequently they can only relate to themselves if, and to the extent in which, other people relate to them. The isolated individual and the solitary subject are deficient modes of being human, because they fall short of likeness to God. Nor does the person take priority over the community. On the contrary, person and community are two sides of one and the same life process.[75]

Accordingly, just as the unity among the trinitarian persons does not take precedence over the distinction among the three persons, the human community shaped by the likeness of God does not take precedence over its individual members. In other words, trinitarian fellowship does not commend homogeneous human communities that erase personal differences. Rather, it fosters human fellowships of "diversity in unity" in which individual potentials are realized and differences may abound.[76] On the basis of Moltmann's conception of *imago Dei*, McDougall affirms, "Sociality and right relationships with one's neighbors belong to the essence of what it means to be human."[77]

As argued above, Moltmann has made an important point by his conception of *imago Dei* as *analogia relationis*: Human beings are social beings, who are supposed to live in and through their fellowship with others, reflecting the social trinitarian fellowship. We will take this aspect of *imago Dei* as *analogia relationis* to the next step: What does it mean for Korean-North American women to live as *imago Dei* mirroring the social trinitarian fellowship in their context today?

Social Trinitarian Praxis for Korean-North American Women in the Multicultural, Multiracial, and Pluralistic Context Today

According to Moltmann, true human fellowship is founded on the essence of trinitarian fellowship, which involves "openness to one another,

---

75. Moltmann, *God in Creation*, 223.

76. McDougall, "The Return of Trinitarian Praxis?," 196. See also Moltmann, *The Spirit of Life*, 219–20.

77. McDougall, "The Return of Trinitarian Praxis?," 192.

Social Trinitarian Understanding of the Cross

sharing with one another, and respect for one another. It is the reciprocal communication of all that one has and is."[78] Moltmann names this true human fellowship "open friendship." Human beings embody this principle of trinitarian fellowship in the Christian life through "open friendship." In contrast to the exclusive friendship of people which are based on utilitarian purposes or for pleasure or between people who are alike, Moltmann finds the opposite picture of friendship in the self-giving love of Christ in the gospels. For instance, in the Gospel of Luke Jesus is called "the friend of sinners and tax collectors" (Luke 7:34).[79] John 15:13-15 makes clear that the friendship of Christ shapes the Christian concept of open friendship: "Jesus' surrender of himself to death is presented as love for his friends . . . In the community of Jesus, the men and women disciples are no longer God's servants. They are friends of God."[80] Later, the community of Christ, Moltmann insists, drew from the open friendship of Jesus their basic principle to "accept one another as Christ has accepted you, for the glory of God" (Rom 15:7). This self-giving love of the "Other" in "open friendship" is expressed in the forms of compassionate fellowship, solidarity with those who are in the margins, forgiveness, and acceptance of others in their diversity. It is noteworthy that in the gospels, the early Christian community remembers Jesus as often rebuking and challenging the teachers of the Law and the Pharisees who showed social prejudice toward the poor, children, women, and Gentiles. In contrast, with his boundless life-giving love, Jesus himself welcomed everyone regardless of their race, culture, status, or gender into trinitarian fellowship. Christian believers are, therefore, charged to practice such open friendship in the world.

This "open friendship" through which human beings embody the principle of trinitarian fellowship sets up the vision of Korean-North American women building a community which mirrors the trinitarian fellowship among people in the world. Today, the world is marred by intolerance and oppression in the forms of injustice like sexism, racism, classism, and religious persecution. In such a world, how could Korean-North American women emulate the trinitarian fellowship in their private and social spheres of Christian life toward this vision? Before discussing trinitarian praxis in their context, I will look into Andrew Sung Park's *han*

---

78. Moltmann, "Fellowship of the Holy Spirit," 57. See also Moltmann, *The Spirit of Life*, 219.

79. Moltmann, *The Spirit of Life*, 257–58.

80. Ibid., 258.

theology in comparison to Moltmann's conception of sin and critique both to see in what respect each of their harmatology fails to reflect the spirit of *analogia relationis*.

Practical Relevance of the Social Trinitarian Theology of the Cross: A Critique of Andrew Sung Park's *han* Theology and Moltmann's Conception of Sin

In chapter 1, I analyzed the *Sitz im Leben* of the Korean-North American immigrant women. Up until the 1970s, Korea had been striving to stabilize the country politically and grow economically through industrialization. In those days, women were, generally speaking, supposed to sacrifice their own interests: In family settings, daughters and wives were often told and expected to yield for the common welfare of family. In social settings, women were often required to yield their opportunities for self-improvement and success to men. The central minority thrived and succeeded by taking advantage of the weaker and the marginalized. The androcentric, collective socio-political condition caused helpless victims to develop *han*, which is defined as "the accumulated feeling of powerlessness and despair." [81] In this situation, Korean theologians developed a unique Korean theology called *Minjung* theology.[82]

However, as I have already investigated in chapter 1, the politico-social milieu of Korea has changed drastically.[83] The majority of Korean women today do not consider themselves as "*han*-ridden" people. Korean-North American immigrant women who experienced the change of socio-political milieu in Korea as well as those who are educated in the North American context cannot be treated as a monolithic group of victimized

---

81. Nam–Dong Suh, "Towards a Theology of *Han*,"58.

82. *Minjung* refers to the people who are politically oppressed, socially alienated, economically exploited, and kept uneducated in cultural and intellectual matters. See Moon, "A Korean *Minjung* Perspective: The Hebrews and the Exodus,"241.

83. In December, 2012, Miss Park, Keun Hye (the oldest daughter of the ex-president, Park, Jung Hee who was in presidential office for 18 years from 1961–1979) was elected to be the president of South Korea. She was inaugurated on the 25th of February in 2013 as the president of the South Korea. It is a history-making incident because she is the first female president of South Korea, and also she is a daughter of the ex-president Park who is known as dictator. The fact that the Korean people elected a female president reflects how they have changed in their view of gender.

people irrespective of their varied socio-cultural, religious, political and economic differences.

In view of this changing milieu of Korea as well as the North-American context where they now live, I will critique Andrew Sung Park's *han* theology. I am fully aware of the socio-political situation of South Korea when Park wrote his monograph, *The Wounded Heart of God* in 1993. For the last two decades, their living condition has drastically improved; therefore, I will argue, Korean liberation theologians including feminist theologians should not stay with a theology of *han* which divides people into the simplistic dichotomy between the oppressed (*han*-ridden) and the oppressors (sinners), but move to an approach which is holistic and inclusive. I would argue that we are called to construct a theology which recognizes their interconnectedness and need to live together with others in mutuality and reciprocity so that all people can thrive together for the glory of God.

Andrew Sung Park in his *The Wounded Heart of God,* innovatively constructs a doctrine of sin from the perspective of *han*. He distinguishes *han* from sin, *han* for the oppressed, and sin for the oppressor. He insists that sin may be forgiven by the repentance of the oppressor, whereas *han* can be resolved through reconciliation of the oppressor and the oppressed by means of the healing of the latter.[84] Without the forgiveness of the wronged, reconciliation between the wronged and the wrongdoers is incomplete.[85] Furthermore, Park criticizes Moltmann's understanding of the cross as "the divine passion for sinners" as being one-sided. He quotes Moltmann's contention that "What happened on the cross must be understood as an event between God and the Son of God . . . He is acting in himself in this manner of suffering and dying in order to open up in himself life and freedom for sinners."[86] Park is concerned that Moltmann overlooks the other side of the cross, the side that epitomizes *han*, the agony of the victims of sinners. Park here misunderstands the breadth of Moltmann's concept of "sinner" which does not only refer to oppressors but also to the oppressed. For Moltmann, the death of Jesus on the Cross is for both the godless (the sinners who suffer their own turning away from God) and the godforsaken (those who are the innocent victims of pointless sufferings). The resurrection of Jesus, for Moltmann, represents salvation for both the godless and the godforsaken

---

84. Park, *The Wounded Heart of God*, 78.
85. Ibid., 85.
86. Ibid., 120. Park here quotes Moltmann, *The Crucified God*, 192.

because Jesus died for them and identified with them in their suffering of God's absence.

Interestingly, in his *Spirit of Life* which was published in 1992, a year earlier than Park's *The Wounded Heart of God*, Moltmann develops his harmatology, and there he differentiates the perpetrator and the victim. Moltmann understands sin here in terms of "violence committed by people against other people, and by human beings against weaker creatures, and a crime against life."[87] In this way, Moltmann recognizes that violence always has two sides, the perpetrator and the victim; an act of violence that destroys life on both sides but in different ways, the perpetrator through the evil committed and the victim through suffering. When he talks about structural sins, Moltmann recognizes that "we human beings are both the perpetrators and the victims."[88] There are vicious circles of poverty, racial and cultural alienation, and progressive destruction of the environment, in which "human beings are both the perpetrators and the victims of these vicious circles and their deadly spirals . . . ."[89] In his recent book, *Sun of Righteousness, Arise!*, Moltmann shows his far more developed harmatology. He mentions that "victims can become perpetrators too, and in many people the perpetrator side and the victim side are inextricably intertwined."[90]

Nevertheless, by remaining only in the politico-social framework which divides people into perpetrators and victims, Moltmann, like in the case of Park's *han* theology, fails to recognize sufficiently the insight that each individual can potentially be both a perpetrator and a victim concomitantly in their interpersonal as well as social relationships. The oppressed are not only sinned against, but they are also potentially sinning against others. In many cases, oppressors are *han*-ridden. The *han*-ridden also oppress others in different cases. Furthermore, if we keep the dichotomy between *han* for the oppressed and sin for the oppressor, human beings tend to categorize themselves as the victim or the oppressed, and do not responsibly face sin, evil, and injustice.

At its deepest level, sin is not merely a transgression against either a moral or social code. Sin needs to be defined in terms of social trinitarian fellowship. Sin, I propose, is the breaking of fellowship with the triune God. If sin is the breaking of fellowship with the triune God which is expressed

---

87. Moltmann, *The Spirit of Life*, 132.
88. Ibid., 139. See also Moltmann, *Sun of Righteousness, Arise!*, 138.
89. Moltmann, *The Spirit of Life*, 139.
90. Moltmann, *Sun of Righteousness, Arise!*, 138.

Social Trinitarian Understanding of the Cross

in various forms of broken relationships, then we can take *han* as a form of sin, because *han* is originated and prolonged by broken fellowship with God and others. *Han,* as a form of sin, needs to be forgiven and healed also because *han* is often expressed in resentment, hatred, violence, and antagonism toward others. In this respect, sin needs to be defined as "a personal or systemic distortion of trinitarian fellowship." McDougall affirms, if we define sin as "a personal or systemic distortion of trinitarian fellowship," it will provide a suggestive metaphor in which the disparate manifestations of sinfulness among human beings can be described.[91] For instance, sin as broken fellowship encompasses both the classic Augustinian notion of sin as "pride" as well as contemporary feminist reconstruction of sin as "self-loss" or "lack of self-esteem."[92]

By defining sin as "a personal or systemic distortion of trinitarian fellowship", I argue, we can talk about the remedies of sin in terms of reconciliation of human relationships to God and to one another. Reconciliation is made possible through acts of confession, repentance, forgiving, and being forgiven and healed. However, this dimension of God's active forgiving and people's repentance is not emphasized in Moltmann's theological works. We find the reason in his conception of the incarnation and the "surplus of grace." Moltmann finds that the rationale of the incarnation is not in sin but in creation. He views the incarnation as the perfected self-communication of the triune God to his world and a step taken for the sake of perfecting creation.[93] The incarnation of the Son is more than what he calls, "an emergency measure" on God's part, taken in order to counter the emergency of sin in the world.[94] God's love goes beyond the measure of human need because, Moltmann argues, "Ultimately, love cannot be content simply to overcome sin. Love arrives at its goal when it has also overcome the conditions that make sin possible." [95] Accordingly, the Son of God did not become man simply because of the sin of men and women, but rather

---

91. McDougall, "The Return of Trinitarian Praxis?," 202–3. In fact, Moltmann once mentioned briefly that sin is a perverted relationship to God in his book, *God in Creation*, 233–34.

92. McDougall, "The Return of Trinitarian Praxis?," 201. McDougall develops the doctrine of sin within this frame of Trinitarian fellowship specifically as forms of "un-faith, un-hope, and un-love" in her *Pilgrimage of Love: Moltmann on the Trinity and Christian Life,* 236–37.

93. Moltmann, *The Trinity and the Kingdom*, 116.

94. Ibid., 114.

95. Ibid., 116.

The Liberative Cross

for the sake of perfecting creation. The cause of the incarnation is the triune God's inward passion and interest for God's creation.[96] As we understand the incarnation as a step taken by the triune God for the sake of perfecting creation, the incarnation of the Son has a significance of its own. In other words, the Son of God would still have become incarnate even if Adam had never sinned. Consequently, Moltmann dismisses the theological position that regards the incarnation of the Son as the functional presupposition for the atoning sacrifice made necessary by sin.

Another reason why this aspect of forgiveness and repentance is not emphasized in Moltmann's theological works is found in his conception of the "surplus of grace." For Moltmann, the justification of sinners is more than merely the forgiveness of sins: through his resurrection, Christ brings about "the new righteousness, the new life, and the new creature (Rom 4:25)."[97] Expanding on the idea of the crucifixion as "more than" justification, Moltmann talks about the "surplus of grace" over and above the forgiveness and the reconciliation of sinner. This "surplus of grace" which represents the power of the new creation consummates creation-in-the-beginning. It is this "surplus of grace," which will eventually fulfill the eschatological vision in that "human beings shall become truly and finally free" and do what is good just because it is good" without "the torment of choice."[98] Ansell explains how this eschatological vision of perfect freedom becomes possible for Moltmann: the conditions which make sin possible will be transformed with the "*annihilatio nihil*" (the annihilation of hell). Ansell states:

> With the *annihilatio nihili* which is the annihilation of hell (objective genitive)—a hell that begins for Moltmann before creation when God forsakes space so that there may be a world—the annihilation of hell (subjective genitive)—which includes, or comes to expression in, our present tendency to annihilate ourselves in sin-comes to end.[99]

---

96. Ibid., 115–16. Moltmann sees the "*imago Dei*" in Genesis 1: 26–27 as both promise and destiny, and insists that in Christ we have the fulfillment of the promise made to man that he will be "the image of the invisible God." It follows from this that Christ is "the true man," and in fellowship with "the true man" believers discover the truth of human existence.

97. Ibid., 116.

98. Ansell, "The Annihilation of Hell and the Perfection of Freedom," 437–38. See also Moltmann, *God in Creation*, 88.

99. Ibid., 437. See also Moltmann, *Sun of Righteousness, Arise!*, 141.

According to Moltmann, Ansell explains, "With the *annihilatio nihil*, the dangerous space, distance, and distinction that exist between God and creation will be closed, and mutual indwelling will come to characterize the relationship not just between creatures but also between God and creation."[100] In this way, Moltmann offers a theology of hope on the basis of this eschatological vision on the grace of divine nature.[101]

As mentioned above, Moltmann insists that the Son of God did not become man simply because of the sin of men and women, but rather for the sake of perfecting creation. In light of this conception of the incarnation, Moltmann talk about the "surplus of grace" which represents more than the justification of sinners in terms of forgiveness and reconciliation. It represents the power of the new creation, which consummates creation-in-the-beginning. This "surplus of grace" will eventually fulfill the eschatological vision in that "human beings shall become truly and finally free."[102] Accordingly, it is God's "surplus of grace" that will bring about the "universal glorification of God."

Nevertheless, I argue, we are still "on the way" to the eschaton. Until the eschaton, we cannot overemphasize how important it is for human beings to repent their sins and be assured of God's forgiveness so as to be restored to the trinitarian fellowship. I concur with McDougall as she insists that it is by confessing our sins and asking for the forgiveness of God and being reconciled to one another by forgiving and being forgiven that we would hasten "'the return of trinitarian praxis'—of drawing all things into deepening fellowship with God and one another."[103]

So far, in this section, by critiquing Park's *han* theology and Moltmann's conception of sin, I have opposed the dichotomous structure between the oppressed (*han*) and the oppressor (sin), and argued for an inclusive, holistic approach which recognizes their interconnectedness and embraces the need of interdependence regardless of gender, generations, ethnicity, and race. Defining sin as "a personal or systemic distortion of trinitarian fellowship," I have also argued that we need to emphasize the importance of repentance, forgiveness, and reconciliation in our relationships with God and others as we are still on the way to the eschaton.

---

100. Ibid., 437.
101. Ibid., 438.
102. Moltmann, *God in Creation*, 88.
103. McDougall, "Return of Trinitarian Praxis?," 203.

In the following section, I will explore how the concept of *perichoresis* can be applied in Korean-North American women's interpersonal, social relationships. The concept of *perichoresis*, I have argued, can be applied to human community only in an analogous rather than a univocal sense because the world is affected by sin.[104] In other words, the perfectly loving mutuality of the Trinity can be appropriated only in a creaturely way within the conditions of history, and specifically speaking, through *imitatio crucis*. Korean-North American women *as imago Dei* mirror the perichoretic inner life of the Trinity in their contemporary social relationships only through living in *imitatio crucis* and *imitatio relationis*.

Practical Relevance of the Social Trinitarian Theology of the Cross: Living Perichoretic Life in the Private and Social Spheres of Christian Life as Korean-North American Women

By his particular use of the concept of *perichoresis*, Moltmann provides Korean-North American women with a social trinitarian model of human relationships. It signifies the "social unity" that is constituted by the reciprocal self-giving love among the Father, the Son, and the Spirit in freedom.[105] Moltmann insists that the freedom in which the divine persons of the Trinity exercise their perichoretic fellowship is a contrast to the Enlightenment ideal of freedom as autonomy which leads to the potential domination of others. The concept of freedom as "the individual's independent right of disposal over his own life and his own property," atomizes society into a collection of solitary and competing individuals. [106] "Such a model of human freedom," McDougall points out, "at its worst, leads to the subjugation of the weak by the dominant and the dissolution of all true bonds of community."[107] Freedom as domination or lordship over other people is

---

104. See section I.2 above. Here I employed Volf to argue that the Trinity should serve as a model for human relationships, however, in a creaturely way only within the conditions of history. See Volf, *After Our Likeness*, 198–200. See also Volf, "The Trinity is Our Social Program."

105. Moltmann, "Creation, Covenant and Glory," 125–42. See also Moltmann, *The Trinity and the Kingdom*, 129–50.

106. Moltmann, *The Spirit of Life*, 115.

107. Moltmann, *God for a Secular Society*, 156. Cf. McDougall, "The Return of Trinitarian Praxis?," 198.

Social Trinitarian Understanding of the Cross

possible only at the expense of someone else. This model of human freedom has the potential to willfully crush the weak.

In contrast to the definition of freedom as autonomy which leads to the potential domination of others, the social trinitarian model of Christian fellowship promotes a freedom in reciprocal giving and receiving, mutual recognition, and acceptance. This "communicative freedom," according to Moltmann, promotes "a freedom for and with another person." To explain the "communicative freedom," Moltmann quotes the Reformer, particularly Luther's treatise *On the Freedom of a Christian* (1521): Faith makes people "free lords of all things and subject to no one": but love makes them at the same time "perfectly dutiful servants of all subject to all."[108] Accordingly, a society mirroring the social trinitarian model of human relationships is neither a collective society where individuals' potentials and differences are suppressed, nor an individualistic society where fierce competition is engendered among individuals to subjugate others for their own benefits. Rather, it is the society where individuals are free to realize their potential and to serve one another by using their various gifts in love and trust.

In light of the vision for such a society, we need to discuss how Korean-North American women could embody and reflect the trinitarian fellowship which has been concretely demonstrated through the cross. My social trinitarian view of the cross is in contrast to that of feminist theologians' who are concerned that the cross signifies self-abnegation for women. I will argue here that Korean-North American women will achieve their self-worth and self-respect by looking to the cross in faith and living *imitatio crucis* and *imitatio relationis*.

In chapter 2, I demonstrated how feminist theologians like Nakashima Brock and Delores Williams critique the cross as a symbol of violence against the powerless and wish to remove the cross from their Christology. In contrast to the feminist theologians who regard the cross as victimization of the helpless Son, I argued that the cross of Christ, as a trinitarian event, signifies the divine act of love in solidarity with all those who cry out to God in their abandonment. I also discussed how some feminist theologians like Valerie Saiving, Judith Plaskow, and Daphne Hampson critiqued the cross as a symbol of self-abnegation for women. They are afraid that by embracing the "selflessness of love," women will wrongly try to strangle any impulse in them toward a healthy sense of self-differentiation and self-concern. Thus, the feminist theologians focus on how to empower women

---

108. *LW* 31:364. Moltmann quotes this in *The Spirit of Life*, 115.

The Liberative Cross

by emphasizing women's sin as underdevelopment or negation of the self. In so doing, they tend to evade the fact that women are also potentially responsible for social evils. In response to their critique, I argued that women are not excluded from responsibility from perpetration of various forms of oppression. The death of Jesus on the cross does not address only men and their sins but it embraces both men and women in their sins. Therefore, it calls both men and women into *metanoia* from their sin.

Korean-North American women will experience empowerment as they, by looking to the cross in faith, serve others with awareness of their interconnectedness with others and in solidarity with those who suffer. One may ask how Korean-North American women could help others unless they have a healthy sense of self. According to feminist theologians like Valerie Saiving, Judith Plaskow and Daphne Hampson, women need to learn first to reclaim their own autonomy and to be aware of their own distinct desires and needs. I agree that women need to have a healthy sense of self in order to serve others in relationship. However, I also contend that they will come to have self-worth and self-respect as they reach out to others in love. On the basis of the social Trinity, Wilson-Kastner rightly insists that the more women reach out to others and are accepting of connections, the more they will come to consciousness and possession of their selves. She states, "The divine persons of the Trinity are three centers of divine identity, self-aware and self-giving in love, self-possessed yet freely transcending the self in eternal trinitarian interconnectedness."[109] In the Trinity both "the self-focused, the self-conscious dimension" and "the self-transcending, other-directed, outward oriented dimension" nourish each other.[110]

The Diakonia Sisterhood in Korea is a great example which demonstrates how their self-giving love in humility empowers themselves and others in margins. The sisters demonstrate in their life and ministry that it is not by claiming power and accumulating it to themselves that they are empowered. It is rather by their self-giving love in *imitatio crucis* and *imitatio relationis* that they are empowered. The Diakonia Sisterhood in Korea, a Protestant monastic community was established in 1978 under the guidance of a *Minjung* theologian, Ahn, Byung Mu solely for the purpose of helping the poor, the sick, and the uneducated in the margins. Sister Han, Eun Sook, one of the first members of the sisterhood received an E.H. Johnson award from the Presbyterian Church of Canada in 2012 on behalf

---

109. Wilson-Kastner, *Faith, Feminism and Christ*, 126.
110. Ibid.

Social Trinitarian Understanding of the Cross

of the Diakonia Sisterhood.[111] She exemplifies the humility and self-giving Spirit of the Cross in her life journey and work. The sisters living in monastic style and in self-giving service have helped numerous people in the margins, young and old, by providing them with shelters, clothes, food, health services, and education. Their voluntary self-giving life in *imitatio crucis* and *imitatio relationis* is born out of the inner strength drawn from God and their spiritual discipline. It is in contrast to the androcentric, *han* sacrifice of Korean women who were forced into the situation where they had no choice but submission to men. The members of the Diakonia Sisterhood are free in spirit to serve others, seeking to live in solidarity with those who suffer, and have a strong sense of personal empowerment.

The sisters, by choosing to live the simplistic, self-giving, communal life, challenge the individualistic, materialistic world today, and call Korean women to *metanoia* for their tendency to turn Christian faith into *cultus privatus* as a means for their personal comfort and success. Christian faith as *cultus privatus* has caused them to be less concerned for social problems but encouraged triumphalism which motivates them to rule over instead of reaching out to those in the margins with the spirit of solidarity.

The social Trinitarian perspective of the cross, which promotes *imitatio crucis* and *imitatio relationis,* puts into question their very motivation to be rich and powerful. They are challenged to ask, "Do we seek power and prosperity 'to rule over and control others' or do we seek to serve in *imitatio crucis* and *imitatio relationis* to participate in the self-giving love of triune fellowship in every situation (Matt 20:25-8; Mark 10: 45)?" Moltmann rightly insists that power itself (capacity for fulfillment) is not sin; the misuse of power is sin (domination over others).[112] When power is given, it is not to rule over but rather to serve the oppressed, the marginalized, and the weak in solidarity with them in *imitatio crucis* and *imitatio relationis*.

---

111. Sister Eun Sook Han graduated from Han-shin seminary in 1974, and involved in the urban mission for the poorest in Seoul by establishing a credit union for homeless families to save up to rent a place, a nursery for young mothers to be free from babysitting so that they could go to work. She also planted a church for the women and taught them how to read. After many years of urban mission, she cooperated with professor Ahn, Byung Mu (a *Minjung* theologian) to establish a Diakonia sisterhood in Korea to do the social works more effectively with other women who have the same vision in 1978. For her dedication and works, Sister Han received an E. H. Johnson award at the annual conference of the Presbyterian Church of Canada conference held in 2012 at Durham, Ontario in Canada.

112. Chapman Jr., "Hope and the Ethics of Formation: Moltmann as an Interpreter of Bonheoffer," 456.

This social trinitarian model of human fellowship which I propose for Korean-North American women embraces both those who suffer and those who thrive. No matter what situation Korean-North American women may be in, they will always find some who are in need of their help. The privileged are called to serve those who are less privileged than they are. However, even those who are considered less privileged can serve others who may need their help. Through living in *imitatio crucis* and *imitatio relationis*, Korean-North American women will be restored to self-worth and self-respect.

In the following section, I will discuss how Korean-North American women could participate in building an ecclesial community that is modeled after the trinitarian fellowship. The social trinitarian praxis should be applied not only within the church but also beyond the boundaries of the church. However, in the following I will limit my scope within the ecclesial community and discuss their participation in the ecclesial community rather than ecclesiology or missiology *per se*. Within this scope, I will explore how the social, ethical and moral implications of the social Trinity can be applied for the ecclesial life in the spheres of church structure and leadership, Christian mission, and interfaith dialogue.

Praxis of Trinitarian Fellowship at the Corporate Level: The Leadership and the Structure of the Church

We cannot deny that the church is a distinctive form of human community in need of structure and leadership. What does a church look like when it mirrors the trinitarian fellowship in terms of its leadership and structure? In this regard, Moltmann puts forward a notion for non-hierarchical church structures, which reflect his egalitarian model of the Trinity.[113] This aspect of trinitarian fellowship implies that a church should be free of structures of domination and subjugation, and that only reciprocal friendship and spirit of love and freedom should govern in the church.

Volf, who is greatly influenced by Moltmann, attempts to "develop a non-hierarchical but truly communal ecclesiology based on a

---

113. Moltmann, *The Trinity and the Kingdom*, 70. Moltmann writes here that, in the Trinitarian kingdom, God is not the Lord but the merciful Father. In this kingdom there are no servants but only God's free children. He emphasizes that what is required in this kingdom is not obedience and submission but love and free participation.

non-hierarchical doctrine of the Trinity."[114] He argues that the different views on the trinitarian unity have an implication for ecclesial structures. Volf states:

> The structure of the Trinitarian relations is characterized neither by a pyramidal dominance of the one (so Ratzinger) nor by a hierarchical bipolarity between the one and the many (so Zizioulas), but rather by a polycentric and symmetrical reciprocity of the many . . . the symmetrical reciprocity of the relations of the Trinitarian Persons finds its correspondence in the image of the church in which all members serve one another with their specific gifts of the Spirit in imitation of the Lord and through the power of the Father. Like the divine persons, they all stand in a relation of mutual giving and receiving.[115]

Volf rejects both Ratzinger's trinitarian unity of the persons based on the dominance of the one substance of God and Zizioulas's unity of God grounded in the monarchy of the Father.[116] By the notion of *perichoresis*, Volf insists, "The unity of the triune God is grounded in their mutually interior being."[117]

Volf, however, grounds his proposal for the unity of the church not in the mutual *perichoresis* of human beings, but rather the indwelling of the Spirit common to everyone that makes the church into a communion corresponding to the Trinity.[118] He explicates the reason by saying that "there can be no correspondence to the interiority of the divine persons at the human level."[119] The interiority of the divine persons is strictly reciprocal, which is not the case in the relation between God and human beings. He affirms that human *perichoretic* unity does not necessarily follow from divine *perichoretic* unity. Volf confirms the point by exegeting John 17:21, "That they may all be one, as you, Father, are in me and I am in you." He argues:

> This "as" (καθώς) may not be interpreted in the sense of identity, but rather must be interpreted in the sense of similarity . . . The statement "as you, Father, are in me and I am in you" is continued not by "may they also be *in one another*," but rather by "may they

---

114. Volf, *After Our Likeness*, 4.
115. Ibid., 217, 219.
116. Ibid., 201.
117. Ibid., 210.
118. Ibid., 213.
119. Ibid., 210.

also be *in us.*" Human beings can be in the triune God only insofar as the Son is in them (John 17:23; 14:20); and if the Son is in them, then so also is the love with which the Father loves the Son (John 17:26).[120]

Volf concludes that "because the Son indwells human beings through the Spirit, the unity of the church is grounded in the interiority of the Spirit and with the Spirit also in the interiority of the other divine persons, in Christians."[121] Thus, the human *perichoretic* unity does not necessarily follow from divine *perichoretic* unity. It is through the Spirit who indwells the members of the church that they are united to serve one another with their specific gifts of the Spirit.[122]

Volf, in this way, presents an ideal model of the church shaped after divine *perichoretic* unity. The church, according to him, is "a community of men and women whom the Spirit of God has endowed in a certain way for service to each other and to the world in anticipation of God's new creation."[123] However, in reality, I experience in my ministry that the church as a community of forgiven sinners often suffers because of the inner struggles caused by themselves in broken relationships. For that reason, many Korean-North American immigrant churches consume tremendous amounts of energy amending their brokenness and catering to their needs. Consequently, the churches become inert and unable to reach out to the world in anticipation of God's new creation. What I encounter in ministry again and again is the fact that human beings have been affected by sin and that the fullness of restoration of the *imago Dei* is an eschatological reality. The church is on its way toward eschatological reality. The true community of the cross will let the Spirit guide them to continually engage with others in *imitatio crucis*. Without their painstaking engagement of endless love with others in relationships, no changes, no transformation can be expected in the others.

How can Korean-North American women work toward building such a church where the trinitarian fellowship is expressed in a creative mutual partnership between men and women in their service and leadership? First of all, they need to understand Christian leadership from a social trinitarian perspective. In patriarchal structures, the term, "leadership" has

120. Ibid., 212, 213.
121. Ibid.
122. Ibid., 217, 219.
123. Ibid., 231.

Social Trinitarian Understanding of the Cross

often been understood as authority exercised over community. In contrast, leadership which models the trinitarian fellowship demonstrated through the economy of salvation is not authority exercised over community but authority exercised in community for community. In the Gospels, Jesus is presented as one who sought to overturn religious and political leadership as domination. Jesus sympathizes with the suffering through his life and ministry. Through his death on the cross he protests against the injustice in human history. Through his open table fellowship, Jesus invites into the trinitarian fellowship those who were excluded by dominant powers, people like tax collectors, prostitutes, women, children, Gentiles, and so on. In the ministry, Jesus exercised authority by calling and empowering those in the margins to be leaders. Jesus in his leadership demonstrated that power is not something to be accumulated at the top but to be shared and thus multiplied with those in the margins. Therefore, patriarchal styles of leadership dominate the weak and the powerless, but leadership defined by the social trinitarian perspective of the cross seeks to empower the powerless so they can also become leaders to serve others.

In view of the leadership modeled after the trinitarian fellowship, I will expose the patterns of domination and subordination in the ecclesial structure of leadership in Korean churches in both Korea and North America. In so doing, I will review Elisabeth Fiorenza's reconstructed life and practice of woman disciples in the earliest churches as well as LaCugna's social trinitarian perspective on theological feminism.

In chapter 1, I discussed a parallel situation between the early Christian churches in the Roman world[124] and the early Christian church in Korea. The very first recipients of the gospel in Korea were women and children, and women took leadership at the early church not only in ministerial works but also preaching and teaching. However, as intellectual men of higher social class began to join the church, naturally the shifts of leadership took place from women to men and from men of lower classes to intellectual men of higher classes. Thus, patriarchal ecclesial structures were developed, and they were reinforced by patriarchal injunctions in the Scriptures, which are remarkably similar to the patriarchal teachings of Confucianism (Eph 5:21-33; Col 3:18-4:1; 1 Tim 2:10-15; Titus 2:3-5).

Through her reconstructed life and the practices of woman disciples in the earliest churches, Elisabeth Fiorenza exposes an important fact—that patriarchal structures are not inherent in Christian community. Women

---

124. Schüssler Fiorenza, *In Memory of Her*, 251–84.

The Liberative Cross

are welcome by Jesus into a discipleship of equals.[125] Yet, as I have already argued in chapter 1, the household codes of the Pauline and the post-Pauline epistles were developed as a patriarchal reaction to the surrounding cultural norms, which eventually established an order of subordination in the church.[126]

Interestingly, a trinitarian proposal for church leadership and structure seems to have been overlooked by feminist theologians except for LaCugna.[127] LaCugna, like Moltmann and Volf, rejects all forms of inner-trinitarian subordination and the monarchy of the Father. Through the social trinitarian perspective, LaCugna exposes all androcentric biases in complementarian theologies.[128] According to her, the Father of Jesus as the trinitarian God is a relational personal God who does not discriminate based on sex, social status, or ethnicity.[129] In the person of Jesus, God has broken down the barriers, or "the dividing walls" (Eph 2:11-22; Col 1:19-20), and called both men and women, Jews and Gentiles, slaves and free to be one in Jesus Christ so that they may live together harmoniously as one in the new household of God. For LaCugna, this view of the trinitarian God has obvious implications for the shaping of church structures, that there should no longer be structural discriminations between male and female members. She insists that church members are an icon of the Trinity when they live together *perichoretically* in mutual giving and receiving without separateness, or subordination, or division.[130] The human community is to mirror the "divine community of three coequal Persons."[131] Accordingly, in the egalitarian church which reflects the divine sociality in equal mutuality, women are not excluded from

---

125. Russell, *Church in the Round*, 61. Russell explores through the Pauline letters that Paul also explicitly mentions women as his missionary co-workers, with the same terms being used for women and men in this regard: Prisca as co-worker; Junia as apostle; Apphia as sister (Rom 16:3, 7; Phlm 2). Especially in Rom 16:1, Phoebe is called not only *diakonos* (minister, missionary, servant), but also *prostatis* (leading officer, president, governor, superintendent). In comparison to the ministry of deaconess in the later church, Russell affirms, their ministry was not limited to ministry with women or to specific roles or functions.

126. Schüssler Fiorenza, *In Memory of Her*, 285–334

127. LaCugna, *God for Us*, 267–70. See also LaCugna, "God in Communion with Us: The Trinity," 83–108.

128. Ibid., 267–70.

129. LaCugna, "God in Communion with Us: The Trinity," 85–91.

130. LaCugna, *God for Us*, 402.

131. Ibid., 278.

acting in *persona Christi* for the preaching of the Word and administrating church ordinances, baptisms, and the Lord's Supper.

Korean-North American immigrant churches have become much more receptive to women's ordination than before. However, some conservative churches still reject women's ordination on the basis of the theology of complementarity, reinforced by the traditional Confucian perspective of women as subordinate to men.[132] This theology of complementarity is accepted and preached by conservative Korean pastors, who do not acknowledge the cultural conditioning of the biblical text by context in their hermeneutics. According to Werner Neuer, a prominent proponent of this theology of complementarity, women possess the full image of God; however, they were created to be subject to men. The fall, according to Neuer, resulted from the man listening to the woman and submitting to her leadership. He also contends that the fact that Adam named the woman "Eve" confirms his superiority over her (Gen 2:23). Neuer favors the teachings of Paul (i.e., 1 Cor 2:3; Eph 5:12; Col 3:18; Titus 2:5), through which the subordination of women to men is emphasized in comparison to the relationship of the Son to the Father.[133]

In response to this theology of complementarity, LaCugna rightly argues that the subordination of woman to man, as a consequence of the fall, does not belong to God's divinely decreed plan. She states:

> Redemption means bringing to fruition and completion God's providential plan, revealed in Christ, that male and female, Jew and Gentile, free and slave shall dwell together as one in the new household of God. The church is to be the visible sign and witness to this reign of God in which all the false rulers in the world are exposed and overturned—including the false rule of the *pater* over women, slaves and children.[134]

With regard to the doctrine of the Trinity, LaCugna also persuasively points out that theologians who make complementarity argument do not realize that the church also tried to overcome the very heresy of Arianism to

---

132. Neuer, *Man and Woman in Christian Perspective*, 34–41. See also LaCugna, "God in communion with Us: The Trinity," 94–99. Cf. Horowitz, "Aristotle and Women," 183–213. See also Ruether, "Misogynism and Virginal Feminism in the Fathers of the Church," 150–83.

133. Ibid., 112.

134. LaCugna, "God in Communion with Us: The Trinity," 98.

eradicate all subordination between the Father and the Son.[135] LaCugna concludes: "The doctrine of the Trinity not only supports the full equality of male and female but also there is no intrinsic reason why men should be correlated with God the Father and women with God the Son."[136]

As argued above, both Jesus' discipleship of equals and the doctrine of social Trinity assume equality for women in all orders of the church. The conservative Korean churches which reject women's ordination can no longer argue from either a biblical or theological standpoint. They are left only with the traditional or cultural view of women, which has also lost its stronghold. The change of the socio-political milieu in Korea and the egalitarian society of North America, where they now live, are certainly at odds with the prejudice they hold toward women today. Church leadership, therefore, needs to be molded into a social trinitarian model of leadership which values equality and reciprocity among members.

According to this model, I have argued that the patterns of domination and subordination in ecclesial leadership and structure are not inherent in Christian community. Jesus' discipleship of equals and the doctrine of social Trinity assume equality for women in all orders of the church, including preaching the Word and administrating church ordinances. However, I also emphasize that it is not only ordained women but all women who are called to act in *persona Christi* by serving others with their different gifts. This conception of the call for all women to act in *persona Christi* in service leads appropriately to the next topic: The different ways in which the church, as an expression of God's life-giving, acts as a liberating instrument to the world when implementing the praxis of Trinitarian fellowship.

Praxis of Trinitarian Fellowship at the Corporate Level: Mission

The perichoretic relationship of the three divine "persons" provides the foundation for a missional understanding of the church. The concept of *perichoresis* signifies trinitarian fellowship, which is constituted by the reciprocal self-giving love among Father, Son, and Holy Spirit. The Trinity, however, is not a closed circle, but an "open and inviting" communion,

---

135. Athanasius and the Cappadocians struggled vigorously against Arianism to eradicate all subordination between the Father and the Son.

136. LaCugna, "God in Communion with Us: The Trinity," 98.

Social Trinitarian Understanding of the Cross

desiring to share itself freely with its creation.[137] According to Karl Rahner, the unique relationship of the three divine persons, which is revealed through Jesus Christ (economic Trinity), grants us a picture of the divine inner life of God (immanent Trinity).[138] Moltmann, in agreement with Rahner, states that "the relations between the discernible and visible history of Jesus and the God whom he called 'my Father' correspond to the relation of the Son to the Father in eternity."[139] In other words, for Moltmann, "The *missio ad extra* reveals the *missio ad intra*. The *missio ad intra* is the foundation for *the missio ad extra*."[140] In a similar line of thought, Fensham insists, "If the economic Trinity (God's loving mission to the world) shows us the immanent Trinity (who God is in God-self), then the very nature of God's relationship with creation is missional and aimed at drawing all into a loving and diverse community."[141]

In the missional relationship which the triune God has with creation, the church finds the reason for its existence. The church exists as God's life-giving instrument to the world. As Fensham argues, "The church is not the whole mission of God, but has a role to play in joining God's life-giving and liberating mission for God's creation."[142] Mission is then the work of the triune God for the sake of God's own creation, and the church is privileged to participate in this liberating mission of God (*missio Dei*). Moltmann affirms, "It is not the church that has a mission of salvation to fulfill in the world; it is the mission of the Son and the Spirit through the Father that includes the church."[143] In this respect, the church can never be considered the author of mission.

If the church is called to participate in the history of God's dealings with God's own creation, we need to know in what ways we can exercise the calling of God to be a missional church. Moltmann shows us the ways in which God's church participates in God's mission in his monograph, *The*

---

137. Moltmann, "The Inviting Unity of the Triune God," 87. See also Moltmann, *The Trinity in the Power of the Spirit*, 56.

138. Rahner, "Remarks on the Dogmatic Treatise *De Trinitate*," 87. See also Moltmann, *The Crucified God*, 240.

139. Moltmann, *The Church in the Power of the Spirit*, 54.

140. Ibid.

141. Fensham, *Emerging from the Dark Age Ahead*, 17–18.

142. Ibid., 18.

143. Moltmann, *The Church in the Power of the Spirit*, 64.

The Liberative Cross

Church in the Power of the Spirit.[144] As the fellowship of love, the missional church participates in the uniting of humanity, in the uniting of society with nature, and in the uniting of creation with God. As "the church under the cross", it also participates in the history of God's suffering.[145] At the same time, the missional church participates in the history of the divine joy. It rejoices over every conversion and liberation because the church is itself the fellowship of the converted and liberated.

Among these marks of the missional church, I will focus on "the church under the cross," and through it, challenge Korean-North American women to have a new understanding of the mission. Triumphalism prevails among Korean churches today, thinking of mission as "Christianity triumphing over others."[146] However, in the New Testament, the church is often defined as a community of the cross (Rom 5:1-5; 2 Cor 4:5-11) that carries its mission with servitude (Matt 20:28). Thus, a distinct mark of true Christian mission is not triumphalism but servitude, humility and respect for others. The most prominent mark of the true church, Douglas Hall insists, is her suffering nature and participation in the suffering of the Crucified in the life of the world.[147] In discussing the apostolic vocation of the church today, Fensham rightly engages Martin Luther's theology of the cross. Martin Luther in Heidelberg Disputation argues that God is to be known in the pain and suffering of the cross. In contrast, "the theology of glory" is a theology based on human achievement and the ability by which people discern God and are justified. Fensham argues, "This paradoxical quality to the knowledge of God can be extended to an understanding of the church that lives most truly in suffering and humility."[148] In view of this mark of a missional church, churches seeking power and prestige today are called to repentance. Douglas John Hall, as a prophetic voice, invokes these existential questions which arise out of the first Christendom:

> If it gives comfort to crusading Christian conservatives to think that the future still holds a longed-for triumph of the Christian religion, then they had better think again about the actual history of Christian triumphalism in Western (Northern) experience. Do they really wish to become an intolerant, authoritarian, violent

---

144. Ibid., 65.
145. Ibid.
146. Fensham, *Emerging from the Dark Age Ahead*, 58.
147. Hall, *The Cross in Our Context*, 140.
148. Fensham, *Emerging from the Dark Age Ahead*, 64.

religion, ready to go to war not only with Iraq but with Islam and many other religious alternatives that can now no longer be nicely confined to specific territories? Do they really want a Biblicism that is basically uninformed by historical and linguistic research and that dismisses not only complex modern scientific theories like evolution but even much of the ordinary science on which our daily lives are not based? Would they welcome a moral ethos in which not only gays and lesbians but also divorced people were consigned to hellfire, and the psychologically ill were considered demon-ridden?[149]

Hall concludes with this assertion: "We in the once-powerful, now-reduced churches of the West must work out our future in relation to our own peculiar past and present, from which there is no turning back to some earlier religious mentality or form of church and society."[150]

In light of Hall's assertion, Korean-North American churches are pressed to ask whether they desire the power and prestige Christendom represents or a faithful life in *imitatio crucis*. Triumphalism prevails among many Korean churches today as they boast in the size of their membership and the grandeur of their buildings rather than celebrate in the conversions and liberations of people, made possible only through a humble participation of the cross. Their desire for triumphalism instead of humble servitude has caused competition and rivalry among Korean-North American churches. Mega-churches, having greater facilities and better programs, always win in the competition to accommodate more members into their own. Such rivalry and competition among Korean-North American churches have brought them a reputation of being contentious and incapable of working together. It has also caused smaller churches to struggle and suffer greatly for mere survival. Korean-North American churches need to seriously consider the self-emptying, self-giving nature of God which is demonstrated concretely in the economy of relationship within the triune God. In so doing, they will take part in the *missio Dei* as the apostolic church, the church being sent to draw others into the triune fellowship through conversions and liberations in *imitatio crucis*.

The missional church "under the cross" is also characterized by the "open friendship" to everyone. Jesus Christ demonstrates the essence of trinitarian fellowship through his infinite self-giving love in his ministry and death on the cross. According to Moltmann, the infinite self-giving

149. Hall, *The Cross in Our Context*, 164.
150. Ibid., 165.

love of Jesus Christ takes on a visible form in the "open friendship." In his compassion and solidarity, Jesus offered the "open friendship" to everyone. This "open friendship" was especially offered to those in the margins of society, the sinners, the poor, and the outcast.[151] Jesus recognized their dignity as people and did away with the social prejudice they suffered. This "open friendship" is particularly demonstrated by Jesus' attitude toward Samaritans in the gospels. In contrast to the prevailing negative attitude that the Jews have toward Samaritans (John 4; John 8:48; Luke 17:11-19; Luke 10:29-37), Jesus welcomes them to celebrate the messianic feast of grace together as a way to extend his offer of "open friendship." Following the example of Jesus, the apostle Paul also emphasizes that there should be no discrimination between Jews and Gentiles in the new community of Christ (Gal 3:26-29). He explains that Christ has broken down the dividing wall of hostility between Jews and Gentiles through his life, ministry, and death (Eph 2:11-22). Therefore, Gentiles and Jews should be able to worship the same God through Christ who is open and inviting toward those who are radically "Other." In the New Testament, we witness that Jesus and his followers did not aim to create a generic community of cultural homogeneity but rather an open, inviting community by respecting each other's differences and being mutually interdependent.

In view of the "open friendship", which respects and accepts each other's differences, Korean-North American women are challenged to overcome the "us" mentality which they develop in living in a foreign country. This mentality arises because the majority of first generation Korean-North American women struggle with a language barrier which prevents them from being open to people of different cultures and languages. Thus, they tend to solely associate and exercise faith amongst themselves. I argue that their boundary of friendship needs to be expanded to embrace all people and not just the ones who resemble them in social status, gender, ethnicity, or religion. This "open friendship" calls them to live with a full awareness of interconnectedness with others. In opening up to all people from different cultures, Korean-North American women will learn to be aware of the various global issues they face today such as the absence of world peace, ecological problems, hardening poverty, waning public health, racism, and sexual exploitation. They will also actively participate in finding solutions and campaign together with people from diverse backgrounds of

---

151. Moltmann, *The Spirit of Life*, 256–58.

Social Trinitarian Understanding of the Cross

ethnicity, culture, and religion to improve the living conditions for all of God's creation.

Generally speaking, mission has been understood by Korean-North American women in the spatial sense: to evangelize all nations according to the Great Commission in Matthew 28:19. However, the spectrum of mission will be expanded if they understand it from a social trinitarian perspective. Mission understood from a social trinitarian perspective includes not only the intercultural, interracial dimension but also the intergenerational dimension. I have already mentioned that the Trinity, Moltmann suggests, is an "open and inviting" communion desiring to share itself freely with all of God's creation.[152] God's creation includes not only all nations, ethnicities, animals, plants and etc., but also the generations to come. The triune God yearns for fellowship even with the generations to come. The eschatological vision, which awaits the full restoration of *perichoretic* fellowship, embraces the generations to come. To participate in this vision, Korean-North American women are sent not only to other nations in the spatial sense but also to the next generations, that is, to the future.[153] The mission which reaches the next generations is founded on God's desire to restore perichoretic fellowship with all of God's creation. It is God's desire that both parents and children come together with one heart to serve God (Mal 4:5-6). On the day of the Pentecost in Acts 2, we witness how the Holy Spirit has brought not only Jews and Gentiles but also the young and old to be one family in God. There, the Apostle Peter interpreted it as the fulfillment of Joel's prophecy (Joel 2:28-32), where God promised to pour out the Spirit on "all people," and their "sons and daughters will prophesy."

Korean-North American immigrant churches have enthusiastically involved themselves with the Korean overseas missionary movement.[154]

---

152. Moltmann, "The Inviting Unity of the Triune God," 87.

153. The SLNG (spiritual leaders for the next generations) movement, which is called in Korean *cha-young-ji* un-dong, has been reaching out to churches in Korea and North America since Rev. Dr. Chun Hoi Heo initiated it in 2004. According to him, this movement is not only to help local churches raise spiritual leaders for the future but also to recover the essence of Christianity today which was initiated by Jesus Christ and preached by the early Christian believers. Here I offer a theological grounding for the movement from a different perspective on the basis of the eschatological vision of the full restoration of perichoretic fellowship which embraces the generations to come.

154. GKYM (Global Korean Young Adult Mission) festival is an English-language movement that encourages second-generation North American Korean young adults to "finish the missional task to reach the unreached, unengaged people groups of the world." See advertisement that appeared in *International Bulletin of Missionary Research*.36,

The Liberative Cross

Every year, English speaking Korean-North Americans celebrate the GKYM (Global Korean Young Adult Mission) festival which draws over two thousand attendants. Many second generation young people aspire to become a professional and go to developing countries in Africa or Asia to share the gospel as well as to help them with their professional knowledge and skills. Within the ethos of Korean immigrant churches, they are often compared to the apostle Paul, who was the first missionary to the Gentiles. The apostle Paul was able to do the foreign mission because he had Roman citizenship and was able to speak Greek. Likewise, the second generation Korean-North American young people, as English speaking Canadian or American citizens, have a great advantage to actively participate in overseas mission.

Whereas mission in this spatial sense, to reach out the tribes and nations who have not heard the gospel, has been emphasized as the primary concern for many Korean-North American immigrant churches, the generational dimension of mission has often been neglected. This is disconcerting because my years of experience of ministry in a Korean-North American context leads me to be convinced that the most urgent missional task is the restoration of perichoretic fellowship with younger generations. In this postmodern, post-Christendom era, many young people leave the church. Korean-North American immigrant Churches are no exception. A lot of the second generation Korean-North American young people leave the church once they reach adulthood. For this reason, it is urgent that Korean-North American women have a sense of being sent to the future by raising spiritual leaders for the next generations. This mission to the future, I propose, can be carried out in the form of "relational praxis." [155] Traditionally, the majority of Korean-North American churches have sought to separate the youth ministry from the adult ministry due to language differences and the belief that youth do not want to be disturbed by their parents. However, I propose a "relational praxis", by which their broken relationships with God and parents will be restored. The "relational praxis" encourages mutual participation between the first and second generations in weekly church activities, mission trips, conferences, retreats, intergenerational worship services, and etc. In this way, the "relational praxis" will increase opportunities for the Spirit to flow from parents to children and

---

no. 3 (2012) 142.

155. I propose a "relational praxis" to increase relationship connections between the first and the second generations through mutual participation in various church activities.

Social Trinitarian Understanding of the Cross

from children to parents, and from leaders to young believers and from young believers to leaders. This "relational praxis" will also increase the mutual understanding between the first and the second generations and strengthen their sense of belonging to the same family of God.

Holistic mission is founded on the essence of trinitarian fellowship, which involves "openness to one another, sharing with one another, and respect for one another."[156] What we need to remember in participating in the mission of God (*missio Dei*) is that it needs to be done with humility in the spirit of the *analogia relationis*. We participate in the mission of God in the manner which the triune God has been engaged in this flawed world; that is, through God's self-giving and self-emptying love, in order to heal, restore, and transform people by drawing them to the triune fellowship. The mission is never carried out in a vacuum: It is always carried out among people from diverse ethnicities, cultures, and religions. In fact, Korean-North American women, living in multicultural, multifaith environments, daily encounter people of different cultures and religions in their own neighborhoods and working places. In addition, many second-generation women and men have married interculturally or interreligiously. This increasing reality of a multifaith environment requires us to discuss from a social trinitarian perspective what kind of attitude Christian believers need in order to live harmoniously with people of different faiths and cultures. We are then appropriately led to the next topic: interreligious dialogue.

Praxis of Trinitarian Fellowship at the Corporate Level: Interreligious Dialogue

Many Korean Christian believers, as I already mentioned in chapter 1, have been theologically influenced by a fundamentalist named, "Hyung-Nong Park who saw other religions as weeds or enemies to be destroyed.[157] Thus, they easily fall into the danger of religious imperialism and arrogance. For instance, on the 26th of October in 2010, a few fundamentalist Christians went into the main lecture hall of a Buddhist temple called Bong-eun-sa and held a Christian worship service.[158] A few other cases similar to this in-

---

156. Moltmann, "'The Fellowship of the Holy Spirit': On Pneumatology," 57.

157. I already discussed Hyung-Nong Park's position and influence on Korean Christians in chapter 1. Still today, his theology prevails among the dominant conservative Protestant churches in South Korea.

158. "Bong Eun Sa . . .," Oct. 26, 2010. www.ohmynews.com (accessed October 26, 2010).

The Liberative Cross

cident have been reported on TV in Korea recently. Some Korean tourists in Islamic countries have been noticed by the public as they were going around mosques praying that Muslims might turn to Christ in repentance. These events have caused people to raise questions about what kind of attitudes Christians should have toward other religions. Because of the exclusivist tendency which these incidents exemplify, Christianity is often misunderstood by nonbelievers in Korea as a foreign religion in conflict with their traditional culture, or as a religion of arrogance and domination.[159]

Having immigrated to multicultural North America, Korean-North American Christian women live in a unique situation where they are daily exposed to people from different cultures and religions. In this pluralistic North American context, there is an urgent need to articulate a proper Christian theology that promotes human solidarity and openness toward other religions. What does a social trinitarian understanding of the cross offer on attitudes that Korean-North American women should have toward people from different cultures and religions? In this section, I will discuss the purpose of interreligious dialogue, and the attitudes which a social trinitarian understanding of the cross encourages for Korean-North American women in dialogue with the religious other.

In discussing the purpose of interreligious dialogue, Moltmann makes a distinction between "direct" and "indirect dialogue."[160] "Direct dialogue," according to him, has to do with the confrontation and comparison of different religious concepts of transcendence and salvation, the understanding of humanity and nature. Here, Christianity comes forward with its trinitarian view of God, theology of the cross, doctrine of salvation, and eschatology. In the same manner, other religions also come forward with their unique faith claims. Each of them must be taken seriously in these convictions. The goal of the "direct" interreligious dialogue, however, is not to arrive at a general consensus among different religions. Rather, it is to express our love in the human situation today. According to Moltmann, those who are engaged in interreligious dialogues come to find where religions harbor forces that are hostile to life and destructive of the world, and what changes are required for them to affirm life and preserve the world.[161]

It is, however, always questionable whether the world religions, through "direct dialogue," can arrive at peace between themselves and

---

159. Park, *Christianity and Encounter of Asian Religions*, 125–26
160. Moltmann, *Experiences in Theology*, 20.
161. Ibid., 21.

Social Trinitarian Understanding of the Cross

make a contribution to the peace of the world. Thus, for Moltmann, "interreligious dialogue must be expanded by dialogue with the ideologies of the contemporary world. Together with them, it must ultimately be related to the people who are living, suffering and dying in the world today."[162] He categorizes this pragmatic aspect of interreligious dialogue as "indirect dialogue" in the sense that those who are engaged in the dialogue do not talk about their own religious beliefs directly. They, rather, talk about their common concerns which involve the social questions and the environmental issues at local or global levels.

With regard to attitudes in interreligious dialogue, Moltmann insists, "To be capable of dialogue means to merit dialogue."[163] Only convinced Christians, Jews, Muslims, and the others, can enter into dialogue. Accordingly, the person who falls in the relativism of the multicultural society does not merit dialogue because the representatives of other religions are only interested in convinced Christians, Jews, Muslims, and others. Thus, Moltmann rejects pluralism. He affirms, "Pluralism is not as such a religion. It is not even a particularly helpful theory for interfaith dialogue. People who begin with this motto soon have nothing more to say, and no one will go on listening to them either."[164]

Even though Moltmann deals with interreligious dialogue in both books, *The Church in the Power of the Spirit* and *Experiences in Theology*, Moltmann does not theologically back up his assertion that pluralism is not a helpful theory for inter-religious dialogue. He does not develop a theology in inter-religious dialogue on the basis of his conception of the social Trinity either. Moltmann just briefly mentions in *The Church in the Power of the Spirit* that we must enter into dialogue with people of a different faith "out of the depths of the understanding of God."[165] He elaborates "the depth of the understanding of God" in terms of God's openness to humanity, God's passion, God's vulnerability, and God's power in weakness. Moltmann states, "The God who wins power in the world through the helplessness of his Son, who liberates through his self-giving and whose strength is mighty in weakness can only be testified to in dialogue and in the wounds and transformations which dialogue brings with it."[166] Nowhere

---

162. Moltmann, *The Church in the Power of the Spirit*, 162.
163. Moltmann, *Experiences in Theology*, 18.
164. Ibid., 19.
165. Moltmann, *The Church in the Power of the Spirit*, 161.
166. Ibid.

The Liberative Cross

in both books mentioned above does Moltmann relate the concept of *perichoresis* to his discussions of interreligious dialogue. Nor does he converse with pluralist theologians who decenter the cross of Christ in Christian faith and theology. According to Harold Wells, pluralist theologians hold that "Christ-centered theologies, operating with high Christologies of a unique and unsurpassable Jesus as incarnation of God, stand in the way of any significant rapprochement."[167] Consequently, they decenter the cross of Christ in Christian faith by claiming that there are many more or less equivalent ways of salvation.[168]

In view of these claims of pluralist theologians, we need to discuss whether a proper attitude for interreligious dialogue can be drawn from a social trinitarian understanding of the cross. I argue that it is neither by relativizing nor by reducing our truth claims that we will be able to avoid arrogance to the religious other. Rather, a proper attitude for interreligious dialogue can be drawn from a social trinitarian understanding of the cross. Fensham affirms, "The dialogical nature of God's mission is emphasized in the recognition of God's unity in diversity."[169] According to him, "Just as *perichoresis* shows the mutual recognition and self-giving nature of the persons of the Trinity, it also grounds the church in constant, self-giving dialogue."[170] The notion of *perichoresis* assures the integrity and the distinctiveness of each person of the Trinity and describes a kind of unity in which the plurality is preserved rather than erased.[171] This mutual indwelling within the Trinity is complete, and yet the integrity of each person is still completely affirmed and maintained as well. When this notion of *perichoresis* is applied in the area of interreligious dialogue, it assures the particularity of each religion (which needs to be protected and maintained) and allows for coexistence through harmony in diversity. Therefore, interreligious dialogue does not aim to be fused or unified into another religion. Rather, it recognizes incommensurable elements between religions. In this respect, people of different religions certainly cannot be relativists. Pre-

---

167. Wells, *The Christic Center: Life Giving and Liberating*, 183.

168. Ibid., 201–10. Wells presents a good debate on the uniqueness and finality of Jesus Christ by critiquing a pluralist, namely, Knitter's position presented in his book *Jesus and the Other Names*, and discusses whether "the pluralist decentering of Jesus" is more respectful of world religions and more life-giving and liberating than the position that asserts the uniqueness and finality of Jesus Christ.

169. Fensham, *Emerging from the Dark Age Ahead*, 152.

170. Ibid.

171. Volf, "The Trinity is Our Social Program," 409.

Social Trinitarian Understanding of the Cross

dominantly in this pluralistic world, Harold Wells recognizes, people run the risk of not taking religious truth claims seriously.[172] In the name of tolerance, they often undermine deep and passionate faith. In such position, any form of commitment cannot be expected. Truth claimers, according to Wells, are inevitably exclusive in some degree. It is not necessarily arrogant to make exclusive/universal truth claims. People make exclusive/universal claims constantly in fields such as politics, ethics, and aesthetics without being accused of arrogance.[173] We must assert our truth claims but do so with humility, acknowledging that others do not share them and allowing them to make different faith statements.[174] One thing we need to recognize in our truth claims is that "truth claims in theology are not universally demonstrable, i.e., we make statements about God, Jesus, salvation, by faith and not by sight (2 Cor 5:7)."[175]

Finally, if Korean-North American Christian women apply this notion of *perichoresis* in the area of interreligious dialogue, they will move away from the religious arrogance and imperialism which they, as ardent Christians, often fall into. A few guidelines for inter-religious dialogue can be drawn on the basis of the perichoretic fellowship of the triune God. First, inter-religious dialogue based on the perichoretic fellowship of the triune God does not seek a single, unified religion. Rather, it recognizes and respects the integrity of the particularity of each religion rather than trying to blend everything together. Secondly, it reflects the self-giving love and humility which the triune God demonstrated through the cross. Fensham insists, like *Dalit* theologians (*Dalit* refers to a group of people traditionally regarded as untouchable in India), our dialogue should begin by first listening to the poor and the marginalized, reflecting the self-giving, the self-emptying love of God.[176] Lastly, it is possible to firmly hold on to our faith in the crucified Christ and yet be open-minded toward the religious "other" because of the universal work of the Holy Spirit.[177] The universality

---

172. Wells, "The Holy Spirit and the Theology of the Cross," 482.

173. Ibid., 483.

174. Ibid., 482.

175. Ibid., 483.

176. Fensham, *Emerging from the Dark Age Ahead*, 70. For Dalit theology, see Lilburn's summary of the 2001 congress of Asian Theologians and his discussion of Wesley Ariarajah's contribution on interreligious dialogue: http://daga.dhs.org/daga/cca/ctc/ctc02-04/ctc0204b.htm (accessed October 7, 2004).

177. Pinnock is a leading evangelical theologian from Canada. He holds to the uniqueness of the person of Jesus Christ by arguing that a high Christology does not

of the Spirit of God, sent from the Father of Jesus Christ, appears in the Scriptures without renouncing the particularity or reducing the scandal of the cross.[178] As Harold Wells argues, even though the universal presence of the Holy Spirit does not establish a natural capacity of human beings to know God, it ensures what kind of attitude we should have toward the truth claiming of other religions. He argues,

> If the Spirit of God, whom Christians also name Spirit of Christ, is present and at work in all creation and with all people, we must eagerly expect to find truth and wisdom in many places. It is not for nothing that God's spirit is omnipresent in the world. The presence of the Lord of exodus and resurrection is always for blessing, and for truth. That is why we listen intently to hear what God's wisdom has taught the Confucians, the Taoist, the Muslim. That is why we thank God for the courage and love of justice which we find in many secular social activists; we may find in them too a risky and

---

necessarily mean exclusivism. According to him, the basis of an open attitude to all peoples theologically is the doctrine of the Triune God and of his prevenient grace. In Christ, "God's secret plan for the creation is disclosed." Therefore the incarnation "does not weaken but seals and strengthens our confidence in the universal salvific will of God." The Logos, which was made flesh in Jesus of Nazareth, is present in the entire world and in the whole of human history. See Pinnock, *A Wideness in God's Mercy*, 77. Pinnock also argues that by acknowledging the work of the Spirit in creation we are actually allowing a more universal perspective of the Spirit's ministry in which the work of preparing hearts to hear the gospel is not set in antithesis to the fulfillment of the gospel in Christ. He insists, "What one encounters in Jesus is the fulfillment of previous invitations of the Spirit." See Pinnock, *Flame of Love: a Theology of the Holy Spirit*, 63. According to his pneumatological theology of religions, religions, rather than being either futile human attempts to reach God or outright obstacles to a saving knowledge of God, can be Spirit-used pointers to and means of contact with God. See ibid., 203. In his book *Meeting of Religions and the Trinity*, 128–32, D'Costa, a Roman Catholic theologian, champions a Trinitarian theology of religions by insisting that the works of the Trinity *ad extra* are undivided, and the presence of the Spirit among other religions also means the presence of the triune God. He also argues that the presence of the Spirit and thus the triune God in other religions also means some kind of presence of the church since in the biblical tradition (especially in the *Paraclete* passages of John 14–16) the presence of the Spirit is connected to the church. See also ibid., 117–27.

178. Wells, "Holy Spirit and Theology of the Cross," 484–92. Wells argues here that as we look at "Spirit of God" and "Holy Spirit" in the Bible we find a dialectic of particularity/universality, and exclusivity/inclusivity. He concludes, "In view of the universality of the Holy Spirit, it is the foolishness of God on the cross which can move Christians to an attitude of vulnerable openness to people of other faiths and of no faith . . . It is this very particularity and scandalously exclusivist/universalist faith in the crucified Christ as Savior of the world which can move us to an attitude of humility in our encounter with others, and to genuine eagerness both to lean and to share." Ibid., 491–92.

Social Trinitarian Understanding of the Cross

visionary thrust toward the future which is indeed an authentic "faith" response to the blowing of God's Spirit in history.[179]

The universal presence and work of the Holy Spirit ensures that we encounter people of other religions with confidence and openness, expecting to find wisdom and truth in them. Because of the universal presence and work of the Holy Spirit, as Wells insists, we can also engage ourselves in interreligious dialogue by recognizing our own vulnerability in faith to find where religions harbor forces hostile to life and destructive of the world, and what changes have to be made for the religions to become a life-giving, liberating power.

As argued above, the social trinitarian fellowship culminated at the cross offers a model for Korean-North American women in interreligious dialogue. Modeling the trinitarian fellowship in generosity and freedom, they will take up an attitude of "open friendship" as they listen to the religious other and share their different faiths and life stories. However, it is not by relativizing or reducing their truth claims that they show open-mindedness toward other religions. Rather, even though they hold on to a faith that is centered on the cross of Jesus Christ, Korean-North American women will face the religious other with confidence and openness because the Holy Spirit is at work in all people. The triune God, who has engaged in creation, is a suffering God who brings life through death and liberates through love. It means Korean-North American women, as *imago Dei*, enter into dialogical relations with attitudes of humility and hospitality toward the religious other.

In chapter 4 I offer the contribution of a social trinitarian theology of the cross toward a feminist Christian praxis for Korean-North American women. This is therefore a contextual and socially located reading of the social trinitarian theology as offered by Jürgen Moltmann and others. I have presented the trinitarian fellowship, which is concretely demonstrated at the cross, as *analogia relationis* to guide human relationships. Korean-North American women are called to mirror the perichoretic relationship of the three divine in various relationships with others. However, because of the gap between the Trinity and sinful, finite human beings, the trinitarian cycle of perfect self-giving love in reciprocity cannot be simply copied in this world marred by evil and sin. Therefore, Korean-North American women are to emulate the suffering love of the triune God to engage in the

---

179. Ibid., 490. For discussion of the Holy Spirit's work in movements for social justice and liberty, see Comblin, *The Holy Spirit and Liberation*, 51–55.

transformation of the deeply flawed world of sin. It is *imitatio crucis* and *imitatio relationis* that they should hold true not only for social knowledge but also for social practice. Nevertheless, *imitatio crucis* and *imitatio relationis* would be impossible without the work of the Holy Spirit through which they come to respond to the triune God. The cross of Christ is the culmination of the self-giving love for the other, and it reveals the essence of trinitarian fellowship in mutuality, reciprocity, equality, and generosity. On this basis, I have explored various ways in which the trinitarian fellowship directs its praxis for Korean-North American women both in the private and corporate levels.

Conclusion

I ENDEAVORED IN THIS thesis to offer both first and second generation Korean-North American women with a theological grounding of the orthopraxy which calls them to live as *imago Dei*, mirroring the triune fellowship. In so doing, I emphasized three elements: First, an appropriate theology of the cross meets the challenges or concerns of developing reality. Second, it is a feminist theology in the sense that I am seeking to retrieve a theology of the cross which is life-giving and liberating for both first and second generation Korean-North American women. Third, it is a social trinitarian approach to the theology of the cross that can reveal the essence of God to be in relation, mutuality and community in diversity.

In seeking for a theology that can meet the challenges of a developing reality, I analyzed the *Sitz-im-Leben* of the first generation Korean-North American women and revealed how the changing milieu of Korea and their life experiences in the multicultural context have influenced them in their understanding of the cross of Christ. I argued that they cannot be treated as a monolithic group of *han*-ridden people because of their varied experiences of power dynamics. Consequently, we should not construct a theology of the cross on the basis of the presupposition that the first generation Korean-North American women are victims in the binary opposition between men and women or between the dominant and the marginal.

I also analyzed how second generation Korean-North American women view Christianity differently from first generation Korean-North American women. Whereas first generations tend to practice Christianity as a means of personal success or as a means to divine salvation which is heavenly and otherworldly, the second generation born and raised in the multicultural society require a new understanding of the Cross that would allow them to envision a new human community based on the values of equality, mutuality, and reciprocity between men and women and between different races and cultures. Both first and second generation Korean-North

American women as "beings-in-the world", having their existence in a network of life, are challenged to move toward an understanding of the cross which allow them to recognize the importance of mutuality and reciprocity in human relationships. Thus, I take it as a prophetic call to retrieve a theology of the cross which provokes both first and second generation Korean-North American women to live in this global world as people fully aware of their need for interdependence, mutuality, and reciprocity, regardless of gender, ethnicity, and race.

In search for a life-giving, liberating symbol of love for women in Christian theology and tradition, I critiqued the theological works of feminist theologians centered on two main issues: first, the male-centered language and symbolism of God, and second, God's relation to the cross. Since exclusive literal patriarchal speech about God has played a role in justifying social structures of dominance, such as the androcentric world view, I have argued that God needs to be spoken of as both male and female in order to relativize undue emphasis on any one image. None of the symbols for God grasps the transcendent; therefore, I have argued that in worship and prayer God should be spoken of in various symbols and images both masculine and feminine as wells as both personal and impersonal.

For the purpose of renewing the idea of God in more inclusive way, I have assessed various attempts that feminist theologians made to expose oppressive theological patterns within theology and tradition. First, I have looked into how they argue against the notion of maleness of God under the categories of the incarnation of the Word in the male Jesus, God understood as a Father, and the Father-the Son-the Holy Spirit language of the Trinity. The incarnation of the Word in the male Jesus has been used to legitimize men's superiority over women. Following Elizabeth Johnson I have argued that it is not Jesus' maleness that is doctrinally important but his humanity in solidarity with the whole suffering human race. In fact, as Johnson argued, God's choice to welcome women and children while incarnated as a man is an intentional and subversive choice that challenges the patriarchal systems of the world. Since I strongly believe that it is necessary to answer the question as to whether we could view the Trinity, God the Father, God the Son, and the Holy Spirit, apart from God's sexuality as feminine or masculine, I argued against the attempts to designate the Holy Spirit as feminine or replace Father-Son-Holy Spirit with other triads of image neither masculine nor feminine. I also looked into Fiorenza's understanding of the life and lordship of Jesus in terms of Sophia as well as Johnson's Sophia-Trinity.

Conclusion

They made great attempts to overcome the weakness of traditional descriptions of God which have reinforced systems of male domination and led to the dehumanization of women. However, I argued that the basic problem causing patriarchal, androcentric mentalities and systems is deeper than language. As LaCugna pointed out, amending religious language in liturgy or theology may raise consciousness about exclusion implicit in language, but it does not immediately overcome all exclusiveness or literalness. In this respect, I argued by agreeing with LaCugna that the Cappadocian concept of *perichoresis* can challenge the Christian imagination to renounce biological, cultural and commonsense notion of fatherhood, including the patriarchal ideal of the self-sufficient father.

I also argued against feminist theologians like Joanne Carlson Brown, Rebecca Parker, Delores Williams and Rita Nakashima Brock who rejected the cross as a symbol of denigration and oppression against women. They argued that the cross promotes an understanding of women as self-sacrificing victims and encourages them to embrace the suffering and oppression in their lives. In contrast to them, Dorothee Sölle in her existential understanding of the cross insists that the cross is neither a symbol expressing the relationship between God the Father and God the Son, nor a symbol of a masochistic God who requires suffering, but is a symbol of how reality can be transformed through true followers of the cross. Reality can be changed through those who exemplify Christ in his suffering for the suffering. In this existential approach to the Cross, however, Sölle missed out on a living sense of God as triune. She restricts the presence of Christ to human involvement. Because Sölle does not view the cross as a triune event, there is no recognition of the work of the Holy Spirit to change, motivate, and empower people to live in solidarity with sufferers. I also critiqued Elizabeth A. Johnson's conception of the cross as the parable that enacts Sophia-God's participation in the suffering of the world. By the cross-resurrection dialectic, Johnson explains that the crucified one is not abandoned but resurrected. The resurrection of Christ becomes the promise of a future for all the dead as well as the whole cosmos itself because "the victory of shalom is won not by the sword of the warrior God but by the awesome power of compassionate love, in and through solidarity with those who suffer."[1] Johnson is right in that she protests against the widespread understanding of atonement that depicts God as an angry Father and judge demanding blood sacrifices before pardoning sinners. However, as Wells

---

1. Johnson, *She Who Is*, 159.

pointed out, a weakness is found in that Johnson's Sophia Christology does not offer an alternative doctrine of atonement. I argued that in order to newly appropriate Jesus' death of atonement, we have to integrate Jesus' death with the whole of his life and resurrection, not to reduce Christ's work to a mere moral example or model for Christian life. Or, if we focus only on the atoning aspect of Jesus' death apart from his life and message, we may present God as so jealous of divine honor that God demands the death of Jesus. Therefore, we should not view Jesus' death apart from his life or resurrection. The death of Jesus is the culmination of his life and message in which he extended God's radically inclusive love to the poor and the social outcasts, the women and the children. The resurrection of Jesus is then the vindication by God of all Jesus did before death. In this respect, I revisited and critiqued Anselm's atonement theory in his *Cur Deus Homo*, to investigate whether Anselm's atonement theory can be incorporated to reclaim aspects of atonement in the feminist theology of the cross and also whether it really has, as feminists argue, promoted an understanding of women as self-sacrificing victims. In so doing, I argued that it does not lead to what feminists term "divinely sanctioned child abuse." However, with regards to whether Anselm's theology of atonement is empowering Korean-North American women today, I argued that even though it does not imply that God is abusive, Anselm's theory of atonement is ahistorical and a-ethical, lacking a social-political dimension by positing a transaction outside of history and involving only the death of Jesus while leaving out the life and ministry of Jesus. In addition, based on the static, hierarchical medieval world view, it is limited and inadequate in relation to the challenges or concerns which Korean-North American women face in the multicultural world today.

In search for a theology of the cross which meets the challenges or concerns of the developing reality for Korean-North American women, I critiqued Moltmann's social trinitarian understanding of the cross as a resource for a feminist theology of the cross. In so doing, I first discussed how Moltmann tries to overcome Luther's theology of the cross. Luther, by affirming a communication of attributes (*communicatio idiomatum*) made it possible to conceive of God in the godforsakenness of Christ and to ascribe suffering and death on the cross to the divine-human person of Christ. Moltmann criticizes Luther's two-nature Christology for leaving out an account of the relationships in which the suffering of the Son is involved

Conclusion

with the persons of the Father and the Spirit. Thus, Moltmann proposes the cross as a trinitarian event.

I argued in this thesis that by viewing the cross from a social trinitarian perspective, we can retrieve a theology of the cross as the basic symbol of Christian faith to be liberating and life-giving. I claimed this social trinitarian approach to the cross as a feminist approach not by adding femininity to the Trinity but by exposing the essence of God to be in relation, mutuality and community in diversity. I discussed how Moltmann, by employing the concept of *perichoresis,* explained that the mutual interpenetration and indwelling of the Father, Son, and Holy Spirit arise from the three persons' eternal acts of self-donation. This triune God, as an "open Trinity" yearning for fellowship with God's own creation, calls human beings to participate in the Trinitarian fellowship through emulating the *perichoretic* love of the Trinity in their relationships with others. The social trinitarian praxis recognizes their interconnectedness and embraces the need of their interdependence regardless of gender, ethnicity and race.

The social trinitarian understanding of the cross embraces Jesus' passion from his birth to his resurrection, and it reveals God as a passionate loving God who suffers in solidarity with the marginalized, the victimized, and the dehumanized. The social trinitarian understanding of the cross, therefore, invalidates traditional descriptions of God which have underwritten male domination and the dehumanization of women. Consequently, the dignity and value of Korean-North American women and their call to live in mutual, reciprocal relationship with others are best promoted by the social Trinitarian approach to the theology of the cross

Finally, I offered in this thesis the contribution of a social trinitarian theology of the cross toward a feminist Christian praxis for both the first and second generation Korean-North American women in their various relationships with others. I argued that they are to emulate the suffering love of the triune God in *imitatio crucis* and *imitatio relationis* and through the aid of the Holy Spirit in this world marred by evil and sin. Based on the social trinitarian model of human fellowship, I called them to envision and participate in building an inclusive society where women and men regardless of gender, race, and ethnicity would be free to realize their potential and serve one another by using their various gifts in freedom and trust. I also discussed how the social trinitarian fellowship demonstrated through the cross calls for an ecclesial reform in the leadership and structure of the church. The Christian church, mirroring the trinitarian fellowship, is to be characterized by reciprocal friendship and self-giving love—regardless of sex, race, or age—among all members of the church. The leadership formed by trinitarian fellowship is to be inclusive, reciprocal, and creative in exercising power to motivate others to be leaders as well. Lastly, the trinitarian fellowship culminating at the Cross contributes to a renewed conception of mission and interreligious dialogue. With regard to mission, I suggested carrying out mission in a larger spectrum from a social trinitarian perspective. The missional church participates in the *missio Dei,* as God's instrument to restore God's perichoretic fellowship with all of God's creation including the generations to come. Thus, I emphasized that it is essential to add the dimension of time and generations to the concept of mission, that is, to prepare the future of Christianity by raising spiritual leaders for the next generations. I also argued that interreligious dialogue based on the *perichoretic* fellowship of the triune God does not seek a single, unified religion. Rather, it enters into dialogue with the attitude of humility and self-giving love to create a world of peace and justice in solidarity with the poor and the oppressed, together.

All in all, I believe that through this social trinitarian understanding of the cross and its praxis, both first and second generation Korean-North American women will be restored to self-respect and self-worth. They will also be empowered to live in mutual, reciprocal relationship with others, protesting against intolerance and oppression in various forms of injustice.

Bibliography

Abetz, Katherine. "Identity for Women: A Proposal for the Gendered *imago Dei* Based on 1 Corinthians 11:1–16." *Pacifica: Journal of the Melbourne College of Divinity* 23 (2010) 15–34.
Adiprasetya, Joas. "Toward a Perchorietic Theology of Religions." ThD diss., Boston University, 2008.
Ahn, Byung-Mu. "Jesus and the Minjung in the Gospel of Mark." In *Minjung Theology*, edited by Yong-bok Kim, 138–54. Singapore: Commission on Theological Concerns, Christian Conference of Asia, 1981.
Althaus, Paul. *The Theology of Martin Luther*. Translated by Robert C. Schultz. Philadelphia: Fortress, 1966.
Aquinas, Thomas. *Summa Theologica*. 2 vols. Translated by Fathers of the English Dominican Province and revised by Daniel J. Sullivan. New York: Encyclopedia Britannica, 1952.
Armstrong, Hilary. "Negative Theology." *Downside Review* 95 (1977) 176–89.
Ansell, Nik. "Annihilation of Hell and the Perfection of Freedom: Universal Salvation in the Theology of Jürgen Moltmann (1926–)." In *All Shall Be Well: Explorations in Universal Salvation and Christian Theology from Origen to Moltmann*, edited by Gregory MacDonald, 417–39. Eugene, OR: Cascade, 2011.
———. "The Annihilation of Hell: Universal Salvation and the Redemption of Time in the Eschatology of Jürgen Moltmann." Thesis, Vrije Universiteit Amsterdam, 2005.
———. *The Annihilation of Hell: Universal Salvation and the Redemption of Time in the Eschatology of Jürgen Moltmann*. Eugene, OR: Cascade, 2013.
Anselm, St. *Cur Deus Homo*. In *Basic Writings*, translated by S. W. Deane, 191–302. 2nd ed. La Salle, IL: Open Court, 1962.
Attfield, D. G. "Can God be Crucified? A Discussion of Jürgen Moltmann." *Scottish Journal of Theology* 30 (1977) 47–57.
Augustine, Saint. *The City of God*. Translated by Marcus Dods. New York: Random House, 1950.
———. *The Trinity*. Translated by Stephen McKenna. Washington, DC: Catholic University of America Press, 1963.
Aulen, Gustaf. *Christus Victor: An Historical Study of the Three Main Types of the Idea of Atonement*. Translated by A. G. Herbert. New York: Macmillan, 1961.
Baer, Richard. *Philo's Use of the Categories Male and Female*. Leiden: Brill, 1970.
Bainton, Roland. *Here I Stand: A Life of Martin Luther*. New York: Mentor, 1950.
Barth, Karl. *Church Dogmatics*. 14 vols. Edited by Geoffrey W. Bromiley and Thomas F. Torrance. Translated by G. W. Bromiley et al. Edinburgh: T. & T. Clark, 1956–69.

Bibliography

Bauckham, Richard. "Moltmann's Eschatology of the Cross." *Scottish Journal of Theology* 30 (1977) 301–31.

———. "Moltmann's Messianic Christology." *Scottish Journal of Theology* 44 (1991) 519–31.

———. "'Only Suffering of God Can Help': Divine Passibility in Modern Theology." *Themelios* 9 (1984) 6–12.

———. *The Theology of Jürgen Moltmann*. Edinburgh: T. & T. Clark, 1995.

Baum, G. "From Solidarity to Resistance." In *Intersecting Voices: Critical Theologies in a Land of Diversity*, edited by D. Schweitzer and D. Simon, 49–66. Ottawa: Novalis, 2004.

Begalke, M. Vernon. "Luther's *Anfechtungen*: An Important Clue to His Pastoral Theology." *Consensus* 9 (1983) 3–17.

Bidwell, Kevin J. *The Church as the Image of the Trinity: A Critical Evaluation of Miroslav Volf's Ecclesial Model*. Eugene, OR: Wipf & Stock, 2011.

Boff, Leonardo. *Church, Charism and Power: Liberation Theology and the Institutional Church*. New York: Crossroad, 1985.

———. *The Maternal Face of God: The Feminine and Its Religious Expressions*. Translated by Robert Barr and John Dierckmeier. Maryknoll, NY: Orbis, 1987.

———. *Passion of Christ, Passion of the World*. Maryknoll, NY: Orbis, 1987.

———. "Trinitarian Community and Social Liberation." *Cross Currents* (Fall 1988) 289–308.

———. "Trinity." In *Systematic Theology: Perspectives from Liberation Theology: Readings from Mysterium Liberationis*, edited by Ignacio Ellacuria and Jon Sobrino, 75–89. Maryknoll, NY: Orbis, 1993.

———. *Trinity and Society*. Maryknoll, NY: Orbis, 1988.

Bonhoeffer, Dietrich. *Creation and Fall: A Theological Interpretation of Genesis 3*. Translated by J. C. Fletcher. London: SCM, 1959.

———. *Letters and Papers from Prison*. Enlarged ed. London: SCM, 1971.

Bosch, David Jacobus. *Transforming Mission*. Maryknoll, NY: Orbis, 1991.

Braaten, C. E. "A Trinitarian Theology of the Cross." *Journal of Religion* 54 (1976) 113–21.

Brecht, Martin. *Martin Luther: His Road to Reformation, 1483–1521*. Translated by James L. Schaaf. Philadelphia: Fortress, 1985.

Brock, Rita Nakashima. "And a Little Child Will Lead Us: Christology and Child Abuse." In *Christianity, Patriarchy and Abuse: A Feminist Critique*, edited by Joanne Carlson Brown and Carole R. Bohn, 42–61. New York: Pilgrim, 1989.

———. *Journeys by Heart: A Christology of Erotic Power*. New York: Crossroad, 1988.

Brown, Colin. "Trinity and Incarnation: In Search of Contemporary Orthodoxy." *Ex Auditu* 7 (1991) 82–104.

Brown, Hunter. "Anselm's *Cur Deus Homo* Revisited." *Eglise et Theologie* 25, no. 2 (1994) 189–204.

Brown, Joanne Carlson, and Carole R. Bohn, eds. *Christianity, Patriarchy and Abuse: A Feminist Critique*. New York: Pilgrim, 1989.

Brown, Joanne Carlson, and Rebecca Parker. "For God so Loved the World?" In *Christianity, Patriarchy and Abuse: A Feminist Critique*, edited by Joanne C. Brown and Carole R. Bohn, 1–30. New York: Pilgrim, 1989.

Brown, Raymond. *The Gospel according to John*. New York: Doubleday, 1966.

Budapest, Zsusanna. *The Spiral Dance: The Rebirth of the Ancient Religion of the Great Goddess*. San Francisco: Harper & Row, 1979.

Bibliography

Bultmann, Rudolf. *Interpreting Faith for the Modern Era*. San Francisco: Collins, 1987.

Buxton, Graham. *The Trinity, Creation and Pastoral Ministry: Imaging the Perichoretic God*. Milton Keynes, UK: Paternoster, 2005.

Calvin, John. *Institutes of the Christian Religion*. Edited by John T. McNeill. Translated by Ford Lewis Battles. 2 vols. Library of Christian Classics 20–21. Philadelphia: Westminster, 1960.

Carr, Anne E. "The God Who Is Involved." *Theology Today* 38 (1981) 314–28.

———. "A New Vision of Feminist Theology: Method." In *Freeing Theology*, edited by Catherine Mowry LaCugna, 5–30. San Francisco: HarperCollins.1993

———. *Transforming Grace: Christian Tradition and Women's Experience*. New York: Harper & Row, 1988.

Castelo, Daniel. "Moltmann's Dismissal of Divine Impassibility: Warranted?" *Scottish Journal of Theology* 61 (2008) 396–407.

Chai, Alice Yun. "Korean Women in Hawaii, 1903–1945: The Role of Methodism in Their Participation in the Korean Independence Movement." In *Women in New Worlds*, edited by H. F. Thomas and Rosemary Skinner Keller, 328–44. Nashville: Abingdon, 1981.

———. "Women's History in Public: 'Picture Brides' of Hawaii." *Women's Studies Quarterly* 1–2 (1998) 51–62.

Chapman, G. Clarke, Jr. "Hope and the Ethics of Formation: Moltmann as an Interpreter of Bonhoeffer." *Studies in Religion and Sciences* 12 (1983) 449–60.

Chapman, Mark D. "The Social Doctrines of the Trinity: Some Problems." *Anglican Theological Review* 83 (2001) 239–54.

Charry, Ellen T. "Is Christianity Good for Us?" In *Reclaiming Faith: Essays on Orthodoxy in the Episcopal Church and the Baltimore Declaration*, edited by Ephraim Radner and George R. Sumner, 225–46. Grand Rapids: Eerdmans, 1993.

Chemnitz, Martin. *The Two Natures in Christ*. Translated by J. A. O. Preus. St. Louis: Concordia, 1971.

Choi, Hee An. *Korean Women and God: Experiencing God in a Multi-religious Colonial Context*. Maryknoll, NY: Orbis, 2005.

Chong, Yo Sop. "Women's Social Status during the Yi Dynasty—from the view point of hope." *Journal of Asian Women* 12 (Seoul: Suk-myong Women's University, 1973) 103–22.

Chopp, Rebecca S. *The Praxis of Suffering*. Maryknoll, NY: Orbis, 1986.

Christ, Carol P. *Diving Deep and Surfacing: Women Writers on Spiritual Quest*. Boston: Beacon, 1980.

———. "Why Women Need the Goddess: Phenomenological, Psychological and Political Reflections." In *Womanspirit Rising*, edited by Christ and Plaskow, 273–87. San Francisco: Harper, 1987.

Christ, Carol P., and Judith Plaskow, eds. *Womanspirit Rising: A Feminist Reader in Religion*. New York: Harper & Row, 1979.

Chung, David. *Religious Syncretism in Korean Society*. Ann Arbor: University Microfilm, 1960.

Chung, Hyun Kyung. "Han-Pu-Ri: Doing Theology from Korean Women's Perspective." In *Frontiers in Asia Christian Theology: Emerging Trends*, edited by R. S. Sugirtharajah, 52–64. Maryknoll, NY: Orbis, 1994.

———. *Struggle to Be the Sun Again: Introducing Asian Women's Theology*. Maryknoll, NY: Orbis, 1990.

Bibliography

Chung, Paul. "The Asian Pursuit of Trinitarian Theology in a Multi-religious Context." *Journal of Reformed Theology* 3 (2009) 144–56.

Cobb, John. *Beyond Dialogue: Toward a Mutual Transformation of Christianity and Buddhism.* Philadelphia: Fortress, 1982.

Coffey, David. "The Holy Spirit as the Mutual Love of the Father and the Son." *Theological Studies* 51 (1990) 193–229.

Collins, Mary. "Naming God in Public Prayer," *Worship* 59 (1985) 291–304.

Collins, Sheila D. "Feminist Theology at the Crossroads." *Christianity and Crisis* 41 (1981) 342–47.

Cone, James H. *A Black Theology of Liberation.* Philadelphia: Lippincott, 1970.

———. *God of the Oppressed.* New York: Seabury, 1975.

Congar, Yves. *I Believe in the Holy Spirit.* Translated by David Smith. New York: Crossroad, 1997.

Conyers, A. J. *God, Hope, and History: Jürgen Moltmann and the Christian Concept of History.* Macon, GA: Mercer University Press, 1988.

Cornelison, Robert T., ed. "The Promise of God's Future: Essays on the Thought of Jürgen Moltmann." *Asbury Theological Journal* 55 (2000) 9–142.

Cunningham, David. S. *These Three Are One: The Practice of Trinitarian Theology.* Cambridge: Blackwell, 1998.

Daly, Mary. *Beyond the Father: Toward a Philosophy of Women's Liberation.* Boston: Beacon, 1973.

———. "Feminist Post-Christian Introduction." In *The Church and the Second Sex*, 15–52. Boston: Beacon, 1985.

D'Costa, G., ed. *Christian Uniqueness Reconsidered: The Myth of a Pluralistic Theology of Religions.* Maryknoll, NY: Orbis, 1990.

———. *Meeting of Religions and the Trinity.* Maryknoll, NY: Orbis, 2000.

———. *Theology and Religious Pluralism: The Challenge of Other Religions.* Oxford: Blackwell, 1986.

DeVries, Mark. *Family-Based Youth Ministry.* Downers Grove, IL: InterVarsity, 1994.

Dostoevsky, Fyodor. *The Brothers Karamazov.* Translated by Andrew R. MacAndrew. New York: Bantam, 1988.

Dunn, James D. G. *Christology in the Making.* 2nd ed. London: SCM, 1989.

———. *The Theology of Paul the Apostle.* Grand Rapids: Eerdmans, 1998.

Ebeling, Gerhard. *Luther: An Introduction to His Thought.* Translated by R. A. Wilson. London: Collins, 1970.

Eckardt, Burnell F. "Luther and Moltmann: The Theology of the Cross." *Concordia Theological Quarterly* 49 (1985) 19–28.

Ekka, Jhakmak Neeraj. *Christ as Sacrament and Example: Luther's Theology of the Cross and Its Relevance for South Asia.* Minneapolis: Lutheran University Press, 2007.

Fabella, Virginia, ed. *Asia's Struggle for Full Humanity.* Maryknoll, NY: Orbis, 1980.

Farley, Margaret. "New Patterns of Relationship: Beginnings of a Moral Revolution." *Theological Studies* 36 (1975) 627–46.

Fensham, Charles. *Emerging from the Dark Age Ahead: The Future of the North American Church.* Ottawa: Novalis, 2008.

Feuerbach, Ludwig. *The Essence of Faith according to Luther.* Translated by Melvin Cherno. New York: Harper & Row, 1967.

Fiddes, Paul. S. *The Creative Suffering of God.* Oxford: Clarendon, 1988.

Bibliography

———. *Past and Present Salvation: The Christian Idea of Atonement*. London: Darton, Longman, and Todd, 1989.

———. "Suffering Divine." In *The Blackwell Encyclopedia of Modern Christian Thought*, edited by Alister E. McGrath, 633–36. Cambridge: Blackwell, 1993.

Forde, Gerhardt O. *On Being a Theologian of the Cross: Reflections on Luther's Heidelberg Disputation, 1518*. Grand Rapids: Eerdmans, 1997.

Fox, Patricia. "The Trinity as Transforming Symbol: Exploring the Trinitarian Theology of Two Roman Catholic Feminist Theologians." *Pacifica* 7 (1994) 273–94.

Fretheim, Terence E. *The Suffering of God: An Old Testament Perspective*. Philadelphia: Fortress, 1984.

Frey, Rebecca. "Why Women Want the Goddess: Experiential and Confessional Reflections." *Lutheran Forum* 5 (1991) 19–26.

Gabriel, Andrew K. "Beyond the Cross: Moltmann's Crucified God, Rahner's Rule, and Pneumatological Implications for a Trinitarian Doctrine of God." *Didaskalia* 19 (2008) 93–111.

Gadamer, Hans-Georg. *Truth and Method*. Translated and revised by Joel Weinsheimer and Donald G. Marshall. New York: Continuum, 2000.

Garcia, Laura. "Femininity and the Life of Faith." In *The Catholic Woman*, edited by Ralph McInerny, 125–30. San Francisco: Ignatius, 1990.

Geertz, Clifford. *The Interpretation of Cultures*. New York: Basic, 1973.

Gibbs, Eddie. "Church Responses to Culture since 1985." *Missiology: An International Review* 35 (2007) 158–68.

Gilbert, Kevin James. "Jürgen Moltmann's Theological Method: Evangelical Options?" *Restoration Quarterly* 41 (1999) 163–78.

Gilkey, Langdon. *On Niebuhr: A Theological Study*. Chicago: University of Chicago Press, 2001.

Goldenberg, Naomi R. *Changing of the Gods: Feminism and the End of Traditional Religions*. Boston: Beacon, 1979.

Grabowski, Stanislaus. *The All-Present God: A Study in St. Augustine*. St. Louis: Herder, 1953.

Gresake, Gilbert. "Redemption and Freedom." *Theology Digest* 25 (1977) 61–65.

Grillmeier, Aloys. *Christ in Christian Tradition*. Vol. 1. Atlanta: Knox, 1975.

Gresham, John L., Jr. "The Social Model of the Trinity and Its Critics." *Scottish Journal of Theology* 46 (1993) 325–43.

Grey, Mary. *Redeeming the Dream: Feminism, Redemption and Christian Tradition*. London: SPCK, 1989.

Guder, D. L. *Missional Church: A Vision for the Sending Church in North America*. Grand Rapids: Eerdmans, 1998.

Hall, Douglas John. *Confessing the Faith: Christian Theology in a North American Context*. Minneapolis: Fortress, 1996.

———. *The Cross in Our Context: Jesus and the Suffering World*. Minneapolis: Fortress, 2003.

———. *God and Human Suffering: An Exercise in the Theology of the Cross*. Minneapolis: Augsburg, 1986.

———. *Lighten Our Darkness: Toward an Indigenous Theology of the Cross*. Philadelphia: Westminster, 1976.

———. "Luther's Theology of the Cross." *Consensus* 15 (1989) 7–19.

Bibliography

———. *Professing the Faith: Christian Theology in a North American Context.* Minneapolis: Fortress, 1993.

———. *Thinking the Faith: Christian Theology in a North American Context.* Minneapolis: Fortress, 1989.

Hampson, Daphne. "Luther on the Self: A Feminist Critique." In *Feminist Theology: A Reader*, edited by Ann Loades, 215–24. Louisville: Westminster John Knox, 1990.

———. *Theology and Feminism.* Oxford: Blackwell, 1990.

Haring, Bernard. *Free and Faithful in Christ.* New York: Crossroad, 1984.

Harnack, Adolf von. *What Is Christianity?* New York: Harper, 1957.

Harrison, Verna E. F. "Perichoresis in the Greek Fathers." *St. Vladimir's Theological Quarterly* 35 (1991) 53–65.

Hart, Trevor. "Person and Prerogative in Perichoretic Perspective: An Ongoing Dispute in Trinitarian Ontology Observed." *Irish Theological Quarterly* 58 (1992) 46–57.

Horowitz, Maryanne Cline. "Aristotle and Women." *Journal of the History of Biology* 9 (1976) 183–213.

Haring, Bernard. *Free and Faithful in Christ.* New York: Crossroad, 1984.

Heo, Chun Hoi. *Multicultural Christology: A Korean Immigrant Perspective.* Berne: Lang, 2003.

Heron, A. "Who Proceedeth from the Father and the Son: The Problem of the *Filioque*." *Scottish Journal of Theology* 24 (1971) 149–66.

Hertig, Young Lee. "Asian North American Women in the Workplace and the Church." In *People on the Way*, edited by David Ng, 105–27. Valley Forge, PA: Judson, 1996.

Heschel, Abraham J. *The Prophets.* Vol. 2. Peabody, MA: Prince, 2003.

Heyward, Carter. *Saving Jesus from Those Who Are Right: Rethinking What It Means to Be Christian.* Minneapolis: Fortress, 1999.

Holmes, Stephen R. "Trinitarian Missiology: Towards a Theology of God as Missionary." *International Journal of Systematic Theology* 8 (2006) 72–90.

Horowitz, Maryanne Cline. "Aristotle and Women." *Journal of the History of Biology* 9 (1976) 183–213.

Hulbert, H. B. *The Passing of Korea.* Seoul: Yonsei University Press, 1969.

Hurh, Won Moo. *Korean Immigrants in America: A Structural Analysis of Ethnic Confinement and Adhesive Adaptation.* Cranbury, NJ: Associated University, 1984.

———. "Religious Participation: Ethnic Roles of the Korean Church." In Won Moo Hurh and Kwang Chung Kim, *Korean Immigrants in America*, 129–37. Cranbury, NJ: Associated University.

———. "Toward a Korean-American Ethnicity: Some Theoretical Models." *Ethnic and Racial Studies* 3 (1980) 444–63.

Hurh, Won Moo, and Kwang Chung Kim. "Religious Participation of Korean Immigrants in the United States." *Journal for the Scientific Study of Religion* 29 (1990) 19–34.

Jaggar, William Leslie. "The Passibility of God as Atonement Motif in the Theology of Martin Luther." PhD diss., Southwestern Baptist Theological Seminary, 1989.

Jensen, Gordon. "The Christology of Luther's Theology of the Cross." *Consensus* 23 (1997) 11–25.

Jeremias, Joachim. *New Testament Theology.* Translated by John Bowden. New York: Scribner, 1971.

———. *The Prayers of Jesus.* Philadelphia: Fortress, 1967.

Johnson, Elizabeth A. *Consider Jesus: Waves of Renewal in Christology.* New York: Crossroad, 1990.

Bibliography

———. "The Incomprehensibility of God and the Image of God Male and Female." *Theological Studies* 45 (1984) 441–65.

———. "Jesus the Wisdom of God: A Biblical Basis for Non-Androcentric Christology." *Ephemerdes Theologicae Lovanienses* 61 (1985) 261–94.

———. "Redeeming the Name of Christ." In *Freeing Theology*, edited by Catherine M. LaCugna, 115–38. San Francisco: HarperCollins, 1993.

———. *She Who Is: The Mystery of God in Feminist Theological Discourse*. New York: Crossroad, 1999.

Jowers, Dennis W. "The Theology of the Cross as Theology of the Trinity: A Critique of Jürgen Moltmann's Staurocentric Trinitarianism." *Tyndale Bulletin* 52 (2001) 245–66.

Jungel, Eberhard. "The Christian Understanding of Suffering." *Journal of Theology for Southern Africa* 65 (1988) 3–13.

———. "The Relationship between 'Economic' and 'Immanent' Trinity." *Theology Digest* 24 (1976) 179–84.

Kadai, Heino O. "Luther's Theology of the Cross." *Concordia Theological Quarterly* 63 (1999) 169–204.

Kang, Don-Ku. "Traditional Religions and Christianity in Korea: Reciprocal Relations and Conflicts." *Korea Journal* 38 (1998) 96–127.

Kant, Immanuel. *Der Streit der Fakultaten (Conflicts of Faculties)*. Hamburg: Meiner, 1959.

Kärkkäinen, Veli-Matti. *An Introduction to the Theology of Religions: Biblical, Historical and Contemporary Perspectives*. Downers Grove, IL: IVP Academic, 2003.

Käsemann, Ernst. *Essays on New Testament Themes*. London: SCM, 1964.

Kasper, Walter. *The God of Jesus Christ*. Translated by Matthew J. O'Connell. New York: Crossroad, 1984.

———. *Jesus the Christ*. Translated by V. Green. London: Burns & Oates, 1976.

Kelly, Robert A. "The Suffering Church: A Study of Luther's *Theologia Crucis*." *Concordia Theological Quarterly* 50 (1986) 3–17.

Kelsey, David. "Whatever Happened to the Doctrine of Sin?" *Theology Today* 50 (1993) 169–78.

Keshgegian, Flora A. "The Scandal of the Cross: Revisiting Anselm and His Feminist Critics." *Anglican Theological Review* 82 (2000) 475–92.

Kilby, Karen. "Perichoresis and Projection: Problems with Social Doctrines of the Trinity." *New Blackfriars* 81 (2000) 432–45.

Kim, Ai Ra. *Women Struggling for a New Life: The Role of Religion in the Cultural Passage from Korea to America*. Albany: State University of New York Press, 1996.

Kim, Andrew E. "A History of Christianity in Korea: From Its Troubled Beginning to Its Contemporary Success." *Korea Journal* 35 (1995) 34–53.

———. "Korean Religious Culture and Its Affinity to Christianity: The Rise of Protestant Christianity in South Korea." *Sociology of Religion* 61 (2000) 117–33.

Kim, Grace Ji-Sun. *Grace of Sophia: A Korean North American Women's Christology*. Cleveland: Pilgrim, 2002.

Kim, Grace Sangok. "Asian North American Immigrant Parents and Youth: Parenting and Growing Up in a Cultural Gap." In *People on the Way: Asian North Americans Discovering Christ, Culture, and Community*, edited by David Ng, 129–45. Valley Forge, PA: Judson, 1996.

Kim, Heup Young, and David Ng. "The Central Issue of Community: An Example of Asian North American Theology on the Way." In *People on the Way: Asian North*

Bibliography

Americans Discovering Christ, Culture, and Community, edited by David Ng, 25–42. Valley Forge, PA: Judson, 1996.

Kim, In Hoe. "Korean Shamanism: A Bibliographical Introduction." Translated by Youngsik Yoo. In *Shamanism: The Spirit World of Korea*, edited by Richard W. Guisso and Chai-Shin Yu, 12–29. Seoul: Asian Humanities, 1988.

Kim, Kristeen. "Christianity's Role in the Modernization and Revitalization of Korean Society in the Twenty-First Century." *International Journal of Public Theology* 4 (2010) 212–36.

Kim, Kwang Chung, and Won Moo Hurh. "Beyond Assimilation and Pluralism: Syncretic Sociocultural Adaptation of Korean Immigrants in the US." *Ethical and Racial Studies* 16 (1993) 696–713.

Kim, Kyoung Jae. "Christianity and Cultures: A Hermeneutic Proposal of Mission Theology as Regards Inter-religious Fusion of Horizons in an East Asian Context." *Journal of Asian and Asian American Theology* 7 (2005–2006) 64–80.

———. *Christianity and the Encounter of Asian Religions: Method of Correlation, Fusion of Horizons and Paradigm Shifts in the Korean Grafting Process*. Zoetermeer, Netherlands: Uitgerverij Boekencectrum, 1994.

Kim, Nami. "'My/Our' Comfort Not at the Expense of 'Somebody Else's': Toward a Critical Global Feminist Theology." *Journal of Feminist Studies in Religion* 21 (2005) 75–94.

Kim, Samuel S. *Korea's Globalization*. Cambridge: Cambridge University Press, 2000.

Kim, Young (Jung) Han. "Christianity and Korean Culture: The Reasons for the Success of Christianity in Korea." *Voices from the Third World* 27 (2004) 7–30.

Kimel, Alvin F., Jr., ed. *Speaking the Christian God: The Holy Trinity and the Challenge of Feminism*. Grand Rapids: Eerdmans, 1992.

Kitamori, Kazuo. *Theology of the Pain of God*. Richmond: Knox, 1965.

Knitter, Paul F. *Jesus and the Other Names: Christian Mission and Global Responsibility*. Maryknoll, NY: Orbis, 1996.

———. *No Other Name? A Critical Survey of Christian Attitudes toward the World Religions*. Maryknoll, NY: Orbis, 1985.

———. *One Earth, Many Religions*. Maryknoll, NY: Orbis, 1995.

Koning, Robin. "Clifford Geertz's Account of Culture as a Resource for Theology." *Pacifica* 23 (2010) 33–57.

Kooi, Cornelis van der. "Herman Bavinck and Karl Barth on Christian Faith and Culture." *Calvin Theological Journal* 45 (2010) 72–78.

Koyama, Kosuke. *Water Buffalo Theology*. Maryknoll, NY: Orbis, 1999.

Kraemer, Hendrik. *The Christian Message in a Non-Christian World*. London: Clarke, 1938.

Kuhn, Thomas S. *The Structure of Scientific Revolution*. Chicago: University of Chicago Press, 1970.

Kuo, Wen H. "Coping with Racial Discrimination: The Case of Asian Americans." *Ethnics and Racial Studies* 18 (1995) 109–27.

Kwok, Pui-lan. *Discovering the Bible in the Non-Biblical World*. Maryknoll, NY: Orbis, 1995.

LaCugna, Catherine Mowry. "The Baptismal Formula, Feminist Objections, and Trinitarian Theology." *Journal of Ecumenical Studies* 26, no. 2 (1989) 235–50.

———. *God for Us*. New York: HarperCollins, 1991.

Bibliography

———. "God in Communion with Us: The Trinity." In *Freeing Theology: The Essentials of Theology in Feminist Perspective*, edited by Catherine Mowry LaCugna, 83–114. San Francisco: HarperSanFrancisco, 1993.

———. "The Trinitarian Mystery of God." In *Systematic Theology: Roman Catholic Perspectives* I, edited by Francis Schussler Fiorenza and John P. Galvin, 149–91. Minneapolis: Fortress Press, 1991.

LaPorte, Jean. "Philo in the Tradition of Biblical Wisdom Literature." In *Aspects of Wisdom in Judaism and Early Christianity*, edited by Robert Wilkens, 103–41. Notre Dame: University of Notre Dame Press, 1975.

Lazareth, William H. *Christians in Society: Luther, the Bible, and Social Ethics*. Minneapolis: Fortress, 2001.

Lee, Jung Young. "The American Missionary Movement in Korea 1882–1945 and Its Contributions and American Diplomacy." *Missiology: An International Review* 40 (1983) 387–402.

———. "Marginality: A Multicultural Approach to Theology from an Asian American Perspective." *Asian Journal of Theology* 7 (1993) 224–53.

———. *Marginality: The Key to Multicultural Theology*. Minneapolis: Fortress, 1995.

Lerner, Gerda. *The Creation of Patriarchy*. New York: Oxford University Press, 1986.

Lienhard, Marc. *Luther: Witness to Jesus Christ*. Translated by J. A. Bouman. Minneapolis: Augsburg, 1982.

Lilburne, Geoffrey R. "Christology: In Dialogue with Feminism." *Horizons* 11 (1984) 7–27.

Loewenich, Walther von. *Luther's Theology of the Cross*. Translated by Herbert J. A. Bouman. Minneapolis: Augsburg, 1976.

Lohse, Bernhard. *Martin Luther: An Introduction to His Life and Work*. Translated by Robert C. Scultz. Philadelphia: Fortress, 1986.

———. *Martin Luther's Theology: Its Historical and Systematic Development*. Minneapolis: Fortress, 1999.

Lossky, Vladimir. *In the Image and Likeness of God*. Crestwood, NY: St Vladimir's Seminary Press, 1974.

Luther, Martin. *Bondage of the Will*. Translated by J. I. Packer and O. R. Johnson. London: Clarke, 1957.

———. *Commentary on Genesis*. 2 vols. Translated and edited by J. Theodore Mueller. Grand Rapids: Zondervan, 1968.

———. *Lectures on Romans*. Library of Christian Classics 15. Translated by Wilhelm Pauck. Philadelphia: Westminster, 1961.

———. *Luther and Erasmus on Free Will*. Library of Christian Classics 17. Edited by E. G. Rupp. Philadelphia: Westminster, 1969.

———. *Luthers Werke: Kritische Gesamtausgabe*. 100 vols. Weimar: Böhlaus Nachfolger, 1883–.

———. *Luther's Works*. Edited by Jaroslav Pelikan, Hilton C. Oswald, and Helmut T. Lehmann. 55 vols. American ed. Vols. 1–30: St. Louis: Concordia; Vols. 31–55: Philadelphia: Fortress, 1955–1986.

———. *Luther's Works: Epistle Sermons*. Vols. 7 and 9. Edited by John Nicholas Lenker. Minneapolis: Luther, 1908.

———. *Sermons on the Passion of Christ*. Rock Island, IL: Lutheran Augustana Book Concern, 1871.

Bibliography

----------. *Three Treatises*. Translated by Charles M. Jacobs, A. T. W. Steinhauser, and W. A. Lambert. Philadelphia: Fortress, 1978.

MacCormack, Carol. P. "Nature, Culture, and Gender: A Critique." In *Nature, Culture and Gender*, edited by Carol MacCormack and Marilyn Strathern, 1–24. New York: Cambridge University Press, 1980.

Madsen, Anna M. *The Theology of the Cross in Historical Perspective*. Eugene, OR: Pickwick, 2007.

Maimela, Simon S. "The Atonement in the Context of Liberation Theology." *Journal of Theology for Southern Africa* 39 (1982) 45–54.

McDougall, Joy Ann. "The Return of Trinitarian Praxis? Moltmann on the Trinity and the Christian Life." *The Journal of Religion* 83 (2003) 177–203.

McFague, Sally. *Metaphorical Theology*. Philadelphia: Fortress, 1982.

McGrath, Alister. *Luther's Theology of the Cross: Martin Luther's Theological Breakthrough*. Oxford: Basil Backwell, 1985.

McIlhenny, Ryan. "A Third-Way Reformed Approach to Christ and Culture: Appropriating Kuyperian Neo-Calvinism and the Two Kingdoms Perspective." *Mid-America Journal of Theology* 20 (2009) 75–94.

McLaughlin, Eleanor Commo. "Equality of Souls, Inequality of Sexes: Women in Medieval Theology." In *Religion and Sexism: Images of Woman in the Jewish and Christian Traditions*, edited by Rosemary Radford Ruether, 213–66. New York: Simon and Schuster, 1974.

McWilliams, Warren. "The Passion of God and Moltmann's Christology." *Encounter* 40 (1979) 313–26.

----------. "Why All the Fuss about *Filioque*? Karl Barth and Jürgen Moltmann on the Procession of the Spirit." *Perspectives in Religious Studies* 22 (1995) 161–81.

Meeks, M. Douglas. *Origins of the Theology of Hope*. Philadelphia: Fortress, 1974.

Migliore, L. Daniel. *Faith Seeking Understanding*. Grand Rapids: Eerdmans, 1991.

----------. "September 11 and the Theology of the Cross." *Princeton Seminary Bulletin* 23 (2002) 54–58.

Min, Anselm Kyongsuk. "Dialectical Pluralism and Solidarity of Others: Towards a New Pluralism." *Journal of the American Academy of Religion* 65 (1997) 587–604.

----------. "The Political Economy of Marginality: Comments on Jung Young Lee, *Marginality: The Key to Multicultural Theology*." *Journal of Asian and Asian American Theology* 1 (1996) 82–94.

Min, Pyong Gap. "Cultural and Economic Boundaries of Korean Ethnicity: A Comparative Analysis." *Ethnic and Racial Studies* 14 (1991) 224–41.

Min, Pyong Gap, and Dae Young Kim. "Intergenerational Transmission of Religion and Culture: Korean Protestants in the U.S." *Sociology of Religion* 66 (2005) 263–82.

Moffat, Samuel Hugh. *The Christians of Korea*. New York: Friendship, 1962.

Moltmann Jürgen. *The Coming of God*. Translated by Margaret Kohl. Minneapolis: Fortress, 1996.

----------. *The Crucified God: The Cross of Christ as the Foundation and Criticism of Christian Theology*. Translated by R. A. Wilson and John Bowden. Minneapolis: Fortress, 1993.

----------. *The Church in the Power of the Spirit: A Contribution to Messianic Ecclesiology*. Translated by Margaret Kohl. London: SCM, 1977.

----------. *Ethics of Hope*. 1st Fortress ed. Translated by Margaret Kohl. Minneapolis: Fortress, 2012.

Bibliography

———. *Experiences in Theology: Ways and Forms of Christian Theology*. Translated by Margaret Kohl. Minneapolis: Fortress, 2000.

———. *God for a Secular Society: The Public Relevance of Theology*. 1st Fortress ed. Minneapolis: Fortress, 1999.

———. *God in Creation: An Ecological Doctrine of Creation: The Gifford Lectures 1984–1985*. Minneapolis: Fortress, 1993.

———. *History and the Triune God: Contributions to Trinitarian Theology*. Translated by John Bowden. New York: Crossroad, 1992.

———. "The Inviting Unity of the Triune God." In *History and the Triune God: Contributions to Trinitarian Theology*, translated by John Bowden, 80–90. New York: Crossroad, 1992.

———. *Man: Christian Anthropology in the Conflict of the Present*. Translated by John Sturdy. Minneapolis: Fortress, 1979.

———. "Reformation and Revolution." In *Martin Luther and Modern Mind: Freedom, Conscience, Toleration, Right*, edited by Manfred Hoffman, 163–90. Lewiston, NY: E. Mellen, 1985.

———. "The Social Doctrine of the Trinity." In *The Christian Understanding of God Today*, edited by James Byrne, 104–11. Dublin: Columba, 1993.

———. *The Spirit of Life: A Universal Affirmation*. Translated by Margaret Kohl. Minneapolis: Fortress, 1992.

———. *Sun of Righteousness, Arise! God's Future for Humanity and the Earth*. Translated by Margaret Kohl. Minneapolis: Fortress, 2010

———. *Theology of Hope: On the Ground and the Implications of a Christian Eschatology*. Translated by James W. Leitch. London: SCM, 1965.

———. *The Trinity and the Kingdom: The Doctrine of God*. Translated by Margaret Kohl. San Francisco: HarperCollins, 1991.

———. *The Way of Jesus Christ: Christology in Messianic Dimensions*. Minneapolis: Fortress, 1989.

Moltmann-Wendel, Elisabeth. *Autobiography*. Translated by John Bowden. London: SCM, 1997.

———. "Is There Feminist Theology of the Cross." In *God—His and Hers*, edited by Elisabeth Moltmann-Wendel and Jürgen Moltmann, 77-91. New York: Crossroad, 1991.

———. *Humanity in God*. London: SCM, 1983.

Mong Ih-Ren, Ambrose. "Approaches to Inter-faith Dialogue: Trinitarian Theology and Multiple Religious Belonging." *Asia Journal of Theology* 24 (2010) 285–311.

Mongeau, Gilles. "Classic Rhetoric and the Control of Elemental Meaning." In *Meaning and History in Systematic Theology*, edited by John D. Dadosky, 354–573. Milwaukee: Marquette University Press, 2009.

Moon, Seungsook. "Overcome by Globalization: The Rise of a Women's Policy in South Korea." In *Korea's Globalization*, edited by Samuel S. Kim, 126–46. New York: Cambridge University Press, 2000.

Muller, Richard A. "Incarnation, Immutability and the Case for Classical Theism." *Westminster Theological Journal* 45 (1983) 22–40.

Nestigen, James Arne. "Luther's Heidelberg Disputation: An Analysis of the Argument." In *All Things New: Essays in Honor of Roy A. Harrisville*, edited by Arland J. Hultgren et al., 147–54. St. Paul: Word & World, Luther Northwestern Theological Seminary, 1992.

BIBLIOGRAPHY

Neuer, Werner. *Man and Woman in Christian Perspective*. Translated by Gordon Wenham. London: Hodder & Stoughton, 1990.

Newbigin, Lesslie. *The Gospel in a Pluralistic Society*. Grand Rapids: Eerdmans, 1989.

Ng, Greer Anne Wenh-In. "Asian Sociocultural Values: Oppressive and Liberating Aspects from a Woman's Perspective." In *People on the Way: Asian North Americans Discovering Christ, Culture, and Community*, edited by David Ng, 63–103. Valley Forge, PA: Judson, 1996.

Ng, Peter Tae Ming. "Timothy Richard: Christian Attitudes toward Other Religions and Cultures." *Studies in World Christianity* 14 (2008) 73–92.

Ngien, Dennis. *The Suffering of God according to Martin Luther's Theologia Crucis*. Vancouver: Regent College, 1995.

Niebuhr, H. Richard. *Christ and Culture*. New York: Harper & Row, 1951.

Oberman, Heiko A. *Luther: Man between God and the Devil*. Translated by Eileen Walliser-Schwarzbart. New York: Doubleday, 1992.

Ochs, Carol. *Behind the Sex of God: Toward a New Consciousness Transcending Matriarchy and Patriarchy*. Boston: Beacon, 1977.

Ogden, Schubert M. "A Priori Christology and Experience." In *Doing Theology Today*, 123–38. Valley Forge, PA: Trinity, 1996.

Otto, Randolph E. "The Use and Abuse of *Perichoresis* in Recent Theology." *Scottish Journal of Theology* 54 (2001) 366–84.

Palmer, Richard E. *Hermeneutics*. Evanston: Northwestern University Press, 1969.

Pannenberg, Wolfhart. "The Religions from the Perspective of Christian Theology and the Self-Interpretation of Christianity in Relation to the Non-Christian Religions." *Modern Theology* 9 (1993) 285–97.

———. "Religious Pluralism and Conflicting Truth Claims: The Problem of a Theology of the World Religions." In *Christian Uniqueness Reconsidered: The Myth of a Pluralistic Theology of Religions*, edited by Gavin D'Costa, 96–106. Maryknoll, NY: Orbis, 1990.

———. "Toward a Theology of the History of Religions." In *Basic Questions in Theology*, translated by G. H. Kehm, 2:65–118. London: SCM, 1971.

Park, Andrew Sung. *Racial Conflict and Healing: An Asian-American Theological Perspective*. Maryknoll, NY: Orbis, 1996.

———. *The Wounded Heart of God: The Asian Concept of Han and the Christian Doctrine of Sin*. Nashville: Abingdon, 1993.

Peach, Lucinda Joy. *Women and World Religions*. Upper Saddle River, NJ: Prentice Hall, 2002.

Pesch, Otto. *The God Question in Thomas Aquinas and Martin Luther*. Philadelphia: Fortress, 1972.

Peters, Ted. "The Atonement in Anselm and Luther: Second Thoughts about Gustaf Aulen's *Christus Victor*." *Lutheran Quarterly* 24 (1972) 301–14.

———. *God as Trinity: Relationality and Temporality in Divine Life*, 1st ed. Louisville: Westminster John Knox, 1993.

Peterson, Daniel. "We Preach Christ Crucified: Rejecting the Prosperity Gospel and Responding to Feminist Criticism Using Luther's Second Theology of the Cross." *Dialog* 48 (2009) 194–201.

Peterson, Mark. "Women without Sons: A Measure of Social Change in Yi Dynasty Korea." In *Korean Women: View from the Inner Room*, edited by Laurel Kendall and Mark Peterson, 37–43. New Haven: East Rock, 1983.

Bibliography

Phan, Peter C. "Jesus the Christ with an Asian Face." *Theological Studies* 57 (1996) 399–430.

Pierce, Andrew, and Gerraldine Smyth, eds. *The Critical Spirit: Theology at the Crossroads of Faith and Culture*. Dublin: Columba, 2003.

Pinnock, Clark. *Flame of Love: A Theology of the Holy Spirit*. Downers Grove, IL: Intervarsity, 1996.

———. *A Wideness in God's Mercy: The Finality of Jesus Christ in a World of Religions*. Grand Rapids: Zondervan, 1992.

Plaskow, Judith. *Sex, Sin, and Grace: Women's Experience and the Theologies of Reinhold Niebuhr and Paul Tillich*. Washington, DC: University Press of America, 1980.

Pless, John T. "Martin Luther: Preacher of the Cross." *Concordia Theological Quarterly* 51 (1987) 83–101.

Prenter, Regin. *Luther's Theology of the Cross*. Philadelphia: Fortress, 1971.

Purvis, Sally B. *The Power of the Cross: Foundations for a Christian Feminist Ethic of Community*. Nashville: Abingdon, 1993.

Rahner, Karl. "Anonymous Christians." In *Theological Investigations*, 6:390–98. Baltimore: Helicon, 1969.

———. "On the Importance of the Non-Christian Religions for Salvation." In *Theological Investigations*, 18:288–95. London: Darton, Longman & Todd, 1983.

———. "On the Spirituality of the Easter Faith." In *Theological Investigations*, 17:8–15. New York: Crossroad, 1981.

———. "Remarks on the Dogmatic Treatise *De Trinitate*." In *Theological Investigations*, 4:77–102.

———. *The Trinity*. Translated by Joseph Donceel. New York: Herder and Herder, 1970.

Ricoeur, Paul. *Interpretation Theory: Discourse and the Surplus of Meaning*. Fort Worth: Texas Christian University Press, 1976.

Ritschl, Dietrich. "Historical Development and Implications of the *Filioque* Controversy." In *Spirit of God, Spirit of Christ: Ecumenical Reflections on the Filioque Controversy*, edited by Lukas Vischer, 46–68. London: SPCK, 1981.

Roetzel, Calvin. "The Grammar of Election in Four Pauline Letters." In *Pauline Theology*, edited by David M. Hay, 2:211–33. Society of Biblical Literature Symposium 4. Minneapolis: Fortress, 1993.

Ross, John. *History of Corea: Ancient and Modern, with Description of Manners and Customs, Language and Geography*. London: Stock, 1891.

Ruether, Rosemary Radford. "Christian Feminist Theology: History and Future." In *Daughters of Abraham: Feminist Thought in Judaism, Christianity, and Islam*, edited by Yvonne Yazbeck Haddad and John L. Esposito, 65–80. Gainesville: University Press of Florida, 2001.

———. "Misogynism and Virginal Feminism in the Fathers of the Church," In *Religion and Sexism: Images of Woman in the Jewish and Christian Traditions*, 150–83. New York: Simon and Schuster, 1974.

———. "A Religion of Women: Sources and Strategies." *Christianity and Crisis* 39 (1979) 307–11.

———. *Sexism and God-Talk: Toward a Feminist Theology*. Boston: Beacon, 1983.

———. *To Change the World: Christology and Cultural Criticism*. New York: Crossroad, 1981.

———. *Women and Redemption: A Theological History*. Minneapolis: Fortress, 1998.

Bibliography

Ruge-Jones, Philip. *Cross in Tensions: Luther's Theology of the Cross as Theologico-Social Critique.* Eugene, OR: Pickwick, 2008.

———. *The Word of the Cross in a World of Glory.* Minneapolis: Fortress, 2008.

Rupp, E. Gordon. "Luther's Ninety-five Theses and the Theology of the Cross." In *Luther for an Ecumenical Age: Essays in Commemoration of the 450th Anniversary of the Reformation,* edited by Carl S. Meyer, 67–81. London: Concordia, 1967.

Russell, Letty M. *Church in the Round: Feminist Interpretation of the Church.* Louisville: Westminster John Knox, 1993.

———. *The Future of Partnership.* Philadelphia: Westminster, 1979.

Ryu, Tong-Shik. *The History and Structure of Korean Shamanism.* Seoul: Yonsei University Press, 1975.

———. *Tao and Logos.* Seoul: Christian Literature Society, 1978.

Saiving, Valerie. "The Human Situation: A Feminine View." *Journal of Religion* 40 (1960) 100–112.

———. "The Human Situation: A Feminine View." In *Womanspirit Rising: A Feminist Reader in Religion,* edited by Carol P. Christ and Judith Plaskow, 23–42. New York: Harper & Row, 1979.

Sanders, John. *Atonement and Violence: A Theological Conversation.* Nashville: Abingdon, 2006.

Sarot, Marcel. "Auschwitz, Morality and the Suffering of God." *Modern Theology* 7 (1991) 135–52.

———. "Patripassianism, Theopaschitism and the Suffering of God: Some Systematic and Historical Considerations." *Religious Studies* 26 (1990) 363–75.

Sasse, Hermann. "*Theologia Crucis.*" *Lutheran Theological Journal* 11 (1968) 115–27.

Scaer, David R. "The Concept of *Anfechtung* in Luther's Thought." *Concordia Theological Quarterly* 47 (1983) 15–30.

Schaab, Gloria Lo. "Of Models and Metaphors: The Trinitarian Proposals of Sallie McFague and Elizabeth A. Johnson." *Theoforum* 33 (2002) 213–34.

Schillebeeckx, Edward. *Jesus: An Experiment in Christology.* Translated by Hubert Hoskins. New York: Crossroad, 1991.

Schleiermacher, Friedrich. *The Christian Faith.* Edited by H. R. MackIntosh and J. S. Stewart. Edinburgh: T. & T. Clark, 1928.

Schneider, Sandra M. *Women and the Word.* 1986 Madaleva Lecture in Spirituality. New York: Paulist, 1986.

Schreiter, Robert J. *Constructing Local Theologies.* Maryknoll, NY: Orbis, 1985.

Schüssler Fiorenza, Elisabeth. *In Memory of Her: A Feminist Theological Reconstruction of Christian Origins.* New York: Crossroad, 1983.

———. "Interpreting Patriarchal Traditions." In *The Liberating Word,* edited by Letty M. Russell, 39–61. Philadelphia: Westminster, 1976.

———. *Jesus: Miriam's Child, Sophia's Prophet: Critical Issues in Feminist Christology.* New York: Continuum, 1994.

———. "The Will to Choose or to Reject: Continuing Our Critical Work." In *The Feminist Interpretation of the Bible,* edited by Letty M. Russell, 125–36. Philadelphia: Westminster, 1985.

———. "Wisdom Mythology and the Christological Hymns of the New Testament." In *Aspects of Wisdom in Judaism and Early Christianity,* edited by Robert L. Wilken, 17–42. Notre Dame: University of Notre Dame Press, 1975.

Bibliography

———. *Wisdom Ways: Introducing Feminist's Biblical Interpretation.* Maryknoll, NY: Orbis, 2001.
———. "You Are Not to Be Called Father." *Cross Currents* 29 (1979) 301–23.
Schweitzer, Don. "Contrasting Approaches to Social Analysis in the Theologies of Douglas Hall and Jurgen Moltmann." *Religious Studies and Theology* 16 (1997) 37–54.
———. "Douglas Hall's Critique of Jürgen Moltmann's Eschatology of the Cross." *Studies in Religion* 27, no. 1 (1998) 7–25.
———. "Jürgen Moltmann's Theology as a Theology of the Cross." *Studies in Religion* 24 (1995) 95–107.
Singh, David Emmanuel, and Bernard C. Farr, eds. *Christianity and Cultures: Shaping Christian Thinking in Context.* Cumbria, UK: Regnum, 2008.
Smith, Susan. "Gospel and Culture." *Missiology: An International Review* 34 (2006) 337–48.
Sobrino, Jon. *Christology at the Crossroads: A Latin American Approach.* Translated by John Drury. Maryknoll, NY: Orbis, 1978.
Sölle, Dorothee. *Suffering.* Translated by Everett R. Kalin. Philadelphia: Fortress, 1975.
Song, C. S. *Jesus, the Crucified People.* New York: Crossroad, 1990.
Southern, R. W. *The Making of the Middle Ages.* New Haven: Yale University Press, 1953.
Stanton, E. Cady, S. B. Anthony, and M. J. Gage, eds. *History of Woman Suffrage.* Vol. 1. New York: Fowler & Wells, 1881.
Starkloff, Carl F. "The Problem of Syncretism in the Search for Inculturation." *Mission* 1 (1994) 76–96.
———. *A Theology of the In-Between.* Milwaukee: Marquette University Press, 2002.
Stassen, Glen H. "Concrete Christological Norms for Transformation." In *Authentic Transformation: A New Vision of Christ and Culture,* edited by Glen H. Stassen, D. M. Yeager, and John Howard Yoder, 127–89. Nashville: Abingdon, 1996.
Steinmetz, David. C. *Luther in Context.* Bloomington: Indiana University Press, 1986.
Stewart, Charles, and Rosalind Shaw. *Syncretism/Anti-Syncretism: The Politics of Religious Synthesis.* London: Routledge, 1994.
Strelan, John G. "*Theologia Crucis, Theologia Gloriae*: A Study in Opposing Theologies." *Lutheran Theological Journal* 23 (1989) 99–113.
Suchocki, Marjorie. "The Unmale God: Reconsidering the Trinity." *Quarterly Review* 3 (1983) 34–49.
Suh, Nam Dong. *A Theology of the Changing Era.* Seoul: Korean Theological Study Institute, 1976.
———. "Toward a Theology of Han." In *Minjung Theology,* edited by Yong-bok Kim, 51–68. Singapore: Commission on Theological Concerns, Christian Conference of Asia, 1981.
Tanner, Kathryn. *Christ the Key.* Cambridge: Cambridge University Press, 2010.
———. "Kingdom Come: The Trinity and Politics." *The Princeton Seminary Bulletin* 27 (2007) 129–45.
———. *Theories of Culture: A New Agenda for Theology.* Minneapolis: Fortress, 1997.
Tappet, Theodore G., ed. *The Book of Concord.* Philadelphia: Fortress, 1959.
Thiemann, Ronald F. "Beyond Exclusivism and Absolutism: A Trinitarian Theology of the Cross." In *God's Life in Trinity,* edited by Miroslav Volf and Michael Welker, 118–29. Minneapolis: Fortress, 2006

Bibliography

Thistlethwaite, Susan. "On the Trinity." In *Lift Every Voice: Constructing Christian Theologies from the Underside*, edited by Susan Brooks Thistlethwaite and Mary Potter Engel, 115–26. Maryknoll, NY: Orbis, 1998.

Thomas, M. M. "The Absoluteness of Jesus Christ and Christ-Centered Syncretism." *Ecumenical Review* 37 (1985) 387–97.

Thompson, Deanna A. *Crossing the Divide: Luther, Feminism, and the Cross*. Minneapolis: Fortress, 2004.

Thompson, John. "Christology and Resurrection in the Theology of Karl Barth." In *Christ in Our Place*, edited by Trevor A. Hart and Daniel P. Thimell, 207–23. Exeter, UK: Paternoster, 1989.

———. "Modern Trinitarian Perspectives." *Scottish Journal of Theology* 44 (1991) 349–65.

Tillich, Paul. *Christianity and the Encounter of the World Religions*. New York: Columbia University Press, 1961.

———. *On the Boundary*. New York: Scribner's, 1966.

———. *The Religious Situation*. 1932. Reprint, Cleveland: World, 1964.

———. *The Shaking of the Foundations*. New York: Scribner's, 1953.

———. *Theology of Culture*. Oxford: Oxford University Press, 1959.

———. *What Is Religion?* New York: Harper & Row, 1969.

Tinder, Galen. "Luther's Theology of Christian Suffering and Its Implications for Pastoral Care." *Dialog* 25 (1986) 108–13.

Tonstad, Linn Marie. "Sexual Difference and Trinitarian Death: Cross, Kenosis, and Hierarchy in the Theo-Drama." *Modern Theology* 26 (2010) 603–31.

Tracy, David. *The Analogical Imagination: Christian Theology and the Culture of Pluralism*. New York: Crossroad, 1981.

Trible Phyllis, *God and the Rhetoric of Sexuality*. Philadelphia: Fortress, 1978.

Vanhoozer, Kevin J. "The World Well Staged? Theology, Culture, and Hermeneutics." In *God and Culture*, edited by D. A. Carson and John D. Woodbridge, 1–30. Grand Rapids: Eerdmans, 1993.

Vercruysse, Joseph E. "Luther's Theology of the Cross at the Time of the Heidelberg Disputation." *Gregorianum* 57 (1976) 523–48.

Volf, Miroslav. *After Our Likeness: The Church as the Image of the Trinity*. Grand Rapids: Eerdmans, 1998.

———. "'The Trinity is Our Social Program': The Doctrine of the Trinity and the Shape of Social Engagement." *Modern Theology* 14 (1998) 403–23.

Walsh, Brian J. "Transformation of Culture: A Review Essay." *Conrad Grebel Review* 7 (1989) 253–67.

Weaver, J. Denny. "Atonement for the Non-Constantinian Church." *Modern Theology* 66 (1990) 307–23.

———. *The Nonviolent Atonement*. Grand Rapids: Eerdmans, 2001.

———. "Violence in Christian Theology." *Cross Currents* 51, no. 2 (2001) 150–76.

Weber, Max. *The Sociology of Religion*. Boston: Beacon, 1963.

Wells, Harold. *The Christic Center: Life-Giving and Liberating*. Maryknoll, NY: Orbis, 2004.

———. "The Holy Spirit and Theology of the Cross: Significance for Dialogue." *Theological Studies* 53 (1992) 476–92.

———. "Korean Syncretism and Theologies of Interreligious Encounter: The Contribution of Kyung Jae Kim." *Asia Journal of Theology* 12 (1998) 56–76.

———. "The Theology of the Cross and the Theologies of Liberation." *Toronto Journal of Theology* 17 (2001) 147–66.

Bibliography

———. "Trinitarian Feminism: Elizabeth Johnson's Wisdom Christology." *Theology Today* 52 (2004) 330–43.

Westhelle, Vitor. *The Scandalous God: The Use and Abuse of the Cross*. Minneapolis: Fortress, 2007.

Wiesel, Elie. *Night, Dawn, The Accident: A Trilogy*. New York: Hill and Wang, 1987.

Williams, Delores S. "Black Women's Surrogate Experience and the Christian Notion of Redemption." In *After Patriarchy: Feminist Transformations of the World Religions*, edited by Paula M. Cooey et al., 1–14. Maryknoll, NY: Orbis, 1990.

———. *Sisters in the Wilderness: The Challenge of Womanist God-talk*. Maryknoll, NY: Orbis, 1993.

Wilson-Kastner, Patricia. *Faith, Feminism and the Christ*. Philadelphia: Fortress, 1983.

Wink, Walter. *Engaging the Powers: Discernment and Resistance in a World of Domination*. Minneapolis: Fortress, 1992.

———. *Naming the Powers: The Language of Power in the New Testament*. Vol. 1. Philadelphia: Fortress, 1984.

Wolfson, Harry Austryn. *The Philosophy of the Church Fathers*. Cambridge, MA: Harvard University Press, 1956.

Wood, James. "Two Kingdoms—in America?" *Currents in Theology and Mission* 14 (1989) 165–76.

Wynne, Jeremy J. "Serving the Coming God: The Insights of Jürgen Moltmann's Eschatology for Contemporary Theology of Mission." *Missiology: An International Review* 35 (2007) 437–52.

Yu, Eui-Young, and Earl H. Phillips, eds. *Korean Women in Transition: At Home and Abroad*. Los Angeles: Center for Korean-American and Korean Studies, California State University, 1987.

Zimany, Roland. "Views and Counterviews: Moltmann's *The Crucified God*." *Dialog* 15 (1977) 49–56.

Zizioulas, John. *Being as Communion: Studies in Personhood and the Church*. Crestwood, NY: St. Vladimir's Seminary, 1985.

Name Index

Adiprasetya, Joas, 126, 126n170, 127n173, 127n175, 141–42, 141n24, 142n26, 191
Ahn, Byung Mu, 162–73, 163n111, 191
Ansell, Nik, ix, 119n135, 121–22, 122n148, 158–59, 159n98, 191
Anselm of Canterbury, 35, 36n100, 77
Aristotle, 60, 60n80, 112, 169n132, 196
Arius, 57
Athanasius, 61, 170n135
Augustine of Hippo, 46, 117, 122, 191, 195
Aulen, Gustaf, 35n99, 80n156, 191, 202
Aquinas, Thomas, 47, 47n28, 60–61, 191, 202

Barth, Karl, 15n42, 16n50, 17–19, 23n73, 116–17, 117n120, 123–25, 133, 143–45, 191, 198, 200, 206
Basil, 57, 100n39, 200
Bauckham, Richard, 72n130, 107–8, 107n72, 108n78, 130n186, 192
Boff, Leonardo, 49–50, 50n34, 58n72, 137–39, 139n11, 192
Bohn, Carole R., 69n114, 192
Bonhoeffer, Dietrich, 150n67, 192, 193
Bottome, Francis, 64
Braaten Carl E., 116–17, 116n114, 192
Brock, Rita Nakashima, 68–76, 69n116, 85, 161, 187, 192
Brown, Hunter, 80, 80n155, 192
Brown, Joanne Carlson, 55n56, 68–69, 69n114, 76–79, 79n149, 85n.173, 86n177, 187, 192
Bultmann, Rudolf, 14, 14n38, 193

Carr, Anne E., 40n5, 47n29, 60, 60n79, 61n86, 75, 75n140, 91, 193
Castles, Stephen, 26, 26n77
Chapman, Mark D., 138n8, 193
Charry, Ellen T., 193
Cho, Yong-gi, 13, 13n37
Choi, Hee An, 28–29, 28n80, 34–35, 193
Christ, Carol P., 42–43, 42n13, 43n19, 193
Chung, Hyun Kyung, 15–16, 16n50, 30n89, 193, 194
Collins, Mary, 49n30, 51n29, 194
Comblin, Jose, 183
Cone, James, 87–88, 88n181, 194
Congar, Yves, 49–50, 49n32, 131, 194
Crosby, Francis Jane (Fanny), 64
Cunningham, David S., 138n7, 194

Daly, Mary, 42–43, 42n15, 43.n17, 194
Dostoevsky, Fyodor, 107n71, 195
Dunn, James, 55n56, 92n4, 194

Eckardt, Burnell F., 118, 118n124, 194

Fensham, Charles, 171–72, 171n141, 180–81, 194
Fiddes, Paul S., 111, 111n90, 120, 138, 194
Fiorenza, Elisabeth S., 31–32, 40–44, 41n9, 52–53, 52n47, 89, 167–68, 167n124, 168n126, 199, 204
Forde, Gerhardt O., 94, 94n10, 195
Frey, Rebecca, 66, 66n105, 195

Gadamer, Hans-Georg, 3–5, 3n6, 4n8, 10n.28, 40, 142n27, 195
Garcia, Laura L., 59n77, 195
Gilkey, Langdon, 65, 195

Name Index

Gregory of Nazianzus (329–390), 49, 57, 61, 126–27, 126n171, 141
Gregory of Nyssa, 57
Gresake, Gilbert, 79n150, 195
Grillmeier, Aloys, 195
Guisso, Richard W., 28, 28n83, 30n88, 198

Hall, Douglas John, xiv, 1, 172, 195, 205
Hampson, Daphne, 42–43, 42n13, 43n18, 66, 68, 161–62
Han, Eun Sook, 162, 163n111
Haring, Bernard, 63, 63n95, 196
Harrison, Verna E. F., 126n171, 127n174, 141n25, 196
Hart, Trevor, 123n156, 124–25, 144, 176, 224
Heschel, J. Abraham, 113, 113n100, 196
Heidegger, Martin, 3
Heo, Chun Hoi, 175n153, 196
Hulbert, H. B., 11, 11n32, 196

John of Damascus (676–754), 100n38, 127, 141–42
Johnson, Elizabeth A., 39, 39n2, 44, 45, 45n24, 47n28, 49, 49n33, 50–56, 61–63, 74–75, 89, 91n2, 162, 163n111, 186–87, 196, 199, 204
Jowers, Dennis W., 114n108, 116n114, 119–20, 197

Kant, Immanuel, 143, 143n34, 197
Kasper, Walter, 79, 197
Keshgegian, Flora A., 83, 83n168, 84, 86, 197
Kilby, Karen, 137–41, 137n5, 141n22, 141n23, 146, 197
Kim, Ai Ra, 24, 197
Kim, Chai-Choon, 16–19, 16n50, 196, 198
Kim, Kyoung Jae, 2, 6–10, 10n27, 16–19, 21, 22, 35, 198, 206
Knitter, Paul F., 198
Kuhn, Thomas, 1, 2, 2n2, 198
Kwak, Pui-lan, 20, 20n66, 198

LaCugna, M. Catherine, 46n26, 51–52, 56–59, 61, 89, 122n149, 131, 137, 144n39, 168–70, 187, 193, 197, 198, 199
Lilbourne, Geoffrey R., 199
Luther, Martin, 47n28, 66n103, 66n104, 80–83, 90–101, 105, 111, 112, 118n124. 172, 188, 191, 192, 194, 196, 199, 201, 202, 203, 204, 205, 206

Madsen, Anna M., 83n5, 95n13, 200
McDougall, Joy Ann, xiii, xiiin2, xviii8, 136n1, 140–42, 140n19, 145–46, 151–55, 157, 159–60, 200
McGrath Alister, 93, 93n8, 95n15, 196, 200
Maximus the Confessor (580-662), 141
McFague, Sallie, 58n71, 200, 204
McWilliams, Warren, 133n198, 200
Moltmann, Jürgen, ix, xiii, xiiin1, xiv, xvi, xviii8, xvii, xviin9, 59, 59n76, 68, 68n111, 70–73, 86n176, 90, 92–95, 96, 96n19, 98, 101–46, 150–64, 168, 171, 173, 175–83, 188–89, 191, 194, 200
Moltmann-Wendel, Elisabeth, 44, 49n31, 67, 67n106, 70n121, 120, 120n139, 201

Neuer, Werner, 59n77, 169, 169n132, 202
Ngien, Dennis, 99, 99n35, 100, 100n37, 101n42, 202
Niebuhr, H. Richard, 17n51, 64n97, 65, 65n99, 66, 195, 202, 203

Pannenberg, Wolfhart, 44, 44n23, 202
Park, Andrew Sung, 27n79, 155, 155n84, 202
Park, Hyung-Nong, 14–17, 19, 23, 14n39, 16n50, 197
Parker, Rebecca, 68–69, 76, 77n143, 79, 85n173, 187, 192
Peters, Ted, 80n156, 82, 82n162, 83, 148, 202
Philo, 54, 54n53, 113, 199
Pinnock, Clark, 181n177, 203
Plaskow, Judith, 43n19, 64n96, 65–66, 68, 161–62, 193, 203
Plato, 112
Popkes, Wiard, 120, 120n140

210

Name Index

Pseudo-Cyril of Alexandria, 126
Purvis, Sally, 67, 67n107, 203

Rahner, Karl, 76, 76n141, 123n156, 124n161, 130–31, 144n40, 171, 171n138, 203
Ramshaw-Schmidt, Gail, 51
Reuther, Rosemary, 43, 43n21, 44, 60, 63n94, 169n132
Ricoeur, Paul, 40n4, 203
Roetzel, Calvin, 93, 93n5, 203
Ross, John, 11, 11n30, 203
Russell, Letty, 51, 51n40, 168n125, 204
Ryu, Tong-Shik, 8n23, 19–21, 19n61, 20n65, 204

Saiving, Valerie, 64–66, 64n
Schleiermacher, Friedrich, 143, 143n35, 204
Schüssler Fiorenza, Elisabeth, 31, 31n90, 41n9, 44, 52n47, 54n49, 167n124, 168n126, 199, 204
Sölle, Dorothee, 44, 71–73, 71n126, 91n1, 108, 120, 122, 187, 205
Song, C. S., 15n44, 205
Starkloff, Carl, 22, 22n71, 205
Steinmetz, David, 92n25, 205
Suh, Nam Dong, 15, 15n43, 16, 16n47, 27n79, 154n81, 205

Tanner, Kathryn, 138, 138n9, 146, 146n53, 147, 147n57, 148, 205

Thistlewaite, Susan Brooks, 51, 206
Thompson, Deanna A., 66n103, 67, 67n108, 96n21, 97n26, 98, 206
Tillich Paul, xvin5, 1n1, 23, 23n73, 64n97, 65n101, 203, 206
Trible, Phyllis, 40–42, 40n6, 206

Volf, Miroslav, xiv, 130n191, 131n191, 137, 137n4, 139n13, 147–50, 164–68, 180n171, 192, 205, 206
Von Harnack, Adolf, 142–43, 142n30, 196
Von Loewenich, Walther, 93n7, 95n15, 199

Weaver, J. Denny, 81, 81n158, 84–85, 85n170, 206
Wells, Harold, x, xvin7, 12, 12n34, 16, 16n48, 21–22, 56n60, 75, 75n138, 89, 98, 98n30, 99n34, 180–83, 180n167, 181n72, 182n178, 186–87, 205, 206
Wiesel, Elie, 72, 72n127, 108, 108n76, 109, 207
Williams, Delores, 68–60, 69n, 113, 161, 187, 207
Wilson-Kastner, Patricia, 58n72, 162, 162n109, 207

Zizioulas, John, 137, 137n4, 165, 207

Topical Index

a-ethical, 87, 90, 188
Against the Robbing and Murdering Hordes of Peasants, 97
agennesia (unbegottenness), 58
a-historical, 87, 88, 90
Alexandrian Christology, 100
analogia relationis, 138, 150, 151, 152, 154, 177, 183
androcentric, 27, 29, 41, 45, 51, 56, 88, 154, 163, 168, 186, 187, 197
Annihilation of Hell, The, 119n135, 122n148, 158, 158n98, 191
anthropodicy, 108
anthropomorphic, 140, 142, 146
apatheia, 100, 101, 112
apophatic, 46, 47, 141
apotheosis, 142
Appeal to the Christian Nobility, 96
Arianism, 57, 61, 169, 170n135
arrogance, 12, 177, 178, 180, 181
atheism, 106, 107
atonement, xv, xvi, 35–36, 74–77, 79–80, 90, 118–21, 120n137, 187–188, 190, 195, 196, 200, 202, 204, 206
Auschwitz, 72, 108, 204
autonomy13, 67, 160, 161, 162
aut poena aut satisfaction, 80

Babylonian Captivity of the Church, 96
beings-in-the-world, 4, 142
Bielian theology, the, 94
black theology, 87, 194
blood, 34, 69, 75, 83, 187
broken fellowship, 157
Brothers Karamazov, The, 72, 107, 107n71, 108, 194

Buddhism, 6–8, 7n21, 12–13, 29, 194
Buma, 72, 108

Cappadocians, xvi, 58, 58n72, 92, 100, 187
cataphatic, 141
Chalcedon, 61, 62
Christus Victor, 35, 35n99, 36, 80n156, 84, 191, 202
circumincessio (to move around), 128, 129
circuminsessio (to sit around), 128, 129
Christendom, 96, 172, 173, 176
Church in the Power of the Spirit, The, 171, 171n143, 179, 179n162, 200
communicatio idiomatum, xvi, 99n35, 100, 101, 111–12, 188
communicative freedom, 161
complementarian, 168
conditio sine qua non, 1
contextual theology, xi, 1
contextuality, xiv, 1
coram Deo, 94, 96
cosmic child abuse, 76
cosmological argument, 106
cross-resurrection dialectic, 74, 187
crucified God, 101, 105, 106, 111
crux sola est nostra theologia, 95
cultus privatus, xii, 23, 36–38, 163
Cur Deus Homo, xv, 36n100, 76–90, 188, 191, 192

De Fide Orthodoxa, 127, 127n175
decrucifying Jesus, 68–71
de-historicize, 87
determinism, 94
Diakonia Sisterhood, 162–63, 163n111
dialectic, 67, 74, 182n178, 187

213

Topical Index

dialectical Christology, the, 104
dichotomy, 14, 155, 156
discipleship of equals, 168–70
diversity, 22, 27, 51, 56, 90, 125, 125n166, 126, 135, 152, 153, 180, 185, 189, 192
domination, 12, 43, 44, 56, 67, 89, 90, 106, 160–64, 167, 170, 178, 187, 189, 207

ecclesial, 41, 45, 55, 96, 98, 138, 148, 164, 165, 167, 170, 189, 192
ecclesiology, 164, 200
economic Trinity, 51, 130–32, 130n191, 131n191, 171
effective history (*wirkungsgeschichte*), 4, 40
efficacy, 69, 117
E. H. Johnson Award, 162, 162n111
emergency measure, 157
empathy, 139, 142, 146
empowerment, 35, 90, 162, 163
enlightenment, 14, 160
epiclesis, 49
epistemology, 95
eros, 71
erotic power, 69–71, 192
eschaton, 107, 159
eschatology, 178, 191, 192, 201, 205, 207
exclusivist, 12, 15, 23, 26, 178, 182n178
existential, xii, 14, 71–73, 172, 187
Experiences in Theology, 102n46, 129n182, 130, 130n187, 178n160, 179, 179n163, 201
expiatory sacrifice, 118

faciendo quod in se est, 94
feudal, 36, 36n100, 60, 79, 90
fiduciary, 80
filioque, 130, 132, 133, 133n198, 134, 134n206, 196, 200, 203
fore-structure (*vor-struktur*) of understanding, the, 5, 9, 10–13
forgiveness, 30n89, 33, 35, 78, 82, 88, 96, 97, 105, 119n135, 150, 155, 158, 159
freedom, x, xvii, 2, 21n68, 35, 62, 67, 79n150, 79n151, 86, 96, 105, 106, 112, 113, 119n135, 121, 149, 155, 158, 158n98, 160, 161, 164, 183, 189, 191, 195, 201

fulfillment theory, 19
fundamentalist, 14, 16n50, 23, 32, 177
fusion of horizons, 5

generations, 25, 159, 175, 175n153, 176, 176n155, 177, 185, 190
GKYM, 175n154, 176
God-man, the, 78, 101, 112
godforsaken, the, 68, 104, 110, 113, 121, 155
godforsakeness, xvi, 70, 92, 104, 111, 121, 188
godless, the, 68, 73, 103, 109, 113, 115, 117, 155
grammatical rule, 140

han/han-ridden, 15n44, 15n45, 27, 29, 30n89, 35, 153, 154–9, 163, 185, 202
Hananim, 6n18, 8n23, 11, 11n33, 12
han-pu-ri, 30n89, 198
harmonious order, 28
headship, 60, 85
Heidelberg Disputation, xvi, 92, 93, 96, 97, 172, 195, 201, 206
hermeneutical, 5, 10, 15, 19, 21, 24, 36, 40, 41, 142–4
hidden God, 93, 101
historically effected consciousness (*Wirkungsgeschichtliches Bewusstsein*), 4
homoousion, 123
hope, 2, 27n79, 31, 31, 35, 70, 72, 94, 97, 102, 104, 104n57, 113n103, 121, 121n147, 157n92, 159, 163n112, 193, 194, 200, 201
household codes, 31, 168
hubris, 67
humility, 62, 68, 95, 162, 163, 172, 177, 181, 182n178, 183, 190
hypostasis, 112, 123

imago Dei, xvii, 50, 136–38, 150–52, 158n96, 160, 166, 183, 185, 191
imitatio Christi, 64
imitatio relationis, xvii, 160–64, 184
immanence, 33, 46
immanent Trinity, 130, 130n191, 131, 131n191, 133, 140, 141, 171, 197

Topical Index

imminence of the kingdom, 105
immortal, 106
immutable, 106
impassible/impassibility, 99, 100n38, 106, 111, 112, 193
in se, 47, 52, 94
incarnation, 17, 21, 21n67, 23, 49, 50, 55, 61–63, 68, 77, 78, 88, 89, 101, 132, 148, 157–59, 180, 182, 186, 192, 201
incommensurable, 180
incommunicable, 123, 124
individualistic society, 161
indwelling, xvii, 59, 92, 127, 128, 136, 141, 159, 165, 180, 189
ineffability, 46
interconnectedness, ix, xi, 27, 136, 155, 159, 162, 174, 189
interpenetration, xvi, 58n72, 59, 92, 126, 127, 136, 141, 144
iron/fire, 92
Isis, 53
iustitia Dei, 94

je-sa, 9

kairos, 102
kenosis, 52, 63, 68, 115, 206
koinonia, 56, 90, 129, 144

leadership, xvii, 25, 31, 32, 41, 51n41, 61, 121, 135, 138, 164, 166–70, 189, 190
liberation theology, 87n180, 192, 200
logos, 20, 20n63, 21n68, 53–55, 100n38, 182n177, 204

maleness of God, 45, 46, 61, 89, 189
medieval, 36n100, 60, 60n78, 79, 90, 96, 98, 99, 188, 200
metanoia, 162–63
methodolatry, 42
minjung, 15–16, 16n46, 27n79, 154, 154n82, 162, 163n111, 191, 205
missio ad extra, 171
missio ad intra, 171
mission, xiii, xvii, 13, 18n59, 19n61, 20, 53, 135, 138, 145, 147, 163n111, 164, 170–2, 175, 175n154, 176, 177, 180, 190, 192, 198, 205, 207

modalism, 124, 126, 128, 144n39
modes of being, 123–25, 128, 143, 144n39, 152
monarchical, 60
monotheistic, 143, 144
mutuality, ix, xii, xiii, xiv, xv, xvii, 38, 39, 56, 58, 58n72, 90–92, 129, 130, 135, 136, 149, 155, 160, 168, 184–86, 189

namjon-yobi, 28
namyo-yubyol, 28
natural theology, 18, 19n59, 106, 107
negation of self, 65
Neo-Confucianism, 8, 9
neo-platonic, 82, 90, 130
Niceno-Constantinopolitan Creed of 381, 133, 133n199, 134
Niebuhrian conception of sin, 65
nondata, 42
Night Trilogy, The, 71, 72
nonquestions, 42
norma normans, 142
nothingness, 106, 109

omnipotent, 93, 99, 106
On the Freedom of the Christian, 96
ontological, 23n73, 61, 62, 123, 124, 131
open friendship, 153, 173, 174, 183
open Trinity, xvii, 129, 136, 189
opera trinitatis ad extra, 132
opera trinitatis ad intra, 132, 171
optimism, 102
opus alienum, 94
orthopraxy, 142, 148, 150, 185
ousia, 57, 123, 124

Paraclete, 49n30, 51, 182n177
paradidonai, 102n49, 114, 120
paradoken, 115
paradoxical, 17, 95, 96, 101, 172
particularity, 180, 181, 182, 182n178
passio activa, xiii, 86, 114, 115, 120
passionate love, 112
passive submission, 82
pathetic theology, 111, 113
pathos, 113
patriarchy, 48, 49, 52, 57, 58, 63, 192, 199, 202, 207

215

Topical Index

Peasant Wars, the, 96
penal substitution, 80–84
perfecting creation, 157–59
perichoresis, xiv, xvi, 59, 92, 122n149, 126–30, 136, 137n5, 139n14, 140–41, 141n19, 136, 137n5, 139n14, 140–141, 141n19, 142, 144, 149, 151, 160, 165,170, 180–1, 187, 189, 196–97, 202
perpetrator, 121, 156
persona Christi, 61, 169, 170
personhood, xvi, 24, 58, 88, 90, 123, 125, 137n4, 144, 207
pluralism, 179, 194, 198, 200, 202, 206
political religion, 104
praxis, ix, xi, xiii, xv, xvi, xvin8, 25, 32, 39, 40n3, 44–47, 90, 92, 130, 130n189, 135–38, 140n19, 142n28, 146n50, 150–53, 151n74, 157n91, 159, 159n103, 160n107, 164, 170, 176, 176n155, 177, 183–84, 189–90, 193, 200
prejudice, 3, 4, 6, 9, 10, 13, 24, 32, 153, 170, 174
prerogatives, 63, 125
projection, 106, 137n5, 138, 139n14, 141n19, 197
prophetic call, xii, 37, 38, 172, 186
Proslogium, 82, 82n163
prosopon, 123
protesting God, 107–9
Pungryudo, 6, 6n18, 7, 7n21, 19n61

ransom, 75, 84
reality of history, the (*Die Wirklichkeit der Geschichte*), 4
reciprocal sacrifice of love, xiii, xvi, 145
reciprocity, ix, xii, xvi, xv, xvii, 38, 39, 92, 112, 129, 130, 135–39, 155, 165, 170, 183–86
reconciliation, 18, 155, 157–59
relational praxis, 176, 176n155, 177
relationality, 51, 123, 202
relativizing, 180, 183
remote Christo, 77
repentance, 10, 37, 155, 157–59, 172, 178
Resolutions, The, 93

restitutio in integrum (restoration to original condition), 118
resurrection, 12, 16, 23, 70, 74–76, 84, 94, 96, 103–4, 114, 116n114, 135, 145–46, 155, 158, 182, 187–89, 206
retribution, 81, 84, 85, 119
revealer of the Trinity, 131, 145, 146
revelation, 15, 18, 18n59, 23, 23n73, 56, 95, 101, 104, 116n119, 117, 119, 130, 133

Sabellian, 124, 126, 144n39
sado-masochistic, 11, 116, 120, 122
salvation, 2,3, 10, 12–16, 20–21, 33, 36, 38, 40, 44, 52, 56, 64, 66, 67, 69, 70, 73, 75, 84–88, 94, 95, 112, 119n135, 120n137, 130–32, 145, 155, 167, 171, 178, 180–81, 185, 191, 195, 203
Sam-sung-gak, 7, 8
Satan, 81, 84
satisfaction atonement, 79, 81, 83
seinsweisen, 123, 143, 144n39, 144n40
self-giving, 50, 86, 117, 131n191, 132, 145–46, 150–53, 160, 162–63, 170, 173, 177, 179–84, 190
selflessness of love, 65, 161
sexuality, 26, 40, 41, 90, 186, 206
Shamanism, 2–3, 6–8, 12, 17, 19, 29–30, 30n88, 198, 204
sin, 156–66, 183–84, 189, 197, 202, 203
Sitz-im-Leben, 27, 154, 185
SLNG (spiritual leaders for the next generations), 175n153
social analogies, 140
social program, 130, 131n191, 139, 139n13, 140, 147n56, 148, 148n58, 149n60, 150n64, 160n104, 180n171, 206
social Trinity, 40n3, 55, 90, 135, 145, 162, 164, 170, 179
social-constructivist, 65
solidarity, 62, 70–75, 89, 91–92, 99, 102, 106, 113, 119, 135, 136, 153, 161–63, 174, 178, 186–90, 192, 200
Sophia, 52–56, 74–75, 89–90, 186–88, 197
Sophialogical tradition, 49, 52, 89
soteriology, 13, 80

Topical Index

Spirit of Life: Universal Affirmation, The, 116n115, 117–19, 133n201, 134n206, 136n1, 151n68, 152n76, 153n78, 156n87, 160n106, 161n108, 174n151, 201
staurocentric, 114n108, 119, 197
structure of the church, 135, 138, 164, 189
subordinationist, 51, 89
substance, 57–58, 122–25, 122n147, 128, 132, 144, 150, 165
substitute, 51, 80, 81
"suffering in suffering," 109
Sun of Righteousness, Arise, 119n133, 128n178, 156, 156n88, 158n99, 201
superfluous, 134, 143
surplus of grace, 157–59
sympathy, 113
syncretism, 12, 12n34, 16n48, 21n67, 22–23, 198, 205, 206

Tao-te-ching, 20
theism, 106–8, 110, 201
theistic religion, 104, 106
theologia cruces, vii, xvi, 92–93, 95, 99, 197, 202, 204, 205
theologia gloriae, 93–94, 100–101, 205
theology of complementarity, 57, 59, 59n77, 61, 169
theology of the two governments, the, 97
theology of the two kingdoms, the, 97, 200, 207
theopaschitic, 115
theory of paradigm, 3

transcendence, 46, 50, 90n35, 178
transience, 112
trinitarian hermeneutics, 142–43, 146
trinitarian history, 51, 145
The Trinity and the Kingdom, 59n76, 112n97, 116–17, 117n120, 122–29, 132n195, 134n203, 137n4, 139, 142n29, 143n35, 144n39, 145n47, 146n51, 157n93, 160n105, 165n113, 201
triumphalism, 163, 172–73

una substantia (homogeneity of substance), 122, 128
underdevelopment, 65, 162
universality of the Spirit, 182n178
universality of salvation, 52

viability, 44
via negativa, 46
victimization, 64, 74, 85, 161
victory of shalom, 74, 187
violence, 34, 37, 44, 69, 71, 74, 81, 81n158, 84–85, 85n170, 97, 119, 150, 156–57, 161, 204, 206
vulnerability, 111, 179, 183

Way of Jesus, The, 49, 114n105, 115n109, 117, 117n122, 121n145, 201
will-to-power, 65–67
Wounded Heart of God, The, 15n44, 27n79, 155, 155n84, 156, 202

www.ingramcontent.com/pod-product-compliance
Lightning Source LLC
Chambersburg PA
CBHW050442240426
43661CB00055B/2477